The Congregational Handbook

How to Develop and Sustain Your Unitarian Universalist Congregation

Third Edition

Edited by Lawrence X. Peers

Unitarian Universalist Association
Boston

Printed in the USA.

ISBN 1-55896-334-0

10 9 8 7 6 5 4 3 2 1
99 98 97 96 95

Acknowledgments

"Criteria for Bylaws" by Robert W. C. Brown. Copyright © 1981 by Robert W. C. Brown.
Reprinted by permission of the author.

"Volunteer Practices Guide" is from *The Church and Its Volunteers, Office for Church Life
and Leadership.* Copyright © 1979 by the United Church of Christ. Used by permission.

Individual reflection exercise in Chapter 2 is used by permission of Gustave Rath and
Norman Shawchuck.

Tips on an annual review process in Chapter 5 is adapted from *Evaluating Ministry: Principles and Processes for Clergy and Congregation* by Jill M. Hudson. Copyright © 1992.
Reprinted by permission of the Alban Institute, 4550 Montgomery Avenue, Bethesda, MD
20814-3341.

The Annual Review of a Congregation's Ministry in Chapter 3 is from "How to Evaluate
Your Church's Ministry" by Catherine Holmes Clark, from *Action Information,* Volume
XVII, No. 1, January-February 1991. Reprinted by permission of the Alban Institute, 4550
Montgomery Avenue, Bethesda, MD 20814-3341.

Contents

Introduction

We stand at a significant juncture in the development of the Unitarian Universalist Association of Congregations. The challenge before us is to become a vital force for spiritual growth and social ministry. This goal can only happen if all of our congregations respond to this call by continually renewing themselves. The process of renewal includes cultivating a clear sense of mission, which articulates why a given Unitarian Universalist congregation is needed. From this ever-renewing sense of purpose comes the inspiration for reviewing and guiding the practices in our congregations. When congregational ideals and practice are aligned in your congregation, it becomes a strong testimony to Unitarian Universalism in the community, which serves not only the local area but Unitarian Universalism as well.

Our congregations, though autonomous in governance, exist as vital links to other Unitarian Universalist congregations around the world. We deserve both to honor our own traditions but also to uphold a set of standards and responsibilities to each other as guardians of this Unitarian Universalist congregational tradition. Our heritage claims the ultimate freedom and autonomy of congregation. Our heritage also claims the ultimate responsibility of a congregation to be a place where our ideals are practiced and made real forces of healing and liberation.

This *Congregational Handbook* is intended as a reference and a guide to member congregations in the Unitarian Universalist Association. While no handbook can guide a Unitarian Universalist congregation in all its practices, this one attempts to make the following available to congregations:

- guidance on the advantages and responsibilities of being a member congregation of the Unitarian Universalist Association
- a list of resources and services available to member congregations
- guidance on major dimensions of congregational life.

The central assumption that guides this *Congregational Handbook* is that a vital congregation continually renews its sense of vision and purpose as it learns from its practice. A feature of this edition of the *Congregational Handbook* is the organization of the material in a way that assumes a congregation has done the foundational work of cultivating a vision (a compelling image of what it ultimately aims to become), articulating a mission (a sense of purpose), and defining a covenant (its guiding values). It is becoming common practice for many Unitarian Universalist congregations to develop a mission statement. This *Congregational Handbook* attempts to place this statement in the operational context of a congregation's life so that it guides and inspires, among other things, programming, budgeting, and outreach.

Hopefully, you will find in these pages both practical advice and inspiration. Many people have contributed their best wisdom and advice to our congregations. This *Congregational Handbook* is a reenvisioning of a project that was first published in 1977. Since then, there have been enduring strengths and significant changes in Unitarian Universalist congregational practice. This edition builds on two previous editions, but is reoriented around central themes and practices of current Unitarian Universalist congregations.

Much gratitude goes to all those who have contributed to this edition. Special appreciation goes to my associate in the Unitarian Universalist Association Extension Department, Simone Gilbert, who managed a tremendous amount of detail and text with great patience and endurance, for us to create this edition.

Lawrence Xavier Peers, Editor
Extension Education and Research Director
Unitarian Universalist Association

February 1995

About the Contributors

Appreciation goes to many Unitarian Universalist Association staff and district services staff, lay leaders, religious professionals, and trustees who have contributed their time and insights to this edition. Rather than list their specific contributions in the *Handbook*, we are listing them here. Some of these contributors also reviewed the entire draft of the *Handbook* and made significant suggestions.

Jory Agate • UUA Department of Religious Education

Julie Parker Amery • UUA Office of Public Relations, Marketing, and Information

Debra Anderson • UUA Department of Religious Education

Marcy Bailey-Adams • UUA Department of Development

Gary Blaine • Tulsa, OK

Ellen Brandenburg • UUA Department of Ministry

Patricia Carol • UUA District Services Consultant

Tom Chulak • Manhasset, NY

Catherine Holmes Clark • Ashburton, MA

Roger Comstock • UUA District Services Consultant

Donna DiSciullo • UUA Department for Congregational, District, and Extension Services

Judith Frediani • UUA Department of Religious Education

Charles Gaines • Acton, MA

William Gardiner • UUA Department of Social Justice

June Gillespie • UUA Board of Trustees

Joan Goodwin • Boston, MA

Harry Greene • UUA Department of Ministry

Robert Gregson • UUA Office for Lesbian, Bisexual, and Gay Concerns

Kristi Heesch • Austin, TX

Patricia Hoertdoerfer • UUA Department of Religious Education

Melvin Hoover • UUA Office for Racial
and Cultural Diversity

Daniel Hotchkiss • UUA Department of Ministry

David Hubner • UUA Department of Ministry

Carolyn Kemmett • UUA Office of Public Relations,
Marketing, and Information

Brian Kiely • Surrey, BC

Carla Kindt • UUA Department for Congregational,
District, and Extension Services

Susan Leslie • UUA Office for Racial and Cultural Diversity

Nancy Bowen Martell • UUA District Services Consultant

John Morgan • Westerville, OH

Diane Miller • UUA Department of Ministry

Makanah Morriss • UUA Department of
Religious Education

Eugene Navias • Boston, MA

Lawrence Peers • UUA Department for Congregational,
District, and Extension Services

Lola Peters • UUA Department of Social Justice

Barbara Prairie • UUA Department of General Assembly

Peter Raible • Seattle, WA

Gustave Rath • Evanston, IL

Meg Riley • UUA Office for Lesbian,
Bisexual, and Gay Concerns

Jeanellen Ryan • UUA Department of Religious Education

Fia Scheyer • UUA Department of Development

William Sinkford • UUA Department for Congregational,
District, and Extension Services

Beverly Smrha • UUA District Services Consultant

Robert Snow • UUA Department of Development

David Tedesco • UUA Board of Trustees

Deborah Weiner • UUA Office of Public Relations,
Marketing, and Information

Barbara Wells • Woodinville, WA

Ed Wiltz • Gaffney, SC

Brenda Wong • UUA Publications Department

How to Use This *Handbook*

This *Congregational Handbook* is both a resource and a guide for Unitarian Universalist congregations. As a resource, members of your congregation may turn to these pages to get information on the services of the Unitarian Universalist Association, a particular committee, or a particular aspect of congregational life. Members of a congregation will find here general guidelines on how to conduct a goal-setting meeting, a long-range planning process, or an annual canvass. The list of resources and guidelines available in this *Congregational Handbook* is not comprehensive, but it is adequate for launching the reader into further resources and services available to Unitarian Universalist Association member congregations.

Each year congregations routinely change some of their leadership on committees and governing boards. This *Handbook* can be useful in:

- orienting new committee chairs to their own and their committee's role
- orienting and developing the skills of lay leaders within the congregation in goal setting, planning, and reviewing the effectiveness of the congregation
- giving members of the congregation processes to enhance the work of their committees or task forces
- informing members about the Unitarian Universalist Association and the services it provides to member congregations through its headquarters, district, and field offices.

In addition, this *Handbook* will be useful to congregations during significant transition points, which can only be defined by a particular congregation. Ordinarily, they occur before or after a significant event in the life of a congregation. Examples include during an interim ministry period, the start of a new ministry, the move to a new building, significant membership growth, change or crisis in the congregation, or decline in membership. In addition to informing your congregation of the services and resources that are available to member congregations of the UUA and UUA districts, there are processes and guidelines here for a congregation to utilize during a transition period. The chapters your congregation may want to review could include:

- Chapter 1: On Being a Member Congregation of the Unitarian Universalist Association
- Chapter 3: Reviewing Your Congregation's Ministry, Minister(s), and Staff
- Chapter 4: Congregational Planning and Goal Setting
- Chapter 6: Religious Professionals
- Chapter 7: Programming for Congregational Growth (The Self Study and Profile of Your Congregation forms provided in Chapter 7 can be used by congregations to gather important data about themselves for planning purposes. The forms may also be used as a profile of your congregation for your leadership, the district office, Unitarian Universalist Association staff, and others who may work with a congregation.

We have drawn from many resources to create this *Handbook*. Use what is here and add new ideas and resources.

Unit I

Being and Becoming a Unitarian Universalist Congregation

One

On Being a Member Congregation of the Unitarian Universalist Association

The Unitarian Universalist Association of Congregations

The Unitarian Universalist Association (UUA) of Congregations is a religious organization that combines two traditions: the Universalists, who organized in 1793, and the Unitarians, who organized in 1825. They merged into the Unitarian Universalist Association in 1961.

Both groups trace their roots in North America to early Massachusetts settlers. Overseas, their heritages reach back centuries to religious pioneers and reformers in England, Poland, and Transylvania.

Organization

Each of the more than 1,000 member congregations in the United States, Canada, and overseas is democratic in polity and operation; they govern themselves. They unite in the Unitarian Universalist Association to provide services that individual congregations cannot provide for themselves and to strengthen and grow Unitarian Universalism and implement its principles. Each congregation is associated with one of the Unitarian Universalist Association's twenty-three districts.

Government

The Unitarian Universalist Association is governed by a board of trustees consisting of district trustees, selected by the various districts and at-large trustees, who are elected by delegates to the General Assembly. The General Assembly is the annual business meeting of the Association, held in various parts of the continent. The board of trustees meets four times each year, three times in Boston and once at the General Assembly.

An elected moderator presides at the General Assembly and at meetings of the board of trustees and represents the Association on special occasions. A financial advisor, elected by the General Assembly, also sits on the board.

An elected president, an appointed executive vice president, a treasurer, vice presidents, and department directors form the executive staff, which administers the day-to-day concerns of the Association.

Unitarian Universalist Association Staff	Scattered throughout North America and clustered in two buildings on Boston's Beacon Hill are 150 people whose full-time concern is service to Unitarian Universalist congregations. The Unitarian Universalist Association and its employees and services in Boston are reachable Monday through Friday at (617) 742-2100, from 9 AM to 5 PM (Eastern time) or by fax at (617) 367-3237. District staff and some other offices of the Unitarian Universalist Association can be reached through their district office or individual offices.
Beliefs	Unitarian Universalism is a liberal religion with Jewish and Christian roots. It has no creed. It affirms the worth of human beings, advocates freedom of belief and the search for advancing truth, and endeavors to provide a warm, open, supportive community for people who believe that ethical living is the supreme witness of religion. The member congregations of the Unitarian Universalist Association covenant to affirm and promote the Unitarian Universalist Association Principles and Purposes, adopted by the 1984 and 1985 General Assemblies.

The Unitarian Universalist Purposes and Principles

Principles	We, the member congregations of the Unitarian Universalist Association, covenant to affirm and promote:

- The inherent worth and dignity of every person;

- Justice, equity and compassion in human relations;

- Acceptance of one another and encouragement to spiritual growth in our congregations;

- A free and responsible search for truth and meaning;

- The right of conscience and the use of democratic process within our congregations and in society at large;

- The goal of world community with peace, liberty and justice for all;

- Respect for the interdependent web of all existence of which we are a part.

Purposes	The living tradition which we share draws from many sources:

- Direct experience of that transcending mystery and wonder, affirmed in all cultures, which moves us to a renewal of the spirit and an openness to the forces which create and uphold life;

- Words and deeds of prophetic men and women which challenge us to confront powers and structures of evil with justice, compassion, and the transforming power of love;

- Wisdom from the world's religions which inspires us in our ethical and spiritual life;

- Jewish and Christian teachings which call us to respond to God's love by loving our neighbors as ourselves;

- Humanist teachings which counsel us to heed the guidance of reason and the results of science, and warn us against idolatries of the mind and spirit.

The Unitarian Universalist Association shall devote its resources to and exercise its corporate powers of religious, educational and humanitarian purposes. The primary purpose of the Association is to serve the needs of its member congregations, organize new congregations, extend and strengthen Unitarian Universalist institutions and implement its principles.

UUA Services and Resources to Congregations

Here is a partial index of services and resources available to member congregations from the Unitarian Universalist Association departments.

Adult Program Materials .... Department of Religious Education

Advertising Consultation .... Public Relations, Marketing, and Information Office

AIDS Projects Support .... Office of Lesbian, Bisexual, and Gay Concerns

Annual Report on Giving .... Development Department

Antiracism and Diversity Resources .... Office for Racial and Cultural Diversity

Archival Research .... Public Relations, Marketing, and Information Office

Beyond Categorical Thinking Program .... Department of Religious Education

Bisexual, Gay, and Lesbian Concerns
    Advocacy and Program Material .... Office of Lesbian, Bisexual, and Gay Concerns

Black Concerns Working Group
    Workshops... Office for Racial and Cultural Diversity

Building Loan Administration .... Department of Finance

Building Loan Guarantee and
    Grant Program....................................... Department for Congregational, District, and Extension Services

Campus Ministry Support .... Department for Congregational, District, and
Extension Services

Canvass Training at the District Level .... Department for Congregational, District, and
Extension Services

Capital Campaigns .... Department for Congregational, District, and
Extension Services

Capital Campaigns Consultation .... Department for Congregational, District, and
Extension Services

Children's Program Materials .... Department of Religious Education

Church Musician's Information .... Department of Ministry

Church Staff Finances .... Department of Ministry

Committee on Ministry .... Department of Ministry

Compensation of Church Staff .... Department of Ministry

Computer-related Advice to Congregations .. Department of Computer Services

Conflict Management for Ministers .... Department of Ministry

Conflict Management with Congregations ... Department for Congregational, District, and
Extension Services

Connections Newsletter .... Public Relations, Marketing, and Information
Office; Publications Department

Continuing Education/Professional .... Development Department; Department of
Ministry

Curriculum Development for All Ages .... Department of Religious Education

Decisions for Growth Program .... Department for Congregational, District, and
Extension Services

Demographic Resources .... Department for Congregational, District, and
Extension Services

Diversity of Membership Initiatives .... Department for Congregational, District, and
Extension Services

Emergency Aid for Ministers .... Department of Ministry

Estate Planning .... Development Department

Ethics and Action Newsletter .... Department for Social Justice

Exhibits of Unitarian Universalist
    Products and Services .... General Assembly Office

Extension Internship Program .... Department for Congregational, District, and
Extension Services

Extension Ministry Program .... Department for Congregational, District, and
Extension Services

Extension Training for Ministers .... Department for Congregational, District, and
Extension Services

Extension Training for Small and
    Mid-sized Congregations .... Department for Congregational, District, and
Extension Services

Ministerial Settlement Processes .... Department of Ministry

Ministerial-Congregational Relations .... Department of Ministry

Ministry Packet .... Department of Ministry

Music Resources .... Department of Religious Education

New Congregation Organizers Training .... Department for Congregational, District, and Extension Services

New Congregations Ministry Program .... Department for Congregational, District, and Extension Services

Newsletter Evaluations for Congregations ... Public Relations, Marketing, and Information Office

Ordinations and Installations .... Department of Ministry

Organizational Development for
    Congregations .... Department for Congregational, District, and Extension Services

Pension Plans .... Department of Finance

Planned Giving Church Kit
    and Workshops .... Development Department

Professional Ethics for Church Staff .... Department of Ministry

Public Information .... Public Relations, Marketing, and Information Office

Public Relations .... Public Relations, Marketing, and Information Office

Racial and Cultural Diversity Speakers .... Office for Racial and Cultural Diversity

REACH: The Religious Education Action
    Clearinghouse Resource .... Department of Religious Education

Religion That Puts Its Faith in You
    Program .... Public Relations, Marketing, and Information Office

Religious Educators, Placement Network
    for Career Oriented .... Department of Religious Education

Resource Bank for People of Color .... Office for Racial and Cultural Diversity

Retirement Planning .... Department of Ministry

Sabbatical Planning .... Department of Ministry

Scouting Programs .... Department of Religious Education

Service of the Living Tradition .... General Assembly Office

Skinner House Books .... Publications Department

Social Justice Workshops for
    Congregations and Districts .... Department for Social Justice

Special Event Fundraising .... Development Department

Student Scholarship Aid and Counsel .... Department of Ministry

Tours of the UUA .... Public Relations, Marketing, and Information Office

Unitarian Universalist Association
     Directory Files .... Department of Computer Services

Unitarian Universalist Association
     Elections (odd-numbered years) .... General Assembly Office

UUA Directory .... Public Relations, Marketing, and Information Office

Video Loan Library .... UUA Bookstore

Ware Lecture .... General Assembly Office

Welcoming Congregation Trainers
     for Districts.. Office of Lesbian, Bisexual, and Gay Concerns

World Circulation.. Department of Computer Services

World Magazine .... Office for the *World*

Worship Resources .... Department of Religious Education

Young Adult Ministries Training
     and Support .... Department for Congregational, District, and Extension Services

Young Religious Unitarian
     Universalist (YRUU) .... Department of Religious Education

Youth Conference, Continental (Con-Con) .. Department of Religious Education

Youth Group Program Materials .... Department of Religious Education

Departments of the Unitarian Universalist Association

Beacon Press

Beacon Press, an imprint of the Unitarian Universalist Association, publishes books that spread values included in the Unitarian Universalist Association Statement of Principles and Purposes to readers within and beyond the denomination. (Skinner House Books, another Unitarian Universalist Association imprint, publishes books whose primary audience is within the denomination.)

All Beacon Press books are available for sale in retail bookstores and at the Unitarian Universalist Association Bookstore.

Unitarian Universalist Association Bookstore

The Unitarian Universalist Association Bookstore sells resources and books published by the Unitarian Universalist Association, Beacon Press, and other publishers. It also maintains the Video Loan Library. The bookstore manager assists congregations and districts in the arrangement of book tables for special events.

Department of Computer Services	The Department of Computer Services provides computer and software support to the Association. It maintains the membership list of the Unitarian Universalist Association, controls the distribution of the *World* magazine, and is responsible for maintaining and verifying data files collected to produce the annual Unitarian Universalist Association Directory.
Development Department	The Development Department raises funds for Unitarian Universalist Association services, programs, and outreach. By working on both the continental and local levels, the department encourages increased generosity among Unitarian Universalists toward all aspects of denominational life. The Development Department also offers consultation and information on fundraising techniques and programs for member congregations.

Services and Programs

Annual Report on Giving
Connections Newsletter
Estate planning
Financial planning
Planned Giving Church Kit and workshops
Special event fundraising

Department for Congregational, District, and Extension Services	The Department for Congregational, District, and Extension Services (created April 1995) combines the functions of the former Department of District and Congregational Services with the Department of Extension.

The staff of this department includes field staff, made up of twenty-seven professional district "executives" (whose titles vary and are determined by the districts), program consultants who are employed jointly by the UUA and the districts, and Boston-based Extension staff.

The director of this department oversees its work; encourages collaboration between the field staff, the Extension staff, and other departments of the Association; and administers the Racial/Ethnic Diversity Extension Program.

The mission of the field staff is direct service to UUA congregations, including consultations on a wide variety of congregational issues, including long-range planning and organizational development, ministerial transitions, leadership training, and conflict management. The district "executive" serves as the UUA's local presence and is the first person you should contact with questions and concerns about UUA services and your relationship to the Association.

The Extension staff works for the development of congregations and other Unitarian Universalist communities committed to growth, and to inspire and support changes that increase membership and diversity in the UUA.

District and Congregational Services

Conflict management
Consultation
Leadership training
Liaison between Unitarian Universalist Association, districts, and
congregations
Organizational development
Religious education and youth programs

Extension Services

Building Loan Guarantee and Grant Program
Campus ministry support
Canvass training at the district level
Consultation for capital campaigns
"Decisions for Growth" Program
Demographic resources
Diversity of membership initiatives
Evangelism and Outreach Training
Extension Internship Program
Extension Ministry Program
Extension training for ministers and new congregation organizers
Extension training for small and mid-sized congregations
Large church consultations
Minister-on-Loan Program
New Congregations Ministry Program
Young adult ministries training and support
International programs

Department of Finance

The Office of the Treasurer and Financial Vice President performs all financial transactions of the Unitarian Universalist Association. It receives and disburses monies, maintains accurate records of the transactions, and manages and accounts for the Unitarian Universalist Association's endowment funds and the Unitarian Universalist pension plan.

Services and Programs

Building loan administration
General Investment Fund
Pension plans

General Assembly Office

The annual General Assembly (GA) of the Unitarian Universalist Association is a six-day convention held in June to conduct the business of the Association and to offer programs and events of interest to congregations and individual Unitarian Universalists. All clergy and members of Unitarian Universalist congregations are eligible to attend, and congregations may be represented by voting delegates. General Assembly is the largest gathering of the Association, drawing approximately 2,500 Unitarian Universalists. The assembly is held in different areas of the United States each year and in Canada every ten years.

Services and Programs

Exhibits of Unitarian Universalist products and services
Over 3,000 programs and events, including lectures, workshops, worship, and meetings
Plenary sessions
Professional meetings
Service of the Living Tradition
Unitarian Universalist Association elections (odd-numbered years)
Ware Lecture

Office for Interfaith and International Relations

The Special Assistant for Interfaith and International Relations represents the UUA President on the council of the International Association for Religious Freedom and on the board of the Holdeen India Program. The Special Assistant serves as a staff liaison to the Canadian Unitarian Council, the British General Assembly of Free Christian and Unitarian Churches, and the Partner Church Council. The Special Assistant is a member of the committee planning a gathering of representatives of Unitarian and Universalist congregations around the world to form an International Council of Unitarians and Universalists, and also serves as a representative to interfaith organizations in the United States.

Office for Lesbian, Bisexual, and Gay Concerns and the AIDS Action and Information Program

The Office of Lesbian, Bisexual, and Gay Concerns fosters the acceptance, inclusion, understanding, and equality of gay, lesbian, and bisexual persons in the Unitarian Universalist Association and its member congregations primarily through the Welcoming Congregation Program.

The AIDS Action and Information Program coordinates, improves, and encourages a Unitarian Universalist response to the continuing AIDS crisis.

Services and Programs

Advocacy
Counseling
Educational, worship, and program materials
Information and referral services
Support for local AIDS projects
Welcoming Congregation Program
Welcoming Congregation trainers for districts
Workshops

Department of Ministry

The Department of Ministry services the needs of congregations, ministers, and the association by providing counsel, leadership, and resources for developing and nurturing a ministry of excellence and effectiveness.

Services and Programs

Assistance with international ministries
Committee on Ministry
Conflict management
Consultation in recruitment, education, certification, and settlement
     processes
Church staff finances
Compensation surveys
Continuing education/professional development
Emergency aid
Financial planning
Insurance and pensions
Interim ministers
Ministerial education
Ministerial fellowship rules and policies
Ministerial settlement
Ministerial-congregational relations
Ministry Packet
Ordinations and installations
Personal and professional counseling
Professional ethics
Research and statistics on ministry
Retirement planning
Sabbatical planning
Student scholarship aid and counsel

Pickett and Eliot Guest Houses

The Operations Department oversees the rental of meeting and function spaces, and is responsible for the operation of Pickett and Eliot Guest Houses, a newly renovated bed-and-breakfast open to the public. Call (617) 742-2100 for reservations.

Public Relations, Marketing, and Information Office

The Public Relations, Marketing, and Information Office promotes the UUA and Unitarian Universalism by communicating with press and media who cover the UUA, disseminating print and electronic media materials that promote the philosophy and goals of Unitarian Universalism, and supporting efforts within and outside the denomination to inform people of the Association's progressive stands on numerous issues.

With the Development and Publications Departments, the office publishes *Connections,* the bimonthly denominational newsletter. In addition, it compiles the annual Unitarian Universalist Association Directory, responds to informational inquiries, and provides archival research and guided tours of the Unitarian Universalist Association headquarters.

Services and Programs

Archival research
Connections newsletter

Newsletter evaluations for congregations
Public information
Public relations and advertising consultations
Public relations and marketing services
"Religion That Puts Its Faith in You" Program
UUA Directory
Video production
Tours of the UUA

Publications Department

The Publications Department produces the Association's workshop and religious education resources and pamphlets, publishes titles under the Unitarian Universalist Association imprint, Skinner House Books, sponsors the Melcher Book Award and the Stansfield Scholarship, and markets titles sold through the UUA Bookstore.

With the Development Department and the Public Information Office, the Publications Department produces and distributes the Unitarian Universalist Association newsletter *Connections*.

Office for Racial and Cultural Diversity

The Office for Racial and Cultural Diversity is responsible for implementing the 1992 General Assembly resolution on racial and cultural diversity in Unitarian Universalism. It works with the Unitarian Universalist board of trustees, committees, congregations, staff, and related organizations in the creation of a more racially and ethnically diverse, multicultural Association.

Services and Programs

Antiracism and diversity resources
Black Concerns Working Group workshops
Consultation and planning
Resource Bank for people of color
Speakers

Registry of Conscientious Objectors

The Unitarian Universalist Association maintains a Registry of Conscientious Objectors and encourages men and women of all ages who are members of Unitarian Universalist congregations to submit statements to this registry on their behalf and in support of draft-age members and their families. Information on how to register is available from the Office of the Executive Vice President, 25 Beacon Street, Boston, MA, 02108. Ask for the Unitarian Universalist Association pamphlet "Facts on Military Service and Conscientious Objection."

Religious Education

The Religious Education Department supports the planning and conducting of congregational programs of religious growth and learning for Unitarian Universalists of all ages. The department's services include consulting, leadership training, and developing curricula and programs.

Services and Programs

Adult program materials
Annual Continental Youth Conference (Con-Con)
"Beyond Categorical Thinking" Program
Children's program materials
Church musicians' information
Consultation and resources for congregational religious education
    programs
Consultation on scouting programs
Curriculum development for all ages
Family programming ideas
Grants and scholarships for religious education leaders
Intergenerational programming
Leadership development for youth and youth advisors
Leadership training for curricula
Loan Library of Unitarian Universalist curricula
Local Youth Group Program materials
Music resources
Placement network for career-oriented religious educators
REACH: The Religious Education Action Clearinghouse Resource
    Packet
Support for district-level youth events
Young Religious Unitarian Universalists (YRUU)
Worship resources

Department for Social Justice

The Department for Social Justice focuses on training, information sharing, networking, and advocacy work. The department's primary purpose is to provide training for ministers, seminarians, and members of local congregations who wish to lead social justice programs in their congregations. The department works with interreligious and secular advocacy organizations for effective impact; gathers and develops educational materials; and encourages the training, organization, and mobilization of local and district social action groups.

The Department for Social Justice also coordinates the Social Action Clearinghouse (SACH), a quarterly roundtable meeting of Unitarian Universalist Association offices, associates, and affiliates whose work involves social justice issues.

The Washington Office for Social Justice provides information and support for Unitarian Universalists who are lobbying on public policy issues. The director of the Washington Office also provides training in lobbying skills.

Services and Programs

Ethics and Action newsletter
GA Resolutions and Resources Handbook
Social justice workshops for congregations and Districts
Study guides for the General Assembly resolutions

The *World* Magazine   The *World* magazine, which reaches more than 100,000 Unitarian Universalist households, is a bimonthly denominational publication with feature articles on Unitarian Universalist's and religious news.

The District as a Resource for Congregations

The twenty-eight UUA district organizations provide direct and easily accessible services to congregations. Each of the districts is staffed by a religious professional, usually called a District Executive. All maintain a district office with administrative support. In addition to this paid staff, the volunteer district boards are charged with planning and communicating information about Unitarian Universalist Association and district programs that can assist congregations in a variety of ways.

Districts usually have committees devoted to religious education, extension and growth, social justice, and other areas. Many districts have teams of consultants who have been trained in conflict management, antiracism work, Safe Congregations, and other areas. Most importantly, the district staff can help direct congregations to the most appropriate and helpful resources the Association has available. Accessing these resources is as simple as a phone call to the district office.

The district executive offers free consultation to congregations on a wide variety of issues, from conflict management and crisis intervention to ministerial transitions and fundraising. The district executive represents the Association's professional staff at the local level. In addition to providing specific information, the district executive can sort out the various elements in congregations' requests and direct them to appropriate people on the Boston-based staff. She or he can help you get the information you need with the least complication and frustration.

Each district publishes a newsletter that is distributed to all congregations. Check with your church office, board president, or minister if you don't regularly see this valuable resource. This district newsletter contains information about upcoming district programs (from religious education to leadership schools) and notification of Unitarian Universalist Association training and educational programs in your district.

Some congregations feel that they are able to deal well with the issues that confront them, and as an association of congregations, we absolutely recognize the right of the individual congregation to manage its affairs and shape its life as a religious community. But it is important for congregations to know that they do not have to operate in a vacuum. Participation in district events can be a valuable source of information and support. So, if you have a question, call the district office.

District Offices

Ballou-Channing
325 W. Elm Street
Brockton, MA 02401
Office (508) 559-6650

Central Mass.\Conn. Valley
219 Overlook Drive
Greenwich, CT 06830
Office (203) 629-3545

Central Midwest
114 S. Marion Street
Oak Park, IL 60302
Office (708) 383-4344
FAX (708) 383-4366

Florida\Mid-South
116 So. Magnolia Avenue
Ocala, FL 34474
Office & FAX
(904) 622-5199

Joseph Priestley
730 Halstead Road
Wilmington, DE 19803
Office (302) 478-1018
FAX (302) 478-5948

Massachusetts Bay
110 Arlington Street
Boston, MA 02116
Office (617) 542-3231
FAX (617) 542-4201

Metro New York
3261 East Blvd.
Bethlehem, PA 18017
Office & FAX (610) 691-0949

Michigan\Ohio Valley
3163 Flushing Road, Suite 108
Flint, MI 48504
Office (810) 239-5815
FAX (810) 239-6539

Mountain Desert
1510 Glen Ayr Dr. #4
Lakewood, CO 80215
Office (303) 238-4051

New Hampshire\Vermont
41-A South State Street
Concord, NH 03301
Office (603) 228-8704

Northeast
227 Industrial Way
Portland, ME 04103
Office (207) 797-3246

Ohio-Meadville
611 Market, Suite #3
Akron, OH 44303
Office (216) 762-8860

Pacific Central
2441 LeConte Ave.
Berkeley, CA 94709
Office (510) 845-6233
FAX (510) 845-6273

Pacific Northwest
Mailing address: P.O. Box 289
Woodinville, WA 98072-0289
Shipping address:
17311 135th NE, #B400
Woodinville, WA 98072
Office (206) 481-6003
Fax (206) 481-6230

Pacific Southwest
12355 Moorpark Street
Studio City, CA 91604
Office (818) 769-5917

Prairie Star
122 W. Franklin Ave., Suite 303
Minneapolis, MN 55404
Office (612) 870-4823

St. Lawrence
695 Elmwood Avenue
Buffalo, NY 14222
Office (716) 882-0430
FAX (716) 882-6637

Southwest
6720 Brentwood Stair Rd.
Ft. Worth, TX 76112
Office (817) 446-0099
FAX (817) 446-1505

Thomas Jefferson\Mid-South
1534 North Decatur Road, NE
Atlanta, GA 30307
Office (404) 377-9275
FAX (404) 377-9203 (Kinkos)

Western Canada
9 Rowand Avenue
Winnipeg, MB R3J 2N4
CANADA
Office & FAX (204) 889-4746

Director for Congregational, District,
and Extension Services
25 Beacon Street
Boston, MA 02108-2800
Office (617) 742-2100, ext. 461
FAX (617) 523-4123

Reporting Membership Figures

Each year member congregations are required to report their legal membership to the Unitarian Universalist Association. Legal membership is defined as the total number of persons qualified to vote at legal meetings of the congregation.

This figure is used in several ways. It is part of the basis for determining the congregation's Fair Share to the Unitarian Universalist Association Annual Program Fund (see the section on the Annual Program Fund within this chapter). Aggregated with data from other congregations in each district, this figure is part of the basis for allocating grants from the Unitarian Universalist Association to each district. Aggregated with data from all member congregations, it is used to measure overall size and membership trends in the denomination. This figure is also published in the annual UUA Directory and is an important component in describing a congregation.

It is contrary to the spirit in which this reported membership figure is used to include persons who were at one time active members but currently have no intention to participate in the congregation's activities or to support it financially, nor any desire to remain members.

However, some congregations have no bylaw provision for removing persons from membership. This creates a dilemma in reporting membership figures if legal membership in that congregation includes anyone who has signed the membership list, whether they are currently present, active, or interested.

For the purpose of reporting membership to the Unitarian Universalist Association, it is recommended that you include persons who have signed the membership list and meet any one of the following three conditions, as well as can be determined by a reasonable effort:

1. The person has participated in an activity of the congregation in the past year.

2. The person has made a recorded financial contribution since the beginning of the previous fiscal year.

3. The person expresses verbally or in writing a desire to remain a member.

The legal definition of membership used by any member congregation need not be affected by following these recommendations.

A congregation's membership committee may take responsibility for determining a current membership figure to report to the Association. During a regular meeting, committee members may informally determine which members of the congregation meet the first condition listed above by going through the membership list and sharing information about known participation.

When in doubt about a member's current participation, the committee may check with the congregation's bookkeeper to see if that member has made a recorded financial contribution since the beginning of the previous fiscal year, thus meeting the second condition.

When in doubt about a member's participation, actively or financially, the committee may telephone or write the member as suggested in the third condition listed above. To avoid the implication of checking up on, or wishing to drop someone, the person telephoning may begin the conversation by saying something like: "I'm on the membership committee, and we're doing our annual membership review. We haven't seen you around lately and thought we'd give you a call to see how things are with you. Do you want us to keep you on the active list?"

Such a call may provide information about life changes the member has not had a chance to share and it may strengthen ties with the congregation. It may elicit information about unmet needs or suggestions of various kinds, which can improve the congregation's program. It will also identify those who no longer wish to remain members. If there is an upcoming congregational event, the caller can issue a special invitation that may get marginal members back into active participation.

Instead of telephoning, the committee may write brief notes along the lines suggested for the telephone call above. It's wise in that case to state clearly, "We'd hate to lose anyone, but we do need to keep our membership list current, so please let us hear from you by (date) if you want to stay on the active list." Include a stamped return postcard or a telephone number to call, to make it as quick and convenient as possible for the individual to respond. The note could include a special invitation to an event if appropriate.

The Unitarian Universalist Association Directory

As a service to its member congregations, the Unitarian Universalist Association publishes an annual directory that contains general information on Unitarian Universalist congregations, ministers, and related organizations. The UUA Directory includes congregation addresses and telephone numbers, when a minister was ordained and the place of his or her current settlement, the certified membership of each congregation, the history and purpose of affiliated organizations, and more.

The UUA Directory is published annually in September and one free copy is mailed to each congregation. Additional copies of the directory can be purchased while supplies last, from the UUA Bookstore, 25 Beacon Street, Boston, MA 02108.

Congregational information for the directory is compiled from a questionnaire that is mailed each year on November 15. This questionnaire is an official document that must be completed, signed, and returned by February 1. Information from this questionnaire is used to:

- Update congregational and ministerial information published in the directory
- Certify each congregation for General Assembly and determine the number of delegates congregations may send to vote on Association business
- Determine each congregation's Fair Share contribution to the Annual Program Fund.

The return date of the questionnaire is specified in the Unitarian Universalist Association Bylaws, which mandates that all Unitarian Universalist congregations must certify for General Assembly by February 1. If a congregation does not return its questionnaire on time, its listing in the directory will not be updated, it will not be able to send delegates to General Assembly, and its Fair Share contributions will not be accurately calculated.

Production of the UUA Directory is carried out by various departments:

- Overall production is coordinated by the Public Relations, Marketing, and Information Office.
- Congregational information (addresses, congregational staff members) is maintained by the Department of Computer Services.
- Ministerial information (personal biographies, credentials, and fellowship) is maintained by the Department of Ministry.
- Certification for General Assembly is determined by the General Assembly Office.
- Affiliation with the Unitarian Universalist Association and congregational status are determined by the Department for Congre-

gational, District, and Extension Services.

* Fair share contributions are determined by the Annual Program Fund Office.

The Annual Program Fund

Significant annual financial support for the programs and services offered by the Unitarian Universalist Association comes directly from member congregations. Congregational contributions to the Annual Program Fund (APF) provide thirty-seven percent of the association's operating budget. The Friends of the UUA program raises additional monies from individual Unitarian Universalists. Together, donations to APF and Friends fund forty-five percent of the annual budget of the Association.

The director and the director's assistant of the Annual Program Fund Office work with a network of volunteers, many of whom are appointed by the UUA board of trustees. Together they manage the program and encourage congregations to give their Fair Share to the Annual Program Fund. Fair Share is a *per capita* dollar amount based on each congregation's certified membership, the number of members reported for General Assembly certification (ability to vote on Association business).

The Unitarian Universalist Association board of trustees determines each year's Fair Share assessment for member congregations and hence the overall APF Fiscal Year Goal. The board is guided by the bylaws of the Association and may not set a new goal in excess of seven percent of the actual APF contributions in the previous year.

District Goals and Grants

The Unitarian Universalist Association redistributes a portion of the Annual Program Fund contributions to all districts. The annual grant awarded to each district, made in the fall of each year, is based on the percentage (up to and exceeding 100 percent) of the Fair Share achieved by the congregations in each district in the previous fiscal year. The total of the Fair Share assessments of all congregations in a given district is that district's Fair Share Goal.

In 1993, the Unitarian Universalist Association board voted to change the district grants formula and designated the following four grants for which districts may qualify:

Basic Grant: One-tenth of the percent of the district Fair Share achieved (not to exceed 100 percent) multiplied by the district's gross contribution to the Annual Program Fund.

Example

District A's Fair Share goal = $145,000.
Gross contribution = $125,000.
District A achieved 86.2% of Fair Share.
The basic grant percentage = 8.62% (one-tenth of 86.2%).
District A's basic grant = $10,766 ($125,000 x 8.62%).

Incentive Grant: Two percent of the district's gross contribution, for a gross increase of ten percent or more over the previous year's gross contribution.

Example

District A's gross contribution = $125,000.
Previous year's gross = $110,000.
Giving increased by 13%. District A is eligible for an Incentive Grant.
Incentive Grant = $2,500 ($125,000 x 2%).

Fair Share Congregation Grants: One of two grants is made to districts based on the percentage of congregations that contributed their Fair Share in the previous year. When seventy-five percent of the congregations in a district are Fair Share contributors, the district will receive a special grant of $1,000; when ninety percent reach Fair Share, the grant is $5,000.

Example

District A has 100 congregations. If seventy-five congregations are Fair Share contributors, then District A will get $1,000; if ninety make Fair Share, the District gets $5,000.

Transition Adjustment Grants: A "transition adjustment" will be given to districts that *maintain or improve* their percentage of district Fair Share relative to their achievement in the fiscal year ending June 30, 1993. The district will receive no less than the sum of the Basic and Incentive Grant amounts awarded from FY 1993. (The Fair Share Congregation Grant is *not* included in the adjustment calculation.)

These adjustment grants will cease after grants are made in fall 1996, based on contributions made to the Annual Program Fund before June 30, 1996.

The APF Continental Committee

The Annual Program Fund Continental Committee includes the director of the Annual Program Fund, a general chair, five regional chairs, four representative liaisons (one each from the Unitarian Universalist Ministers Association, the Unitarian Universalist Association board, Canadian congregations and the District Presidents' Association), and representatives from every district of the Association. The APF Continental Committee meets yearly. Together, it plans and conducts:

- a Fair Share congregation campaign
- visits to individual congregations
- reports of congregations' projected APF contributions
- educational resources and advice about financial matters provided to inquiring congregations.

Questions about your congregation's Fair Share assessment may be directed to the UUA Annual Program Fund, 25 Beacon St., Boston, MA 02108-2800. Telephone (617) 742-2100, ext. 512.

General Assembly

General Assembly (GA) is the six-day annual meeting of the Unitarian Universalist Association, attended by members and religious leaders of all congregations. It is held every June, usually in the continental United States with a location in Canada about every ten years. The purpose of GA is to conduct the business of the Unitarian Universalist Associations, to gather together as Unitarian Universalists, and to share information and experiences through hundreds of programs, workshops, and exhibits. In short, it is an action-packed convention that generates a lot of energy and leaves individuals excited about Unitarian Universalism.

What is General Assembly like?

Everyone who attends GA will give a different description of the experience, as essentially everyone creates his or her own GA. A typical day begins with a worship service, followed by a plenary session, which almost everyone attends. The afternoon and evening are usually devoted to programming, during which up to twenty-five concurrent events may be offered. These include additional worship services, lectures, panel discussions, how-to workshops, hearings on the work of Unitarian Universalist Association committees, annual meetings of Unitarian Universalist related organizations, GA choir rehearsals, and entertainment.

While all this is going on, the display area is open; participants can browse through the UUA Bookstore and Beacon Press book displays, meet Unitarian Universalist Association staff members at their department-sponsored booths, and contact special interest groups. A few large, traditional events are held during the week, such as the Ware Lecture with well-known speakers who are usually not Unitarian Universalists; the Service of the Living Tradition, in which the Unitarian Universalist ministry is honored; the GA choir concert by our annual "pick-up" choir; the Awards Breakfast; and, frequently, an informal banquet featuring regional specialty food and entertainment.

What is a typical site?   General Assembly is usually held in a moderate-size city and may be anywhere in the United States or Canada. The Unitarian Universalist Association board of trustees officially names the site, based on the recommendation of the GA Planning Committee and the GA administrator. A city with a convention center and several nearby hotels is usually selected. Most of the people who attend GA choose one of these hotels located near the major meeting rooms. A range of hotel styles and prices are always available and a car is not needed. Meals are on your own. Exploring local restaurants can be a benefit to the GA experience.

What official business is done?   The business of the Association is conducted by delegates from certified Unitarian Universalist congregations. All UU congregations that have made a financial contribution to the Association the previous fiscal year are given the opportunity to report to the Unitarian Universalist Association and thus become certified for the upcoming GA. About ninety percent of congregations are certified every year and allotted delegates based on their membership.

A plenary or business session at GA is a democratic meeting of more than 1,200 delegates, who may discuss and vote on all business items. Discussion can be very lively and the lines at microphones can get long, but thanks to the skill of the moderator, the cooperation of delegates, and Robert's Rules of Order, chaos is avoided.

General resolutions make a statement of social concern or principle. Individual congregations or districts are invited to submit a resolution every year to the Commission on General Resolutions. This standing committee is elected by delegates to GA and writes up to ten resolutions for the parish poll. Congregations vote, using the parish poll ballot, to select three general resolutions for the GA final agenda. A vote is taken on these general resolutions for one year of study by congregations and districts. After the study year, feedback and proposed amendments, these general resolutions appear on the agenda a second time, for a final vote as Unitarian Universalist Association policy.

Business resolutions directly involve the administration and structure of the Association. They are submitted by congregations, districts, or petitions signed by individual Unitarian Universalists and must appear on the parish poll for a vote by congregations on whether to admit them to the GA final agenda. The topics for business resolutions are many and varied.

In addition to resolutions, the assembly may amend the Unitarian Universalist Association Bylaws. Lest this sound dry and dull, consider that some of the liveliest discussions and arguments at GA can occur over proposed bylaw changes. Proposed amendments can cause Unitarian Universalists to think deeply about their faith and principles when issues such as the Unitarian Universalist Principles and Purposes or governance of the Unitarian Universalist Association are on the floor.

In addition to voting on individual business items, the assembly hears reports from officers and may be informed or entertained by special programs. The sessions are open to everyone registered for GA. Observers may meet between sessions with delegates from their congregations to discuss or influence their votes.

An election for members of Unitarian Universalist Association standing committees and trustees at large is held in odd-numbered years. Every four years, a president and moderator are elected. Voters must be delegates from Unitarian Universalist certified congregations, and absentee votes are accepted.

Who is responsible for General Assembly?

Every UU has the opportunity to contribute to the planning of GA. Individuals, congregations, and districts determine exactly which resolutions and bylaw changes appear on the final agenda. Organizations that are affiliated with the UUA, districts, and departmental staff actually plan and are fully responsible for more than 300 programming events and exhibits, which are open to everyone who attends GA. The Planning Committee, elected by delegates, sets the stage for the entire event and oversees a few of the major presentations. The staff members of the GA Office coordinate the pieces of this large and complex puzzle, making sure the meeting space is assigned and the program is produced.

Resources

For further details on General Assembly, call the UUA General Assembly Office at (617) 742-2100, ext. 209. The GA staff is available to answer your questions, tell you about future GA sites and dates, or send easy-to-use printed material on GA or guides to submitting business items. Information and registration materials may be found in the spring issues of the *World*.

Your Congregation's Bylaws and Congregational Structure

The way in which your congregation is structured should support and enhance its functioning. An effective structure is open and flexible, encourages the active involvement of members, helps people to get things done, enables people to understand and relate easily to their institution, and is congruent with the values cherished by the members.

The bylaws of your congregation state the formal structure and provide for maintaining and changing it. It addition to their usefulness as guidelines for membership, bylaws relate your congregation to the Unitarian Universalist Association and the laws governing nonprofit institutions in your state or province.

Effective bylaws are brief and clearly stated, cover only the "bare bones" of the organizational structure, are reasonably easy to amend, comply with the laws to which your group is subject, and are readily accessible to all members.

In designing or evaluating your organizational structure and writing or revising your bylaws, you need to consider membership and membership responsibilities, leadership and leadership responsibilities, decision-making procedures, and provisions for continuity and change.

Some examples of basic bylaws follow on the next pages. Adapt them to fit your congregation, needs, and ways of doing things. Various alternatives, consequences, and considerations are included parenthetically in each section.

If you have specific questions related to bylaws, write to the Department for Congregational, District, and Extension Services, 25 Beacon Street, Boston, MA 02108. Packets of sample bylaws from several congregations are available on request.

Criteria for Bylaws

Construction of the Bylaws

Clarity: Stating the bylaws in clear and unambiguous language, meeting the test of indisputibility of language, and understandable to the membership at large.

Brevity: Providing *only* the basic rules of the congregation, and only those basic rules considered important enough to protect from easy change by requiring previous notice and two-thirds vote, and doing so in succinct language.

Lawfulness: Conformity not only with the state and provincial law on religious corporations and associations, but with the requirements for member congregations of the UUA, and with the requirements of the congregation's parliamentary authority.

Effective Implementation: Designating a body (e.g., the Board) to be responsible for continuous monitoring of the state for implementation of the bylaws, and taking steps on discovering problems.

Periodic Thorough Reviews: Designating a body (e.g., the Board) to be responsible for a thorough review at stated intervals, so that the bylaws will be adapted to changing conditions and perceptions. Five years is not an inappropriate period.

Ready Amendability: While protecting the bylaws by requiring previous notice and a two-thirds vote in order to change them, the bylaws should also be easily amendable.

Allocation of Authority Within the Congregation

Congregational Polity: An unambiguous statement of the locus of the final authority of the congregation, vested in its legal membership.

Authority to Direct: An unrestricted authority of the congregation, at such times as it seems appropriate, to direct the various constituent organizations and the personnel of the congregation.

Authority to Amend: The authority of the congregation to amend or rescind decisions of the constituent organizations, except when they are in the nature of a contract, or when something has been done that can't be undone.

Exclusive Authority: Designating the areas in which the congregation has the exclusive authority to reach final decisions, including those stipulated by state or provincial law, typically inclusive of adopting and amending bylaws; adopting (except for any limits of authority to adjust the budget given the board) amendments to the budget; electing and removing officers and trustees; and calling and removing the ministers.

Empowering the Board: Providing the board with ample power, so that, even though subject to the direction of the congregation, it has general supervision of the affairs of the society.

Empowering Other Organizations: Providing ample mandates to any congregation council and committees, enabling each of them to function effectively in their particular domain.

Autonomy: Providing for basic independence and autonomy.

Participation in the Decision-Making Processes for the Congregation

Majority Rule: Providing for majority rule for all but a limited and named number of decision areas (such as amending bylaws, calling ministers, and suspending rules of order) and precluding proxy vote.

Access of Agendas: Providing reasonable ready access to the agendas of the key organizational units of the congregation (congregation, board, council) through mailings sent out a week before meetings.

Sufficient Meetings: Scheduling sufficient regular meetings to inform and receive input from the congregation.

Adopting Parliamentary Authority: Adopting such an authority not only for congregational meetings but for the congregation as a whole, and stating that the rules shall govern the congregation except where they are inconsistent with the bylaws.

Participation Through Adequate Access to Information

Regular Reporting: Providing for reporting by both the board and the minister at all regular meetings of the congregation concerning all major decisions taken since the last regular meeting.

Informative Reporting: Providing that when reports include recommendations, or raise issues of potential disagreement, they shall include the advantages and disadvantages of alternative courses of action. This criterion is a universally accepted requisite for rational decision making in all of the generally accepted theories and studies of the decision-making process.

Adequate Consideration of Budget Decisions: Providing sufficient meeting time, participation in preparations, and other steps for the congregation to play an effective role in the many decisions which go into the adoption of an annual budget, and provision of an annual audited statement of the finances of the society. The first part of this criterion may well require two or more congregational meetings in a society of some size.

Open Meetings: Providing that all meetings of the Board, Council, and committees shall be open to all voting members of the society as observers when they are not members, except in the limited cases when these bodies go into executive session. In the latter case, no final or formal actions may be taken while the body is in executive session.

Sufficient Notice: Providing for notices an adequate time before the meetings they apply to, typically ten days to two weeks.

Access to Written Records: Providing on request individual copies of bylaws and the congregation's directory of membership, and, in addition, reasonable access to the rules and records of the congregation.

A "Bill of Rights": To facilitate members' appreciation of their basic rights in the congregation, these rights should be grouped together in the bylaws, similar to the Bill of Rights in governmental constitutions.

Participation in Election and Appointment Processes

Highest Offices All Elective: Providing for the highest offices of the congregation—typically, all officers and trustees, and some other positions, such as the Nominating Committees—to be filled by elections.

Open Nominations: Providing for openness to the candidacy of any voting member, including an invitation to the membership to contribute suggestions to the Nominating Committee; an expressed preference for multiple nominations; and either a requirement for the number of people needed for a valid petition, or allowing nominations from the floor.

Majority Rule Without Exceptions: Providing for run-off elections any time that no candidate receives a majority, or if the election is to fill several positions simultaneously (as for trustees), run-off elections until all those selected have been selected by majorities.

Open Appointments: Providing specific and hence generally known processes for making appointments, including timely arrangements for voting members to make suggestions to those doing appointing.

Rotation of All Offices: Providing a rotation for *all* offices (elective and appointed) with: a) maximum terms for each officer and, b) maximum successive terms before the person must step aside for a stated interval. Recommended maximum terms are three years, maximum periods are six years, rotation intervals are two years. These maximums may be adjusted downward in particular cases.

Membership
Qualifications

Qualifications Based on a Member's Activities: If the qualifications for voting membership require a financial contribution, the amount should be either "any" financial contribution, or one of a modest size, so as not to discriminate by economic status. If a requirement relates to length of membership, it should be of a modest length, not to discriminate against the more mobile members of our society.

Non-Discrimination Generally: Explicitly providing that there shall be no discrimination in either membership or voting membership on the basis of race, sex, color, or national origin.

Freedom of Belief: Explicitly providing that there shall be no creedal test, express or implied, for membership or voting membership.

Suggested Basic Bylaws

These basic bylaws are intended for use by newly organized and smaller congregations who need to review their bylaws at certain developmental stages (e.g., the calling of their first minister). Every congregation should review the criteria for bylaws listed in the previous section. For congregations that need more than these basic bylaws or guidance on a particular article of their bylaws, *A Sample Bylaw Packet* and referral to the bylaws of other congregations similar in size and organization to yours are available from the UUA Department for District, Congregational, and Extension Services or your district office.

Article I.
Name

The name of this religious congregation shall be
_____ *(for example, the Unitarian Universalist Congregation of city, town, or county)*

Article II.
Purpose

The purpose or covenant should be inserted here. This article establishes the group as a religious organization. The wording should be determined by the group as a whole. For example,

The purpose of this congregation is to further individual freedom of belief, discipleship to advancing truth, the democratic process in human relations, brotherhood and sisterhood undivided by nation, race or creed, and allegiance to the cause of a united world community.

or

Love is the spirit of this church and service is its law. This is our great covenant to dwell together in peace, to seek truth in love, and to help one another.

or

We unite in the free quest of high values in religion and in life.

or

In the discipline of truth, irrespective of its source and in the spirit of universal love, undivided by nation, race or creed, we unite to strengthen our convictions in the value and need for liberal religion, and through the strength of unity, to give such expression to these convictions as the congregation decides.

or

The purpose of this church is to foster liberal religious living through worship, study, service, and fellowship.

or

In the love of truth and in the spirit of Jesus, we unite for the worship of God and the service of humanity. Relying upon reason as our guide, and upon freedom as our method, we seek to grow in understanding ourselves and our world, to promote and serve the Universal human family.

or

We are a fellowship of religious seekers united in love of truth and the spirit of Jesus. We are bound together in religious congregation worship of that God which is eternal in every place and time, and we are bound together through service to humanity.

or

The purpose of this congregation shall be the enjoyment and practice of religion founded upon devotion to individual freedom of belief.

**Article III.
Membership**

Any person may become a voting member of this congregation who is in sympathy with its purpose and program, has signed the membership book, and makes an annual contribution of record. It is generally understood that all members should have an understanding of history and the current situation of the Unitarian Universalist Association. It is especially understood that membership is open to all qualified persons regardless of race, color, sex, affectional or sexual orientation, age, or national origin.

Withdrawal of membership may be made by written request to the secretary of the congregation. Such a notice shall be transmitted to the Board of Trustees.

Many bylaws state a minimum age for membership. Some differentiate general membership from voting membership, requiring a voting member to be 18 or older and to have made a financial contribution of record within the past year. Some specify the amount of the minimum contribution ($15 or $30, for example). Some provide for a waiting period between becoming a member and having the voting privilege, typically thirty or ninety days. Voting membership in nonprofit institutions may be defined by state or provincial law, with which bylaws should be in compliance. In some cases state or provincial laws may state that any member of an organization may be an officer. This could be an important consideration in establishing the lower age limits for membership.

In some congregations, bylaws define a procedure for removing a person from membership through that person's written request or the recommendation of the governing board or membership committee when the member has died, moved away, or cannot be located. Bylaws may also provide for official acceptance of new members by formal vote of the governing board and/or the congregation.

**Article IV.
Denominational
Affiliation**

This congregation shall be a member of the Unitarian Universalist Association [Canadian Unitarian Council] and of the _____ District. It is the intention of this congregation to make annual financial contributions equal to its full Fair Share as determined by the Association and the district.

**Article V.
Meetings**

The dates of regular nonbusiness meetings of the congregation shall be determined by the congregation itself, or by any person or persons designated by it. The annual business meeting shall be held each year in the month of _____ at such time and place as shall be fixed by the Executive Committee [Standing Committee or Board of Trustees]. Special business meetings may be called at the written request of any members. The business to be transacted at all meetings shall be set forth in the notice of the meeting, which shall be sent to all members by mail fifteen [15] days before the meeting. Twenty [20] percent of the membership (or _____ members) shall constitute a quorum.

Some bylaws require a larger quorum when certain important decisions are to be made; for example, the purchase or sale of property, the calling or dismissal of a minister. In such cases, a quorum may be defined as forty percent of the voting membership.

Bylaws may also specify when absentee ballots may be used and how they are to be handled.

In some cases, the agenda of the annual meeting is specified in bylaws to safeguard the right of the congregation to hear reports of officers and staff, to elect new officers and nominate committee members, and to adopt an annual budget.

Article VI.
Officers and
Board of Trustees

At each annual meeting officers of the board of trustees shall be chosen, all of whom shall hold their offices for one year and until their successors have been elected and qualified, and who shall perform the duties usually pertaining to these offices. The board of trustees shall be ___ in number. The board of trustees shall have general charge of the property of the congregation and the conduct of all its business affairs and the control of its administration, including the appointment of such committees as it may deem necessary. It may fill vacancies with persons who shall serve until the next annual meeting.

A nominating committee of three members who shall not be members of the Executive Committee shall also be chosen at the annual meeting.

All officers shall be voting members of the congregation.

The decision about how leadership responsibility shall be vested will depend on the congregation's size. The organizational structure should not be unwieldy for the size of the congregation to maintain. In the interest of continuity, the executive committee or board of trustees may be established on a rotating basis with one or more members elected for one year, the same numbers for two years, and the same number for the following years. After the initial election, all officers may be elected for full terms so that only a portion of the executive committee or board of trustees is replaced each year.

The nominating committee is almost always included in bylaws to provide for the continuation of the democratic process in the selection of leadership. Other standing committees may also be defined as desired; however, greater flexibility is allowed when bylaws do not require certain committees.

Basic duties of officers and trustees may be spelled out in bylaws; however, by no means should the entire charge to various committees by included in bylaws. It is far more effective to have such detailed guidelines drawn up separately and reviewed regularly as needs and personnel change.

As a general rule, leaders who are elected by the membership are specified in bylaws, whereas those who are appointed need not be specified. A separate article on committees may follow the article on officers.

Article VII.
The Minister(s)

Once a congregation reaches the point of calling a minister, it is helpful to include in the bylaws an article dealing with the nature of the relationship between congregation and minister, procedures for calling a minister and for terminating a relationship. A sample of such an article follows:

The minister(s) shall be responsible for the conduct of worship within the congregation and the congregation's spiritual interests and affairs. The minister(s) shall have freedom of the pulpit as well as freedom to express his or her opinion outside the pulpit.

Note that such a statement is brief and general. By no means should a full job description be included in bylaws.

The minister(s) shall be an ex-officio *member of the governing board and of such committees as the board shall designate.*

The minister(s) shall be called upon recommendation of the Ministerial Search Committee by a four-fifths majority of qualified members of the congregation present at any meeting legally called for the purpose, quorum for such a meeting is to be constituted by forty percent of the voting members rather than twenty percent of the voting members as called for in Article V.

The minister(s) may be dismissed by a majority vote of the qualified members of the church present at any meeting legally called for the purpose, the quorum for such a meeting to be constituted by forty percent of the voting members rather than twenty percent of the voting members as called for in Article V.

In the event of a minister's dismissal, his or her salary and allowance shall be continued for three months after date of dismissal. Should a minister offer his or her resignation, three month's notice must be given at the time the resignation is made except as the governing board may allow an interval of less time.

Some bylaws specify that the minister(s) must be in fellowship with the Unitarian Universalist Association, as determined by the Ministerial Fellowship Committee. If additional professional staff persons are employed by the congregation, bylaws should cover terms of their selection and dismissal as well.

The article on the minister(s) or the article committees should provide for the selection of a ministerial search committee, usually composed of seven members who are elected at a special congregational meeting called for that purpose, from a slate prepared by the nominating committee, or half elected. The most important consideration in selecting a Ministerial Search Committee is that it have the full confidence of the congregation.

A minister(s) and congregation often agree to establish a Committee(s) on Ministry and may wish to define such a committee in its bylaws.

Article VIII.
Fiscal Year

The fiscal year shall end _____ .

How the fiscal year is defined varies from one congregation to another. The Unitarian Universalist Association fiscal year ends June 30; some convenience is gained when local congregations choose the same arrangement. For a discussion on this see the section, "The Congregational Calendar," in Chapter 5 of this *Handbook*.

Article IX.
Dissolution

In the case of dissolution of the congregation, all of its property, real and personal, after paying all just claim upon it, shall be conveyed to and vested in the Unitarian Universalist Association or its legal successor, or to any Unitarian Universalist related organization, and the board of trustees of the congregation shall perform all actions necessary to effectuate such conveyance.

Article X.
Amendments

These bylaws, so far as allowed by law, may be amended or replaced at any meeting of the congregation by a two-thirds vote of those present and voting. Notice of any proposed change shall be contained in the notice of the meeting.

Two

The Guiding Vision and Mission of a Congregation

Clarifying Your Congregation's Vision and Mission

A biblical writer asserts "Without a vision, a people perish." Indeed, a sustaining and inspiring dimension of a congregation's life is its ability to have a vision of its future. What makes vision more than an idea is the way that vision informs and compels a congregation toward its future.

A vision needs to be empowering, more than the cherished possession of a few—it needs to be a shared vision. A shared vision enables a congregation to move from the status quo towards an overarching goal. A shared vision can create new ways of thinking and acting. A vision statement should be broad enough to provide growing room for a congregation yet be continually renewed as a congregation develops and accepts new challenges. We often limit our vision to what we can conceive as possible or to bring it to the level of the current reality of a congregation. Yet a vision, to be fully empowering, needs to allow us to take a long-term view of ourselves as a congregation.

More than the actual document of a shared vision statement is the process a congregation engages in to create this vision. Peter Senge, author of *The Fifth Discipline: The Art and Practice of a Learning Organization*, writes, "When a group of people come to share a vision for an organization [a congregation], each person sees their own picture of the organization at its best. Each shares responsibility for the whole, not just for their piece." Vision is what takes us beyond the particular dimension of congregational life that is our domain of responsibility to understand how the dimensions and activities of a congregation fit into the larger, overarching aim for the future of a congregation.

An exercise for developing a shared vision statement is presented at the end of this section.

Developing a Mission Statement

A vision statement and a mission statement are distinct but interrelated documents for charting a congregation's future and current plans. A congregation's vision statement gives expression to what it ultimately wants to create as a congregation. It is what it aspires to be as the result of its efforts in ministry, programming, and outreach. To move from having a vision to implementing that vision you need to clarify your mission. Consequently, a mission statement should be informed by the vision of the congregation. A covenant statement is an articulation of the values and qualities that you want to promote in your congregation to enhance and support you in living out your mission.

A mission statement focuses a congregation more explicitly on what it wants to mean to the community where it exists. It orients you in specific ways toward your commmunity and coordinates the various activities and programs toward broader intentions and aims. A congregation often has a mission, whether or not it has been articulated. To engage a congregation in articulating its mission is eliciting the sense of meaning that comes from having a focus, a passion, and a commitment. Generally speaking, a mission statement should answer the following questions:

- If this is our vision, where does this lead us in mission?
- In what ways does our vision lead us in service toward others in the broader community?

Exercises to help you develop your mission statement are included in this section. Sample mission statements are included to give you an idea of how other congregations have articulated their mission. You may want to contact your district office before embarking on a mission-covenant process, because it can assist you with a consultant and other resources.

Criteria for a Useful Mission Statement

John Carver, author of *Boards That Make a Difference*, has developed a checklist to evaluate a mission statement. These criteria are translated here in language that might be useful for your congregation.

1. Does your mission statement address what difference your congregation makes for the broader community or does it merely describe what your congregation is doing?

2. Does the language in your mission statement allow your congregation to accomplish goals rather than state what it intends to do (e.g., using words like "tries" or "seeks")?

3. Is your congregation's mission statement too long? Can it be easily recalled or its essence easily communicated?

4. Is your mission statement too broad or too narrow? (Brainstorm the effects that your congregation might have on the world, then rank order these effects and discuss their relative merit.)

5. How does your congregation's mission statement relate to and differentiate your congregation from other faith communities and Unitarian Universalist congregations?

Developing a Shared Vision Statement

When your congregation decides to engage in the process of developing a shared vision statement and a mission statement, you should recognize that you are beginning a process that has implications for all that you do as a congregation. The goal is not just to have a statement that you can publish in your congregation's membership brochure or order of service cover. The goal is to engage your congregation in a process that clarifies the ultimate and guiding purposes of the congregation. Once your vision and mission statements are articulated, you can move toward a disciplined process of reviewing how to implement these statements in all that you do as a congregation.

Time must be provided for each of these exercises if they are to become the guiding statements for your congregational life. Take the time to prepare your congregation and outline a series of events in the congregation's worship and the committee and program calendar that will enable your congregation to engage fully in this essential process.

Exercises for Creating Shared Vision

Guided Imagery for a Group

Invite participants to relax and use their imaginations to dream of a compelling but practical future for your congregation in ten years. Provide file cards or paper for them to jot down the images, thoughts, feelings, and words that occur to them during the exercise.

Step 1.
Here are some sample words for the guided imagery:

"We all have a vision for our congregation. It informs some of our involvement and continued connection to our life together. This vision, though often unarticulated, exists like a moving picture in our imagination. Allow that moving picture of our congregation to become more explicit. As we engage in this process, relax and allow the vision to appear to you, rather than deliberately trying to create it. As images, thoughts, feelings, or words occur to you, jot them down on the paper, remembering to stay with these images, thoughts, or feelings long enough. Then, even with your eyes half opened, write down the essence of your imaginary experience. Don't interrupt the flow of your imagination to write. Consider that you are taking still frames from the moving picture of your vision and just jot down phrases that describe these still frames.

"In your imagination approach a compelling but practical vision of our congregation ten years from now. What is the feeling of anticipation you experience in yourself as you do this? Imagine yourself approaching the neighborhood or the community where our congregation is located. What do you notice about this surrounding neighborhood or community? Who are the people that live here? What are their needs and desires?

"Approach now in your imagination the actual location where our congregation meets. What does the landscape look like, how does the facility appear on the outside? What does it say about the congregation?

"Now open the doors to the meeting place. What do you notice? Who is gathered there? In what activities are these people engaged? What is the atmosphere like? How does it feel to be there? What are the aesthetics of the place? Tour the building and visit the various activities that are occurring in the building.

"In your imagination allow yourself to get a sense of the worship, education, outreach, and fellowship of this congregation . . . as you deeply hope and imagine it to be ten years from now.

"Stay with whatever images, thoughts, feelings, and events occur to you. Jot down just the essence of what presents itself to you. Spend the next five minutes in this exercise of the imagination."

Step 2
Invite participants to meet with two other people. In groups of three, each person takes five minutes to share their vision with the others. This is not a time to deliberate or discuss. It is a time to listen for some of the common and unique themes that emerge. At the end of fifteen minutes, give the group five minutes to list on a piece of newsprint some of the common and unique themes that they heard among the members of their group.

Step 3
Get back together as a whole group. Invite each small group to share the common themes that they heard in their small group.

Step 4
Solicit some of the common and unique themes for the whole group. Reflect together on this information. Write these on newsprint under the heading "Common Themes" and another sheet, "Unique Themes."

Step 5
Invite a few participants or a task group to take these sheets of com-

mon and unique themes and draft a vision statement that can be circulated among the congregation for thought and reflection before refinement.

Individual Reflection

This vision exercise, proposed by Gustave Rath and Norman Shawchuck, can be incorporated into the worship or spiritual practice of a congregation for approximately a month. At the end of this month, the congregation is then invited to meet in small groups to share some of the common themes of their collective vision.

Step 1

Invite members of your congregation to spend at least a month in individual meditation or reflection on this question: "What is your vision of our congregation ten years from now?"

You might suggest that they spend two brief periods alone each week (e.g., fifteen minutes each time) in addition to a brief period of reflection together in a worship service each Sunday during that month. Toward the end of this period of reflection, they should begin to make a visual representation of their vision and/or a one-page narrative of the images, ideas, and feelings that occurred to them.

Step 2

Hold a congregational meeting in which members in groups of three to five present their vision to each other. Each group should record their "Common Themes" and "Unique Themes" on sheets of newsprint, then present these themes to the whole group.

Step 3

Invite a few of the participants or a task group to take these sheets of "Common Themes" and "Unique Themes" and draft a vision statement that can be circulated among the congregation for further thought and reflection before refinement.

Developing a Mission-Covenant Statement

The process for creating a mission-covenant statement in your congregation should follow the vision statement process. In fact, a mission-covenant statement is a further step toward implementing your vision statement. A mission statement articulates how a congregation should focus its programs and activities in relationship to the surrounding community to fulfill its vision. Mission focuses you "in mission" in the community that your congregation exists. According to Tom Chulak and John Morgan in *Mission-Covenant*, your covenant statement refers to "the promises or commitments that people make to each other in the context of religious community."

Chulak and Morgan explain:

> "Given who we are and where we are, what should we do?"—is a succinct question for understanding mission-covenant as the basis of identity in religious community. There are three components to the question: First, who are we, what is our identity as a religious community? Second, what is the context in which our community is located: its members, its neighborhood, the wider world? And third, what must we do, what is our mission?

Consequently, a mission statement should relate a congregation to the community context by establishing its sense of religious identity, relating it to the needs of those whom it aims to serve and articulating "what must we do" to live out that mission in a particular community.

A covenant statement gives expression to your identity, in particular the qualities that will sustain you in your life together and the "promise" you make to each other in religious community. Covenant is the commitment you make to each other. It is your response to the question: "What are the qualities we want in our life and work together?"

Mission and covenant are very much interrelated dimensions of religious life and support each other. As Chulak and Morgan argue,

> Identity [covenant] is rooted in relationships with the religious community, of commitments people make to each other. Yet, without mission, without outreach and witness, the covenant may become closed. Mission takes the vague sense of fellowship and transforms it into action and wider purpose. On the other hand, a religious community with a clear mission but without covenant runs the risk of broken relationships internally, as factions in the community find no common bond.

An Example of a Process

One model for developing a mission-covenant has been used in a few congregations. There are four phases in the process:

Phase 1
Establish a mission-covenant committee or task force of people who feel a commitment to exploring a congregational mission-covenant and are willing to serve as facilitators. The committee should be representative of the congregation as a whole and be open to anyone. The minister(s) and religious educator of the congregation may be a member of a committee, but should not be its chair. In most cases, a committee chair should be elected.

Make sure that the committee's members and purposes are communicated to the whole congregation, through a special letter, articles in the newsletter, or during a special mission-covenant Sunday service. Make sure that the congregation understands the exploratory nature of the process and that decisions or statements will be made by the whole congregation.

Phase 2

The mission-covenant committee should spend time getting to know one another and planning.

The purpose of the first meeting is to provide background information and to give members of the committee an opportuntity to get to know each other. For example, at the first meeting, spend the first hour in the circle, allowing people an opportunity to discuss their own religious journeys and to present information on the mission-covenant statement process.

Between the first and second meetings of the committee, someone should gather the congregation's present covenant statement and covenants the congregation may have used in the past. These should be reviewed and discussed by the committee at the beginning of the second meeting.

At its second meeting, the committee should focus on the question: "Given who we are, and where we are, what should we do?" Someone should record these comments and provide a written summary at the next committee meeting.

At its third meeting, the committee should begin to address the question of what it wants to do with the congregation and how to proceed. One method is to think in terms of the basic questions on mission-covenant the committee hopes the entire congregation will address.

Phase 3

The mission-covenant committee should begin to carry out the plan for developing a mission-covenant statement in the congregation, which might incude:

- During Sunday services, focus on the process, with sermons and small discussion groups to interpret mission-covenant.

- During the week, schedule small group meetings to focus on the question or questions the committee selected. Committee members should serve as group facilitators and recorders.

When all the questions have been addressed, the committee should meet to share reports. The work of the committee is to identify areas of consensus among small groups.

A committee member should develop a first draft of the mission-covenant statement. All members of the committee should be given the opportunity to review it and make comments. This draft statement should be shared with the whole congregation as a working draft, through written or oral communication, allowing time for congregational review.

The committee takes the suggestions of the congregation and revises the mission-covenant statement. Reproduce this statement and share it with the congregation, with a deadline for receiving additional comments from them.

When all the comments have been received, prepare the final draft. Present this statement to the whole congregation, either as part of the annual meeting or any other special meeting according to the bylaws. Take a vote on the final statement.

If accepted, celebrate the mission-covenant during a special Sunday service. Make final copies of the statement available, and if possible, have a display of the materials developed during the process.

Phase 4
The committee should conclude its work by offering suggestions to the congregation, the board, and committees on ways in which the statement might be used in the life of the congregation: new member recruitment and orientation, public relations, religious education, and community outreach.

Additional Resources for Small Groups

Suggestions for small group work:

Small group pilgrimages. Schedule a session for small groups that enables people to listen to each other, especially about their religious pilgrimages. Allow each person in the group a chance to talk about his or her religious orientation, upbringing, and values. This should be an active listening process in which individuals listen carefully to each other.

Values clarification. Provide participants with index cards and ask them to write down their responses to the following: "Name a religious value that is important to you that is affirmed by this congregation." Go around the group and ask each person to name the value and its importance. Again, this should be a time for active listening rather than debate. When everyone has had a chance, look for common values, themes, and ideas. This session might close with a brief service, at the conclusion of which people would write their values on cards, place the cards in a common bowl or chalice, and have each value affirmed by the entire group.

Build a mission-covenant. Provide the opportunity to develop visual or written materials as a learning strategy. The results of such efforts can be displayed for others to see. Examples are included below.

- Make a "tree of values." Have people list their most important values on a sheet of paper or cardboard, and build a common tree from these.

- Place a mission-covenant bowl in the meetinghouse. Ask people to bring objects, thoughts, or symbols that express their values and place them in the bowl. Over time, collect the results and write them up for use in a special celebration.

- Make a banner or collage that represents the group's understanding of mission-covenant. Each group's banner can be brought together for a final celebration.

- Ask people to make a clay representation of what they mean by mission-covenant and share their models with the group.

- Enlist the aid of artists, poets, musicians, and others to give creative expression to the mission-covenant. Someone might write new words to a hymn, compose a song, or produce a painting. All of these can be used in the final service.

- Create a videotape of the mission-covenant, perhaps using comments from the small groups, songs, poems, etc. These can be shared with the congregation and retained for future use, such as orienting new members or recalling the process.

Developing the mission. Because the development of a mission statement is a new adventure for some congregations, a few suggestions are listed below. Although presented here as a distinct mission exercise, this should be considered part of a process, and a chance to focus more intentionally on the implication of the covenant for mission.

- Ask members of each small group to draw a picture of mission covenant. When the drawings are complete, all should share theirs.

- Take each small group through the mission-development exercise detailed below (used by the Rev. Clark Olsen in groups working on mission statements):

   1. Focus on three questions: What is the mission of our religious community? What is *really* our mission? What are the qualities we want in our life and work together?
      Write these questions on separate flip charts and place them on the wall or where people can see them.

   2. Form subgroups of two persons each. Each person asks the other the three questions above and records the answers. Complete this grouping and questioning process three times. At the conclusion, exchange written answers and have each person circle the responses he or she considers most important. A couple of ground rules: There should be no discussion of the responses and the question must be asked three times.

3. Combine the small groups (two of the two-person groups create a four-person group). Put all responses that were considered most important on a sheet of newprint. The task is to write a mission statement that incorporates the views of the four persons.

4. Write these new mission statements on flip charts.

5. Designate a task group to take all these statements from the groups of four and develop one that incorporates all the others. This statement can be worked on during a break in this meeting or before another meeting of the congregation is held.

6. Reconvene the whole group to review the proposed mission statement. This is a time for clarification, further definition, and explanation, not for writing a new statement.

7. You may wish to make the mission more specific in terms of goals to live out in your community. For example, if your mission is to "transform the world," you might list some of these goals: to survey the needs of the community, to determine where our congregation might be a catalyst for action, to identify and carry out one congregational program or service that fulfills a major unmet community need.

• After going through these exercises, plan for field visits and other community orientation programs. For example, you or members of your small group could schedule interviews with community leaders to get their assessments of unmet needs and a feeling for the area. Or take a walking tour of the neighborhood where your congregation meets, observing housing, public transportation routes, nearby churches, etc. While most of us believe we know the neighborhood where our congregation meets, often we have not observed what is right next door. After conducting interviews and taking a tour, your congregation might consider sponsoring a seminar, forum, or workshop at your facility, bringing in resource people such as community agency directors, city planners, or elected officials to help that congregation focus on its relationship to the community.

Making Mission Statements Work for You

Many congregations participate in a mission statement process, but few congregations take the next steps to implement their mission. The mission statement may find its way into the minutes of a board meeting or an annual meeting or the cover of the Sunday bulletin. Weeks after the excitement of the mission statement process the congregation returns to the same old organizational patterns of behavior. The reason most mission statements fail is because the congregation fails to plan for their effective implementation. The Rev. Gary Blaine has devised some of these methods for planned implementation of a mission statement.

Only by establishing specific, achievable, and measurable objectives can the congregation make its mission statement an effective tool for ministry! Mission objectives are based on the mission statement. The mission statement is an umbrella statement that identifies "who we are" and "what we are about" for the congregation. The mission statement does not explain how that identity and mission will be implemented. The mission objectives clarify how the mission statement is to be implemented over time.

Mission objectives should be limited to three or four (but absolutely no more than five) statements.

Mission objectives usually span a five-year period. Generally it may take up to a year for a board, committee, or task force to develop a complete strategy and budget for the major objective it has decided to implement. A phased implementation of the objectives may be spread across the remaining four years. The congregation can measure the fulfillment of its objectives each year and celebrate its success.

Mission objectives do not curtail ongoing services of the congregation or staff. Worship, religious education, pastoral care, etc., continue. However, they might continue within a different context; they might be challenged to reorient their programs to help the congregation fulfill its mission. Budgets may shift to support the objectives. Staff time might need to be renegotiated. Some congregations will modify their organizatons in concert with the new mission statement and objectives.

Establishing Mission Objectives

After the mission statement has been adopted, select another weekend for the establishment of mission objectives. The mission-objectives process generally takes six to seven hours, including time for lunch and breaks. The participation of a large portion of the congregation is encouraged and childcare will be essential.

Tables and chairs, easels, newsprint, markers, and masking tape are required. Paper and pencils for all participants should be available. You will also need three different colors of adhesive dots.

The Process

1. Review the mission statement. Explain the need for mission objectives and their five-year status. Emphasize that the objectives must be specific, achievable, and measurable. For example, "a more nurturing congregation" fails all three criteria.

2. Ask each person to list the five most important things that the congregation must do in the next five years to implement the mis-

sion statement. Then ask them to scratch off two from their list, leaving three major objectives that are absolutely essential to fulfill the mission.

3. Form groups of four. Each person shares his or her list with the group. After everyone has read the list, the group must come up with a list of three to five objectives on which they can agree.

4. After the groups of four have established their objectives they merge with another group or two (depending on the attendance numbers). These groups of eight to twelve share their subgroup findings. Together they will devise a new list of three to five objectives.

5. Each group presents its objectives to the entire assembly. Many similar objectives can be merged, which is probably one of the most difficult tasks of the facilitator. The entire group may come up with eight to fifteen objectives.

6. Once the master list has been compiled, give everyone one strip of dots in three differnt colors. The dots will be weighted. For example, "gold" is worth three points, "silver" two, and "blue" one. Remind participants to vote for three different objectives, that is, do not put all of their dots on one objective.

7. Tabulate the scores after everyone has voted. In most congregations the top two or three objectives will be very distinct. In some, three or four objectives will be clearly differentiated from the remainder. On the other hand, the value of objectives four, five, six, or more may not be very different. Again, it is important to select three or four but no more than five major objectives. Resist adopting them all. The purpose of objectives is to help the congregation focus its leadership, resources, time, and money to make the mission effective. When these become diluted the impact is minimized.

8. Once the mission objectives have been decided on, the next step is to develop a plan for implementing each objective over time.

Sample Mission Statements

Here are sample mission statements from Unitarian Universalist congregations around the continent.

As a welcoming and accepting, diverse and inquiring religious community, we unite to provide an environment which stimulates a free exchange and exploration of ideas, fosters spiritual and intellectual growth, and serves as a base for active outreach to benefit the world around us.

Unitarian Universalist Church of Corpus Christi, Texas

The purpose of our religious community is to support each other in our various inward journeys toward truth. We will endeavor to do this in an atmosphere of mutual acceptance, openness and friendship. Committed social action on behalf of the local and global communities will be a natural expression of this purpose.

Harrisonburg Unitarian Universalists, Harrisonburg, Virginia

The Dublin Unitarian Universalist Church is a sharing, nurturing, and caring community which promotes spiritual growth and development along with intellectual freedom. We provide an atmosphere of acceptance of one another while seeking to understand ourselves and our universe.

We foster an ethical basis for living and celebrate in life's diversity. We reaffirm our respect for others which empowers us to act on our beliefs to improve our community and relieve social injustice.

Dublin Unitarian Universalist Church, Dublin, Ohio

It is the mission of the First Unitarian Universalist Church of San Diego to become an increasingly diverse community with differing beliefs yet shared values. In joy and mutual support we offer spiritual nourishment, create beauty, affirm the worth of each individual, and honor the democratic process. From this place we encourage all ages to learn and grow together while we labor for compassionate justice in our society and on our planet.

First Unitarian Universalist Church of San Diego, California

Resources

Seuge, Peter. *The Fifth Discipline: The Art and Practice of a Learning Congregation.* New York: Doubleday, 1990.

Morgan, John and Thomas Chulak. *Mission-Covenant Handbook.* Available through the UUA Department for District, Congregational, and Extension Services.

Unit II

Developing Your Congregation's Potential

Three

Reviewing Your Congregation's Ministry, Minister(s), and Staff

What Is the Ministry of the Congregation?

A congregation has a ministry. When that congregation has a minister and other professional staff, the congregation and staff form a partnership with each other in implementing the ministry of a congregation.

Congregation members and professional staff ideally collaborate with each other in performing their ministry. Ministry is a mutual process. Consequently, an evaluation process for a congregation is best done as an evaluation of each partner in the process: professional staff, congregational lay leaders and committees, and the congregation's membership. Jill M. Hudson, in *Evaluating the Ministry*, states: "Ministry is and must be mutual. Therefore, no individual's performance in ministry can be reviewed with fairness apart from the whole."

This philosophy guides the evaluation tools in this section. Congregations sometimes attempt to initiate an evaluation process of a minister or another staff person when members are unhappy. Invariably, this response only exacerbates existing conflict. It is advisable in these circumstances for congregations to consult with their district executive or the UUA Department of Ministry before beginning an evaluation process.

Why You Need to Review the Ministry of Your Congregation

The process for an annual review of a congregation's ministry, which is outlined in this *Handbook*, should determine:

- what is going well
- what needs improvement
- what new goals and directions are emerging in the congregation
- how the minister, professional staff, and congregation can continue to grow together in mutual ministry.

It is important that a congregation approach this annual review of its life together in a way that allows for reflection, learning, and real commitment to its goals. Consequently, some overall guidelines need to be kept in mind as the congregation engages in this process. These guidelines reflect the experiences of many congregations that have used the review process both effectively and ineffectively. In *Evaluating Ministry*, Jill M. Hudson identifies some pitfalls and potholes in the annual review process:

1. Don't procrastinate. Start somewhere. Use the annual review as a way to start a planning process in your congregation, even when you have yet to institute a long-range planning process, vision, or mission-clarification process.

2. Don't tie the annual review process to compensation issues. To ensure that the review process can be an opportunity for growth and learning, keep the compensation review and annual review as separate processes.

3. Keep it simple. Review only a few aspects of ministry at a time rather than the entire efforts of minister, professional staff, and congregation.

4. "Evaluations work best when they are part of a regularly scheduled process of measuring effectiveness."

5. "Comprehensive reviews of a minister's performance are not helpful when major conflicts are present."

6. Focus on positives as well as negatives.

7. Tailor the design to fit the particular situation of your congregation.

An Annual Review Procedure for a Congregation's Ministry

Introduction

This questionnaire is taken from Catherine Holmes Clark's "Annual Church Review Procedure—The Church's Ministry and the Minister." It is part of a self-assessment procedure, which can be used annually to help your congregation review its progress and discern its future directions. You may want to use it in conjunction with the annual meeting of your congregation. If so, then you should send this questionnaire to all members a few months before the annual meeting. You could also use it in conjunction with your annual canvass.

This questionnaire helps analyze the responsibility your congregation takes for its ministry by evaluating how well the congregation is meeting a wide range of goals. Moreover, it can help the congregation understand its own expectations, ask how it is doing, and plan for the coming year.

The questionnaire encompasses four aspects:

1. acknowledging accomplishments
2. reviewing performance
3. noticing specific strengths and weaknesses
4. planning.

Sample Annual Review of a Congregation's Ministry

The purpose of this questionnaire is to help your congregation look at itself as a whole and review its own ministry (not the ministry of the minister or professional staff).

Part 1: Acknowledging What Has Been Accomplished

Think about the goals and plans our congregation made last year. In the space below, list the goals that you recall and rate how well you feel that they have been accomplished. You may add your understanding of why a goal was not accomplished.

Describe Goal or Plan	Accomplished	Partially Accomplished Why?	Not Accomplished Why?
1.			
2.			
3.			
4.			
5.			

Part 2: Reviewing Our Performance

Please rate each skill or quality in the box on the line to its left using the following rating scale:

1 = Exceptional
2 = Better than average
3 = Average
4 = Needs Improvement
5 = Needs a lot of work

The best way to rate these qualities is to move through the form quickly, putting down the first number that comes to mind. Don't worry about whether you really know the facts about a particular item; what is important is to record your perception. As you rate the items, note particular strengths and weaknesses.

Remember, this questionnaire reviews the congregation as a whole (not the minister).

Fulfilling Our Purpose and Mission

____ We have a congregational community that can depend upon each other and take responsibility for each other.

____ We feel a greater unity beneath our diversity, a force which inspires us (some of us call it God, or Spirit, the Holy; others, Love). We pay attention to it and we celebrate it.

____ We are devoted to our larger purposes as a congregational community.

____ We know our congregation's sense of mission and it helps to order our responsibilities and priorities.

Comments:

Inspirational Leadership

____ Congregation members show concern for our essential values by asking questions and discussing issues in depth.

____ Members of our congregation share their deepest experiences.

____ Members of our congregation live out their religious values in a way that provides role models for others.

____ Members speak out in congregational meetings and committees.

Comments:

Practical Leadership

____ People think about the needs of the congregation as a whole. They offer suggestions and request programs that they like. They organize the activities they want to happen.

____ Lay leadership cooperate with the minister.

____ Lay leadership cooperate with the religious educator.

____ Lay leadership cooperate with other professional staff.

Comments:

General Staffing

___ Members volunteer for committees and positions to staff our ongoing work. They follow through with their responsibilities.

___ Members of committees cooperate well. They understand the whole job and coordinate their individual roles.

___ Members care about their work for our congregation. They anticipate problems and find solutions.

___ We pitch in and support the initiatives of our congregational leaders.

Comments:

Taking Care of Facilities

___ Our congregation's buildings and grounds are maintained properly.

___ The interior of the church is comfortable, beautiful, and inviting.

___ Furnishings are appropriate for the use of the space.

___ Supplies are well provided.

Comments:

Finances

___ We allocate funds appropriately so that working budgets adequately cover expenses as they occur.

___ Budgeting allows for items that may not be practical necessities, but have esthetic or human value.

___ We canvass effectively, reaching everyone in our congregation.

___ We pledge financial support and we meet our commitment.

___ We design effective fundraising projects, staff them with enough people, and bring in the funds that we need.

Comments:

Budgeting Time and Energy

___ The congregation uses its human resources wisely, prioritizing projects and distributing responsibility widely.

___ We have procedures for handling the recurring situations in our life as a congregation so that committee members don't have to reinvent the process each time.

Comments:

Communication Process Skills

___ People communicate ideas and feelings relevantly and appropriately.

___ We think about the needs of others and support others' goals, which arise from deep values.

___ The congregation facilitates communication and cooperation among members and builds team spirit.

___ In meetings we do business efficiently while paying attention to cooperative values such as sharing leadership and listening to those who want to speak.

Comments:

Worship Services

___ Our congregation regularly provides worship services that are appropriate to the congregation's needs.

___ The subject and styles of our worship services address the needs of the whole person.

___ We seek out all sources for inspiration and guidance.

___ Lay people participate in a variety of roles in the worship services.

___ Musical elements of the worship services are satisfying.

___ The congregation attends worship services.

Comments:

Religious Education for Children and Youth

___ Programs are well balanced, relevant, and involving. They stimulate personal, emotional, and spiritual development.

___ Teachers' attitudes are supportive, caring, and open minded. They have good rapport with children and youth.

___ Programming and staffing are appropriate: Teachers are good at what they do; there are enough teachers and classes are the right size.

___ Parents support the religious education program by getting their children there regularly.

___ The congregation supports the religious education program for children and youth by volunteering services.

___ Children and young people support their religious education programs with attention, feedback, and suggestions.

___ Youth take charge of activities for themselves; teachers and staff empower them and support their leadership.

Comments:

Adult Religious Education Program

___ Adult religious education programs are well balanced, relevant, and involving. They stimulate our personal and spiritual growth.

___ The congregation supports adult religious education with feedback and suggestions.

___ The congregation supports adult religious education through sharing leadership and resources.

Comments:

Outreach

___ We create a climate of acceptance and friendliness at our congregation. The place looks inviting and it is easy to find one's way around.

___ We have an active program for welcoming and orienting new members.

___ Congregation members greet new people and follow up with contact.

___ We provide activities for assimilating new members into our congregational community.

___ We publicize our activities to let the wider community know what we are offering.

___ We tell our friends what we like about our church and invite them to come with us.

Comments:

Fun and Fellowship

___ People keep in touch with each other.

___ We take advantage of social functions to nurture relationships informally.

___ We support the congregation's need for social fellowship with attendance at social events.

_____ We pay attention to individuals' needs and create a sense of community, caring, and mutual concern within the congregation.

Comments:

Social Justice

_____ Congregation members take an active part in community affairs, express a concern for social well being, and get involved in social issues.
_____ We take part in interfaith social projects and events.
_____ We offer educational programs on social justice issues.

Comments:

Denominational Affiliation

_____ We inform ourselves about the history, issues, and values of our religious heritage. We keep in touch with current developments in our continental association.
_____ We get involved, both as a church and as individuals, in denominational activities in our district.

Comments:

Attitudes

_____ We remember to emphasize the positive. We offer constructive feedback and give credit for jobs well done.
_____ We respect differences, particularly the diversity of our membership.
_____ We believe in each other, our essential unity, and our ability to work together with good will when we differ.
_____ We keep a sense of humor.
_____ We cultivate enthusiasm and zest.
_____ We respect the goodness in everyone.
_____ We believe people have the power and responsibility to make their own decisions and encourage them to find their own wisdom and their own source of guidance.
_____ We believe that people deserve to be happy as well as good. We give friendship, share our sources of spiritual strength, and listen to them well.

___ We believe in ourselves and in the value of the work that this congregation does.

**Part 3:
Noticing Specific
Strengths and
Weaknesses**

Strengths

List specific areas in which you feel our performance as a congregation has improved in the past year.

**Areas That Need
Strengthening**

List in priority order specific areas where you feel our performance as a congregation particularly needs improvement.

**Part 4:
Planning**

What projects or programs would you like to see the congregation initiate in the coming year?

What suggestions do you have for improving the congregation?

What would you like to see accomplished? List and indicate importance with "1" being most important, "2" next important, etc.

Another Sample Review of Your Congregation's Ministry

The following discussion guide was designed by the Committee on Ministry of the First Unitarian Church of Oakland, California. It is based on the philosophy that the work of the committee on ministry is to strengthen the quality of ministry in the congregation. The committee addresses responsibility and accountability of both the laity and clergy in the congregation.

Procedure

Distribute the following questions to members of your congregation in advance of meeting and invite them to consider and jot down their responses. Arrange for members to participate in small groups to discuss their responses; meetings can be held in members' homes or at the church. A facilitator of each group should have the main role of keeping the discussion on track and flowing. A recorder in each group should record the responses of the individual group members.

Our Understanding of Ministry

- What is ministry?

- How is it being lived out in our congregation?

- How do you see your role?

- How well are we doing?

- Where do we need to improve?

Your Involvement in This Congregation

- How long have you been involved with this congregation?

- On the average, how many times each month did you attend Sunday services during the past year?

- Are you now involved in church activities such as serving on a committee, teaching religious education (adult or children), singing in the choir?

- Have you been involved in church activities in the past?

- Do you think that these activities are a good way for you to get involved? Or are there other ways?

Religious Faith

- Is our congregation a place where you are encouraged to articulate your religious beliefs? Have you heard others do so? Where has it happened? Where do you think it can happen most effectively?

- Are people encouraged to share openly the deeper dimensions of their lives?

- Do we make congregational decisions (in committee, board, and congregational meetings) based on our understanding of our religious faith?

- Do the sermons given by our minister(s) or others speak to religious beliefs? Do they call on you to act on those religious beliefs? Do they move you to act on those beliefs?

- Does our congregation have a shared vision? Is that vision widely shared among the members? Do you share that vision?

- Is the adult religious education program sufficient to help us on our religious journeys?

- Is the children's religious education program designed to help them on their religious journeys? Is it effective?

Fellowship

- How well have we created a congregation where all members and friends feel accepted?

- Are some members more valued than others?

- Have we created a congregation where all children feel accepted?

- Do newcomers experience friendliness and warmth when they first step in the door?

- Do we seem willing to give each other the emotional support we need in times of crisis?

- Do we promote an environment where we are emotionally supportive of each other? Does lay leadership promote this environment? Does the professional leadership promote this environment?

- Do we deal openly and honestly with conflict?

Social Service and Ministry

- Are you satisfied with the way that we as a congregation work with the surrounding community?

- What social service projects or ministries are we known for in our community?

- Are we working sufficiently toward bringing hope, justice, and peace to people's lives? Does our church leadership encourage us to do so?

Ministry

- What is your definition of ministry?

- Is our church a place where this happens? Do you feel empowered to minister (based on your own definition) to others in the congregation?

- Are your religious needs ministered to by this congregation?

Other Comments   Please submit other comments that would be relevant to this discussion.

Evaluation Of Church Staff

The challenge of evaluating the work of the minister(s) or other congregation staff is best undertaken as part of a process that includes mutual goal-setting and evaluates the shared ministry of the congregation, including both professional and lay leaders. It is only through the combined efforts of both sets of leaders that congregations identify and make progress toward goals.

The Unitarian Universalist Ministers Association *Guidelines* say: "Essential to any healthy relationship are periodic reviews of the contributions all parties make to it. In the case of the minister and church, such shared reviews can benefit the personal and professional growth of the minister, can give strength and sense of direction of the congregation and can broaden areas of communication and action between them."

The Unitarian Universalist Association Committee on Ministerial and Church Staff Compensation and the Director of Ministerial Development are drafting evaluation procedures for Unitarian Universalist congregations based on the above approach. Under such a plan procedures would be put in place periodically to review the progress of professional staff, committees, and congregations as a whole toward mutually agreed-upon goals. Existing models from Unitarian Universalist congregations and other denominations are being reviewed.

Please get in touch with the director of Ministerial Development for information on this effort and to give suggestions about evaluations.

Resources

Clark, Catherine Holmes. "Annual Church Review Procedure—The Church's Ministry and the Minister." Bethesda, MD: The Alban Institute, Inc., 1986.

Hudson, Jill M. *Evaluating Ministry: Principles and Processes for Clergy and Congregation.* Bethesda, MD: The Alban Institute, Inc., 1992.

Oswald, Roy. "Alban Institute Approach to Assessment," *Clergy Assessment and Career Development.* Nashville, TN: Abingdon, 1990.

Four

Congregational Planning and Goal Setting

Why Your Congregation Needs to Engage in Annual and Long-Range Planning

In every congregation's life occasions occur in which evaluation and planning seem essential. When a congregation is in a period of significant transition or change, these are times to conduct a thorough long-range planning process to provide a new sense of direction for the congregation. It could be after a new minister has arrived or during a period of intensive growth or steady decline in membership. These transition points might include when something new is about to happen, for example, when a congregation is going to call its first minister or begin a capital campaign. It could also happen after a significant event to understand the implications of the change, for example, after a minister has been settled or a congregation has moved into a new facility. A long-range plan typically outlines strategies for moving a congregation toward its preferred future over five years. In the intervening years, the plan is reviewed and revised as necessary.

In addition to these critical periods in a congregation's life, almost every congregation engages in an annual process of evaluation and planning. For some congregations this process is disciplined and formal, for others it is sporadic, routine, and brief.

If a congregation is to learn from its experience and create opportunities to become continually engaged in effective mission in the community, there needs to be a process that brings together long-range planning and annual evaluation and planning. An effective congregation attempts to learn about itself and utilizes that learning to create its future.

The previous chapter, "Reviewing Your Congregation's Ministry, Minister(s), and Staff," gave guidelines for evaluating a congregation. Included in this section are guidelines and processes for planning.

The Planning Process

A good planning process includes an assessment of where you are as a congregation. Consequently, evaluation and planning are interrelated. A planning process that does not include assessment can result in goal setting that is not informed by the reality of your congregation. It can also result in plans that seem too ambitious for your congregation.

Kennon Callahan, a church consultant on long-range planning and author of several books (see "Resources" at the end of this chapter), recommends that a congregation build on its strengths. Consequently, a congregation needs to discern three categories in its assessment:

1. What areas of its life are strengths?
2. What areas are potential strengths that require further work?
3. What areas are limitations that require extensive work?

Planning would proceed in such a way as to build on current strengths and to change potential strengths into real strengths. This process, in Callahan's estimation, helps build the morale of a congregation and makes its planning manageable.

Other planning models are included in this chapter. In evaluating which planning model is most useful and appropriate for your congregation, consider how much time you can invest in the process and your overall aims. Some congregations that have never engaged in planning may need to start by incorporating aspects of evaluation and planning into their congregational and committee life before attempting to launch a more extensive long-range planning process. This procedure builds planning skills and awareness in a congregation.

The tone of your planning process is an important consideration. For example, some congregations engage in planning based on reviewing past and present problems, which can inhibit planning a preferred future. Lyle Schaller, in *Effective Church Planning*, distinguishes between a problem-based approach and a potentialities-based approach to planning. In a problem-based approach a congregation tends to be oriented toward the past, to list problems, to be occupied with liabilities, and to look only at institutional needs. In a potentialities-based approach, a congregation tends to look for new opportunities, to build on assets, and to anticipate the unmet needs of people in the congretaion and the wider community.

To avoid some of the tendencies of problem-based planning, initiate a process that moves your review of your congregation into a planning process that builds on strengths and is "potentialities" based.

A Planning Retreat for Your Congregation's Leadership and Membership

A retreat is an opportunity for a congregation's leadership or membership to put aside its routine agenda and business to look at the big picture. A retreat can be an annual time to share visions and goals and assess a congregation's progress. It is a time to remember the overarching purpose of the congregation and how its committees further that purpose. Moreover, it is a time to nurture relationships between people who will serve together on the board or in other leadership capacities in the congregation.

Preplanning the Retreat

A successful retreat requires preplanning; the outcomes that are sought should inform the design. Do an informal survey of the participants in the retreat that includes these questions:

1. What outcomes do we seek for this retreat?
2. What have we done to achieve these outcomes?
3. What usually gets in our way of achieving these outcomes?
4. What are our priorities for this retreat in terms of our accomplishments and our relationships with each other?

Such input from the group allows those who are planning the retreat to communicate with its facilitator. It also allows priorities to surface that may not have occurred to the planners.

Arrangements for the Retreat

Special arrangements need to be made to allow for a day or weekend away for the participants. These arrangements vary according to your needs and will usually require an investment of financial resources. Most congregations find that this investment is usually returned in the level of enthusiasm, focus, and direction that emerge from the retreat.

Going to a setting other than the usual meeting place helps to communicate that the intent of a retreat is to take a broader perspective than the typical committee meeting allows. Some congregations go to a nearby retreat or conference center. Other congregations meet at another church facility for the event.

Arrangements should be made well in advance of the event to make good attendance possible. Good snacks and meals can enhance the experience of the retreat. You will also need to consider providing childcare or subsidizing private childcare.

Who Should Be Invited?

Many congregations schedule an annual retreat at the time that new leaders are selected. These retreats might include new and continuing board members and committee chairs. Some congregations include just the board and staff and others include committee chairs as well.

In smaller congregations, the entire congregation might be invited to a combination of activities focused on planning for the congregation as well as community building.

How Long Should the Retreat Last?	In congregations that have never had a retreat, some members usually resist the idea. It might be best to start with a one-day retreat, evaluate the experience, and assess whether your group would want to spend more time in retreat in the future. Congregations that have a regular annual retreat have found that a Friday night through a Saturday afternoon gives them ample time to accomplish many goals of a retreat. A shorter time frame might not allow for the getting acquainted and other team-building dimensions of the retreat.

Other congregations find that a full weekend—that is, a Friday evening through a Sunday noon, is best, particularly if they meet in a pleasant environment that allows for recreational, reflective, and informal conversation time. Once a congregation has developed the practice of a regular retreat, the value of the experience usually speaks for itself. |
| **Who Should Facilitate the Retreat?** | The advantage of having a leader for the retreat come from outside your congregation's membership is that it allows you to have a fresh perspective. Such a facilitator should talk with the retreat planning team. Some of the information from a preplanning survey may assist in the design of the event. Please inform this facilitator of (a) specific outcomes you seek for the retreat; (b) what you've already done as a congregation or board to support these outcomes; (c) resistances as a board or congregation; and (d) any routines that need to be scheduled (e.g., an opening or closing worship service, extended break times, meal times, etc.).

Your district services staff or district office may suggest someone in your area to facilitate. You should expect to offer a fee to someone who is not a Unitarian Universalist Association staff member. |
| **What To Do At the Retreat.** | What you do at a retreat depends on the nature of the retreat and the specific needs of your group. Included in this section are some options from which to choose according to your particular needs. |

An Information Gathering and Goal-Setting Session

At significant transition points in a congregation's life, it is helpful to gather information about the congregation that can lead to a goal-setting session informed by a wide range of insights about the congregation. These transition points might include when a congregation calls its first minister, is about to embark on a ministerial search after a crisis, at the start of a capital campaign, or a move to a new facility. Some consultants to congregations propose that these moments of transition are the most teachable moments in a congregation's life, the times in which a congregation is most able to reflect critically on its life together and consider change.

Robert Craig and Robert Worley suggest in *Dry Bones Live: Helping Congregations Discover New Life* that it is most effective to have congregations set goals by first gathering information about the congregation from active and less-active members. At different times in the life of a congregation, the kind of questions the congregation's board and committee chairs ask will vary according the emerging issues in the life of the congregation. Generally, the questions should focus on:

- what members feel is going well in the congregation
- what concerns members have about the congregation
- what members feel the priorities should be for the congregation in various aspects of congregational life: ministry, relationship and mission to the surrounding community, programs of the congregation.

A Suggested Format for Focus Groups

A series of home meetings or small group meetings at the congregation may be used to gather this information. A special attempt should be made to invite and include as many people as possible. Those who facilitate the meetings should have an orientation session to help them clarify their role and the process that they will use to facilitate meetings.

A focus group differs from a structured interview in that the goal is to facilitate discussion among participants rather than primary interaction with the interviewer. It allows participants to reflect on their experiences together and to prompt each other into further articulation and elaboration of the commonalities and differences of their experiences. In a focus group, other questions or themes may emerge as significant to the discussion. Consequently, the leader needs to be flexible enough to include these as well.

Sample Format for Focus Groups

1. Introductions: Invite participants to pair up and introduce themselves to each other. Each person introduces his or her partner to the whole group.

2. Share the purpose of the meeting.

3. Gather information.

Prepare a list of focus questions in advance and write them on a sheet of newsprint so that members of the group can see them and the general outline of the session.

Focus questions might include any of the following or others you decide upon before the session:

- What about our congregation are you most proud of ?
- What hope do you have for our congregation that is still unrealized?
- What changes would you like to see in our congregation?
- What sustains your involvement in our congregation?

- What inhibits your involvement in our congregation?
- How should we be living out our mission as a congregation in the surrounding community?

Following the discussion, the facilitator should summarize some of the most important ideas and feelings expressed in the session.

Moving from Information to Goals

After informational sessions are held and their results summarized, lessons can be drawn from them by answering the following questions:

- What are the most important areas of congregational life expressed in the focus groups, which should be included in our goals?

- What areas of congregational life are people most concerned about?

- What are the priorities that emerge from the discussions?

Procedure

Team up with two other group leaders and share your responses to these questions. Make a list of common responses on newsprint.

In the whole group, compare and contrast lists. Develop a list of priority goals stated in ways that are broad and inclusive.

The board and committee chairs may want to review this document along with these questions: What is feasible? What is a priority? Once the goals are stated, you may ask: How do these priorities align with our overarching vision of this congregation and our mission?

Following these questions, the board and committees should develop specific objectives for each goal. A plan will emerge for the congregation that will include a list of prioritized goals and an action plan for each goal.

The Long-Range Planning Process

Different kinds of planning occur systematically or spontaneously in a congregation. Annual planning focuses on the yearly plans, goals, and budgets. Issue planning occurs when a specific issue (e.g., moving to having two services) needs careful consideration before implementation. Long-range planning is designed to help a congregation clarify its preferred future and to determine the steps it needs to take to get there. Yet long-range planning can also provide a broader perspective for the annual budget or for issue planning that routinely take place within a congregation.

An effective long-range planning process serves two purposes: It articulates what a congregation will look like in a given period of time and it outlines the strategies a congregation needs to take to get there (referred to as strategic planning).

Stages in the Long-Range Planning Process

Planning to Plan

- Design the long-range planning process for your congregation.

- Develop a timetable for the long-range planning process.

- Build commitment among your leadership, staff, and the congregation's membership for engaging in a long-range planning process.

Clarifying the Vision and Mission of Your Congregation

- Facilitate a process for the congregation to articulate a vision for its preferred future.

- Lead the congregation through a mission-statement process.

Exploring Present and Future Strengths and Challenges

- Determine the opportunities and challenges (or threats) that your congregation faces within the community that you aim to serve

- Assess the strengths and weaknesses of your congregation in the face of your vision, mission, opportunities, and challenges.

Identifying Critical Issues

- Discern what critical issues, scenarios, or goals your congregation needs to resolve and plan for.

- Engage your congregation in feedback on the critical issues, scenarios, and goals.

Developing a Long-Range Plan

- Prepare a report of your recommendations.

- Decide on the report and its implementation.

Ongoing

- Monitor the plan and revise it annually.

Determining Your Congregation's Planning Process

An effective long-range planning process has to consider the needs, style, and capacity of the congregation. Typically a long-range planning process requires a timetable of a full calendar year. In some cases, a shorter time frame, such as a church year, work as well. To succeed there has to be some sensitivity to the congregation's culture, style, and way of doing things.

Rather than impose a series of extra meetings upon a congregation, one must consider how some of the steps of the long-range planning process can be incorporated into ongoing activities. Review the congregation's calendar and plan ways to incorporate some of the processes of long-range planning into your worship services, committee meetings, neighborhood or cottage meetings, every-member canvasses, and weekday or after-service programs. Moreover, consider ways to use ongoing activities to facilitate the planning process.

For example, before a vision exercise, have the theme of a worship service be vision. In this service, include statements from members and professional staff on the vision they have for your congregation and a meditation for participants in the worship service. You may want to use cottage meetings or neighborhood meetings to discuss vision or evaluate your congregation or discuss particular options. Involve groups of people on a committee in your congregation to do surveys of community leaders about current and future community needs.

Procedures

There are a variety of procedures for each stage of the long-range planning process. Consultants and resources are available through the district office and the UUA Department for Congregational, District, and Extension Services to help you in the procedures you use.

The Benefits of Long-Range Planning

There are implications for your long-range plan on various aspects of your congregational life: the work of the board and the church committee, the budget, staff, and programming.

The long-range process can benefit your congregation by (a) improving your effectiveness as a congregation, (b) helping you address directly some of your critical issues, (c) being a wise steward of your resources, and (d) making decisions based on your priorities.

Ongoing Process

Without an ongoing monitoring and revising of your long-range plan, it becomes a historical document and not a working document that informs your year-to-year operations. Consequently, a long-range planning committee should have the role of raising these questions to the board, leadership, and congregation:

- Are we meeting our goals? If not, why not?
- Are our vision and strategies for the future still sound? If not, what changes are needed?

A good long-range planning process will inform the ongoing work within a congregation, help to focus its efforts, sustain momentum of its vision, and build its sense of confidence.

Resources

Callahan, Kennon. *Twelve Keys to an Effective Church*. San Francisco: HarperSan Francisco, 1983.

Craig, Robert and Robert Worley. *Dry Bones Live: Helping Congregations Discover New Life*. Louisville, KY: Westminter/John Knox Press.

"Long-Range Planning for Unitarian Universalist Congregations." Available from the UUA Department for District, Congregational, and Extension Services.

Schaller, Lyle. *Effective Church Planning*. Nashville, TN: Abingdon Press, 1991.

Long-Range Planning Consultants are available in some Unitarian Universalist Association districts. Please contact your district office.

Unit III

Effective Congregational Governance and Practice

Five

The Roles and Responsibilities of Committees

A Congregation's Committees

Committees are the vehicle for congregations to accomplish their mission both in the congregation and in the community that they aim to serve. Since ministry is a shared endeavor that engages members in distinct ways in the work of the congregation, congregations need committees that channel the individual talents and qualities of their members into their common work.

Congregational polity is a vital part of the Unitarian Universalist tradition. It informs and inspires our understanding that a congregation is not a geographical parish but a group of people who have covenanted to walk together the path of faith. Congregations are responsible for making decisions that determine their direction. Moreover, congregations must be responsible stewards of their resources and provide opportunities for "promoting the spiritual growth of its membership, and engaging its membership in an effective witness and service to our Unitarian Universalist values within the community."

Without a way to channel the ideals, talents, and responsibilities of its members, a congregation may never act upon its rhetoric.

One role of a congregation is to develop leadership, service attitudes, and skills among its membership for the sake of the congregation and the community that the congregation aims to serve. Committees are a way to help develop leadership, an undertaking that is often undervalued when a congregation focuses only on its needs and does not claim its full mission in the contexts of other institutions.

Vision and Mission

Once a congregation has clarified its vision and mission and outlined ways it will live them out, each committee needs to clarify its own role and relationship to the overarching purpose and mission of the congregation. Without this connection to the overarching purpose, a committee can lose focus and feel disconnected or unclear.

Consequently, a process important to each committee is to answer these questions:

- What is the role of our committee in furthering the vision and overall purpose or mission of our congregation?

- What is our purpose and charter as a committee?
- How will we know that we have accomplished this purpose?
- What is the specific role of our committee in the life of the congregation?

Goals

After developing a mission statement or charter of a committee that is informed and inspired by the overall mission and vision of a congregation, the committee should ask the following:

- What are the various tasks and responsibilities of our committee that express our charter?
- What are the continuing responsibilities of our committee?
- What are the longer-term goals of our committee?
- What are the goals for this year?
- What are the specific strategies for achieving the longer-term and yearly goals of our committee?

Responsibilities and Roles

With charter and goals clarified, a committee can clarify its responsibilities. These tasks include:

- establishing the roles and responsibilities of the committee
- determining what short-term or intermittent task groups need to exist in or outside the committee membership to accomplish routine and special projects
- recruitment of new members for the committee or task groups.

Structure of the Committee

In the process of clarifying its goals and responsibilities, the committee can determine the frequency and length of committee meetings, its responsibilities between committee meetings, and how the committee will communicate with other committees.

A Circular Process

This movement refers to these steps:

- relating the committee's charter to the congregation's vision and overarching purpose or mission
- determining the longer-term and yearly goals of the committee in relationship to this charter
- deciding on the committee's responsibilities and roles
- determining an appropriate meeting schedule.

Though a cascading effect may be the ideal, the reality is that committee work is often a circular process. By working on tasks, a committee often becomes clearer about its purpose. Committee members may bring skills and insights that shape the goals and strategies of the committee. Nevertheless, a dynamic and effective committee can foster connections among the congregation's overall vision and mission, the committee's charter, and the roles and responsibilities of the membership.

Determining Your Congregation's Committees

Congregations have several options when determining what committees they need to do their work. One method is by default, that is, by continuing with committees a congregation already has. Though this may be appropriate in most circumstances, a lack of continual assessment may overburden a congregation and promote complacency or burnout. Another approach is to start or discontinue a committee randomly. Either approach has its pitfalls.

Assess existing committees in your congregation by asking yourself the following:

- Do our congregation's committees express our overarching mission as a congregation?
- Is each committee clear about its own purpose and charter?
- Do the committees function and operate to achieve their purpose?
- Have we placed our resources (financial and volunteer) in a way that expresses our mission initiatives and priorities as a congregation?
- Would it be best to restructure some committees into task forces?
- Are leadership and service opportunities available to members of our congregation?

Possible Committees

This section includes descriptions of various committees that operate in many Unitarian Universalist congregations. They can help you clarify your congregation's committees and establish new ones.

Volunteer Practices Inventory

An assessment of a congregation's current volunteer practices may reveal a congregation's strengths, the strengths it needs to develop, and obstacles it needs to overcome. The following is a useful questionnaire developed by the United Church of Christ.

Directions: Have a group or team in your congregation assess current volunteer practices by checking "Yes" or "No" for each item. In a group or team, share your responses, then answer the questions at the end of this checklist.

(Yes/No)

Mission

____ ____ Does your congregation have a mission statement?
____ ____ Do volunteers know of your congregation's mission statement?
____ ____ Do volunteers understand how their work furthers the mission of your congregation?
____ ____ Does your congregation regularly establish goals for itself?

Expectations of Volunteers

___ ___ Is there a list of all volunteer positions in the congregation?

___ ___ Do people have a good idea of what is expected of them when they accept a volunteer position?

___ ___ Are there written descriptions for most of the significant volunteer roles?

___ ___ Are members aware of what other members are doing in their volunteer positions?

Identifying Volunteers

___ ___ Are members of the nominating committee aware of the interests, talents, and availability of new members?

___ ___ Have members been given a specific invitation to volunteer for a task or committee that is suitable for them?

___ ___ Is any record kept of what members would like to volunteer to do?

___ ___ When a person completes a volunteer responsibility, is there a process to help them evaluate the experience and make recommendations for a successor?

___ ___ When a person completes a volunteer responsibility, is there someone who talks to them about what opportunity they would like next?

Matching Volunteers with Positions or Tasks

___ ___ Has the volunteer work been shared by many members rather than only by a few who do most of the work?

___ ___ Do people have an opportunity to change their volunteer positions?

___ ___ Do you make members of your congregation aware of volunteer positions in the community surrounding the congregation?

Recruiting Volunteers

___ ___ Is a face-to-face conversation used for asking people to serve in volunteer positions?

___ ___ Is everyone asked to participate in a volunteer position given an accurate description of how much time and effort the position will take?

___ ___ Are volunteers given enough information to do the task well?

___ ___ Are people told why they were asked to undertake a particular volunteer role or task?

___ ___ Is there a clear understanding of who is responsible for recruiting members for volunteer positions in your congregation?

___ ___ Are the best persons for each job being asked to volunteer in their area of expertise?

___ ___ Is there a definite and clear time limit to the responsibility that the person is agreeing to do?

Training Volunteers

___ ___ Is there an orientation session for new members of a committee?
___ ___ Are training opportunities available in your congregation or district to help people carry out their volunteer position?
___ ___ Does your congregation provide leadership training for potential as well as current lay leadership?
___ ___ Is someone responsible for making people aware of training opportunities or planning for them?

Supporting Volunteers

___ ___ Is someone available to support, assist, and encourage volunteers?
___ ___ Are volunteers regularly acknowledged and thanked by the congregation for their service?
___ ___ Do volunteers have adequate resources to do tasks?
___ ___ Are members recognized by the congregation when they have completed a term on a committee?

Evaluating the Committee and Volunteer Work of Your Congregation

___ ___ Are volunteers given an opportunity to express their feelings and thoughts about a particular volunteer position and an opportunity to make recommendations?
___ ___ Are criticisms and suggestions taken seriously and acted upon?
___ ___ Is evaluation of a committee's work seen as a way to improve the quality of a congregation's life?

Learning From Your Assessment

1. List the areas in which your congregation has strengths in its volunteer practices.

2. List the areas in which your congregation needs to improve its practices.

3. What are some specific steps that your congregation can take to improve the way it structures and implements its volunteer responsibilities?

Developing Effective Committee Meetings

- Develop an agenda for the meeting and share it in advance with participants.

- **Ask that reports be prepared in advance in writing.** If the business of the meeting becomes too extensive, written reports can help reduce the time needed for meetings.

- **Schedule important items early in the meeting.** Participants are usually fresh when you address these issues.

- **Begin with a centering exercise, song, reading, or silent meditation.**

- **Consider the effect of seating arrangements, chairs in blocks, in a circle, or around a table.** Be mindful of participants' proximity, so that people are neither sitting too close nor too far apart for comfortable interaction.

- **Use methods that will allow committee members to participate.** Occasionally, allow committee members to discuss in subgroups. Invite reticent members to participate and perhaps more importantly, invite reticent members to take responsibility for being sure that they receive a fair hearing.

- **Committee members need to be conscious of the important roles they play in the group.** Study the different roles people can play, analyze the roles each plays, and consciously choose roles that are helpful to the committee's process.

- **Provide periodic opportunities for the committee's ongoing evaluation of its process with evaluation sheets, process reports, subgroup discussions, etc.** Such evaluation is best done often, briefly, and well.

- **The committee needs to be mindful of the needs of individual members.** Participants need to get acquainted with each other as persons. Allow some time at each meeting for the development of feelings of interpersonal support within the group. If negative feelings develop, discuss them as openly as you can, trying to resolve them.

- **Consider your committee's needs for greater flexibility or greater structure.** Is your committee hindered by too strict adherence to formal procedures or would greater attention to formalized procedures make it healthier and more productive?

- **When a decision needs to be made, ask whose responsibility it is.** Is this question best decided by the chair, the executive committee, by another committee or subcommittee, or the whole group? If the whole group, is it sufficiently weighty to require consensus? Will voting do? Is a formal vote needed to achieve validity, even if consensus has been reached?

- **A committee's success is largely a reflection of the proportion of participants who take responsibility for its success.** What proportion of the group identifies with the committee and its goals? While it is neurotic to assume that if the committee fails, it's your fault, it is equally ineffective to assume that the committee's ineffectiveness is the result of other participants' behavior. Rather than searching for someone to blame, energy is better spent asking "How is our interaction effective?" and "How can I add energy to what is effective and withdraw it from what is ineffective?"

Congregational Meetings

The practice of congregational polity dictates that the business of our congregations take place at congregational meetings. Most congregations hold an annual meeting to hear reports from the minister and the officers, to elect new officers and board members, and to approve the annual budget. Other business may also be scheduled at the annual meeting.

In addition, from time to time congregations will hold special congregational meetings to consider significant issues in the life of the congregation. Typically, these meetings must be advertised well in advance (usually a period of time specified in the bylaws) and its business is limited to the subject(s) advertised. Special congregational meetings should be called whenever significant congregational business needs to be conducted.

The annual meeting is typically the only congregational meeting in the year that is open to any business members wish to discuss.

Leadership Roles

The president (or the vice president) of the board usually presides as moderator. The secretary of the board records the minutes. Most congregations' bylaws call for the use of Robert's Rules of Order (the most recent edition); therefore, it is advisable to have present a parliamentarian who is familiar with Robert's Rules and can advise the moderator on questions of procedure. A few congregations have written rules for operating the meeting by consensus.

The president may also wish to use a timekeeper and/or process watcher. The timekeeper's task is to keep the meeting on schedule, and to time individuals' comments when needed. The process watcher is charged with observing how people interact in the meeting, whether one or a few dominate the conversation, and whether the group functions smoothly or gets bogged down. Typically, the process watcher says nothing during the meeting but makes a report of her or his observations to all at the end of the meeting.

Planning the Meeting

The board president should prepare a detailed agenda and time it. The times may be written on the agenda or kept by the president and timekeeper. In either case, speakers should be notified in advance of the amount of time available to them and asked to hold to those limits.

Congregational meetings should be advertised well in advance in accordance with the times stipulated in the bylaws. In the case of a special meeting, the agenda should be published with the advertisement. For the annual meeting, agendas known in advance should be publicized.

Written reports should be prepared in advance, but handed out after the meeting unless the speaker(s) plans to speak directly to the contents of the report (a proposed budget, for example).

Written ballots should be prepared in advance for any issues that will require a vote.

Conducting the Meeting

It is important to pay attention to the comfort of participants. Seats should be comfortable and accessible for the physically challenged. The room should be neither too hot nor too cold. Everyone should be able to see the head table and visual aids used in presentations. Amplification should be provided for those who are hearing impaired.

The board president and other officers responsible for the conduct of the meeting should be seated so that they are visible to those in attendance. The president should have a gavel or gong to gain the attention of participants (nonverbal signals work better than verbal ones). Begin with a centering exercise: a reading, song, or period of silence to remind everyone that this a congregation meeting.

Ideas for Large Meetings

The most effective way to arrive at decisions is in small groups that allow for sufficient discussion and dialogue. In larger groups (over forty), it may not be possible to give everyone enough speaking time to achieve consensus, unless the issue is significant enough for several meetings.

What follows are some suggestions for running large meetings using Robert's or Bourinot's Rules of Order while providing for a maximum of fairness and communal feeling. Robert's Rules provide that any meeting may adopt its own rules, which supersede those presented in Robert's. Such suggestions can be presented by the moderator at the beginning of the meeting as methods of operation that she or he proposes to use in the absence of objections. Most groups will readily accept such suggestions.

1. No one will be called upon to speak for the second time before everyone wishing to speak has spoken once.

2. People are asked to speak for themselves, not for what they think others think. Also, people are asked to be mindful of the feelings of others in the way they phrase their remarks. (It may be necessary for the moderator to monitor this requirement.)

3. People are asked to limit their comments to a specified number of minutes, usually two or three. If the issue is likely to be difficult, the moderator may devise a method of warning the speaker when a minute remains.

4. The moderator will try to call on people with differing points of view alternately.

5. If parliamentary maneuvering gets complicated through the use of amendments, substitute motions and so forth. The moderator can declare the meeting to be in a "committee of the whole." In this status, the issues can be discussed and a consensus reached without the need for motions. Then the moderator can declare the formal meeting resumed and the appropriate motions to ratify the consensus can be made and voted upon.

6. The motion to "call to (for) the question" is legitimate under Robert's Rules, but can often destroy a congregation's community. It requires *immediate* cessation of debate and a vote on whether to continue debate. The majority rules on such a vote. If the debate is terminated in this manner, people often leave the meeting feeling disenfranchised and angry. Instead, the moderator can announce before the meeting begins that she or he will not accept a call to the question. A request to consider whether to end debate would result in a show of hands of those wishing to continue the discussion. Then the moderator can do one of two things: (1) make a judgment as to whether sufficient interest exists to continue (even when such interest is in the minority); or (2) allow each person whose hand is raised to make his or her statement and then end the debate. Experience shows that use of this adaptation of the rules generally avoids unhappiness about the procedure.

7. When routine business is being conducted, such as the election of officers, such rules generally are not necessary. They are helpful when controversial issues must be discussed.

The Congregational Calendar

From time to time, congregations consider changing the calendar of events in congregational life. Usually major events are specified in the bylaws so a change in calendar requires a change in bylaws. Here are points to consider when making such a change.

Three Kinds of Years

Three "years" need to be considered: the congregation program year, the fiscal year, and the calendar year.

In most congregations, the "program year" begins in September and runs through June. Such congregations hold no programs, or only a limited number, during the summer. For some congregations (commonly in vacation areas), the program year starts in the late spring and runs through September or October. For others, it starts in the fall and runs to early spring. Such congregations are affectionately called "sunbird" or "snowbird" congregations, respectively.

The "fiscal year" is the year for which the budget is made up. Fiscal years can start in any month of the year. The Unitarian Universalist Association and many of its districts use a fiscal year that begins on July 1 and ends on June 30 of the following calendar year.

The "calendar year" begins January 1.

Factors in Setting the Congregational Calendar

Two major factors need to be considered for establishing the congregational calendar: the term of office for officers and board members and the timing of the budget.

The congregational organization runs most smoothly when the officers and board are elected at the beginning of the congregation *program* year. Thus, in congregations with a September-to-June program year, officers will be most effective if they take office in early summer. This time frame allows the new board to select its team of committee chairs, to hold a retreat, and to set goals before the program year begins. This method holds true whether the terms are for one, two, or three years. Usually, officers and board member are elected at the annual meeting. Thus, in most congregations the annual meeting would be held in late spring.

"Sunbird" congregations may elect new leaders in the early spring so they are in office during the peak times in the summer. Similarly, "snowbird" congregations may consider early fall elections.

In setting the time for elections of officers, some leaders want the new officers and board to participate in the preparation of the budget for the year in which they will hold office, which is rarely possible. Most budgets are for a period of twelve months and require three to nine months to prepare. Thus, the period of time for which a particular year's budget is being considered and used spans from fifteen to twenty-one months.

Setting the Fiscal Year

The calendar year is the most commonly used fiscal year by businesses because taxes are usually paid on a calendar-year basis. Because congregations do not pay taxes, the calendar year has little significance. In a congregation, the timing of the fiscal year should be related to the timing of the annual canvass.

Experts tell us that April is the best month for raising money because people have their affairs in order for income tax purposes and they are considering the tax effect of charitable giving. The same experts say that October and November are the worst months because folks are worried about paying Christmas-time bills. However, in "snowbird" and "sunbird" congregations, it is better to canvass when the most members are present.

Consequently, a fiscal year that begins in the summer is usually best. It is also consistent with the fiscal years of the Unitarian Universalist Association and most districts.

Changing the Fiscal Year   When a congregation changes its fiscal year, it must consider whether to have a "short" year or a "long" one. For example, a congregation with a fiscal year beginning January 1 that wishes to change to a July 1 fiscal year, a short year would be six months. A long year would extend to eighteen months.

For the short year, it would be necessary to run two fund drives: one in the fall for the year beginning January 1 (for six months) and another in the spring for the new year beginning July 1 (for twelve months). For the long year, members would be asked to pledge once for an eighteen-month period. Experience indicates that the short year generally produces more income, though doing two canvasses requires more work.

The Governing Board

The governing board of Unitarian Universalist congregations is referred to in a variety of ways: "the board," "The Board of Trustees," and even "the Standing Committee" or "the Parish Committee" in some older congregations. The responsibilities of the board and its composition are outlined in each congregation's bylaws. In general, a governing board of a congregation develops administrative policy, is accountable for the business affairs of the congregation, and is the trustee of the property of the congregation.

Whenever appropriate, the governing board should consult directly with the congregation, staff, council, or committee chairs in making its decisions. Congregations allow for such consultation in a variety of ways. At least three models of board and committee interactions are operative in our congregations.

Administrative Board   In this model, the governing board is composed of officers, trustees at-large, and committee chairs. The terms of office are arranged so that continuity and turnover are provided for. Communication between the committees and the board is direct. Coordination of program policy and budgetary responsibility is built into this model. A disadvantage is that committee chairs have to attend board as well as committee meetings, which can overburden them as well as the board with responsibilities best worked on in committee.

Policy-Making Board   In this model, the governing board is composed of officers and trustees elected by the congregation on a rotating basis, so that some members are replaced each year. Some or all board members may serve as liaisons to one or more committees. An advantage of this model is that board members are freed to attend to overall policy decisions and financial matters. They attend committee meetings as necessary but are not expected to be working members of other committees. A disadvantage is that communications between the board and committees may be haphazard. Consequently, this model depends on committee chairs and members interacting with the board as necessary.

Board-Council Model   In this model, the governing board and officers are elected by the congregation, as in the model for a policy-making board. The council is composed of chairs or representatives of the committees and may meet three or four times a year or monthly. The vice president sometimes also chairs the council.

An advantage of this model is that it provides for program coordination without overburdening board members or committee chairs. This model is particularly appropriate for middle-sized and larger congregations that have several active programs. Large congregations may have several councils, each including representatives from committees that are closely related (e.g., Education Council, which includes Children's Religious Education Committee, Adult Religious Education Committee, Youth Adult Committee, Young Adult Programs).

As a congregation grows in size, it may change models to allow for a greater distribution of responsibility among the committees and the council.

Whatever model a congregation adopts, the governing board in a local congregation is entrusted with the responsibility of making policies that are consistent with and help to further implement the congregation's mission and stated direction. The board in any congregation lives in the tension between governing and managing the congregation's affairs. It is easy for a board to get caught up in administrative details or to do the work that should be delegated to the committee or staff responsible for that area.

A board can often lead best by knowing when to engage the congregation's committees, staff, and membership in their conversation. Generally, in a congregation that draws on congregational polity, it is the congregation that convenes to make large policy decisions. Consequently, in addition to its role to set policy, the board has the responsibility of incorporating the congregation's decisions in its work as well as presenting major decisions to the congregation.

Membership Committee

One of the most important committees in a congregation is the membership committee. Because of the mobility of our society, we must continually seek new members to maintain the size of our congregations. If we want to grow, we must clearly intend to do so, plan carefully, and follow through with a membership program.

Although the charge of the membership committee varies from one congregation to another, it is usually responsible for contacting potential new members, welcoming newcomers, and recognizing and helping to integrate new members into the life of the congregation. It works closely with publicity and hospitality committees and with the minister (if there is one).

The typical membership committee's job is:

- for each committee member to be well versed in the principles of Unitarian Universalism, the nature of the local congregation, its programs and emphasis, and to be able to formulate reasons for people to join;

- to welcome newcomers and help them get acquainted;

- to survey the community to discover areas (geographic, economic, social, and political) in which potential new members might be found;

- to search out potential new members;

- to develop means of approaching nonchurch-affiliated persons who might find a focus and association in Unitarian Universalist religion;

- to plan programs of orientation for those new to Unitarian Universalism;

- to plan with the minister and the congregation president or worship committee for suitable recognition of new members;

- to examine the membership roll, assisting in keeping it current and to maintain contact with those whose participation may be waning.

Ideally, every member of the congregation is on the membership committee. Realistically, the committee should have at least three hard-working members for a small congregation and five to seven for a congregation of 150 or more. The size of the committee also depends on the responsibilities of the committee.

Members of the committee should be personable, outgoing, articulate, and enthusiastic Unitarian Universalists. A good balance of age and gender helps the committee be more effective in working with a variety of newcomers. It is also valuable to have at least one brand-new member on the committee as well as others who are longer-term members.

The ways in which a committee carries out its responsibilities also vary from congregation to congregation. Generally, the committee members discover newcomers, greet them, and introduce them to members who can be counted on to help them get acquainted and answer their questions with friendly intelligence. Committee members encourage newcomers to sign a visitors book (making it clear that it is not the membership book) or to fill out a pew card.

The committee may be responsible for maintaining a rack of pamphlets about Unitarian Universalism and preparing an attractive brochure about the local congregation to be added to the pamphlet rack. The committee selects a way to follow up with visitors—a personal note, a telephone call, or a special invitation to a congregational event—and see that their names are added to the mailing list if they wish to receive the congregation's newsletter.

At least once a year, more often for large or rapidly growing congregations, the membership committee should sponsor an orientation for newcomers who wish to know more about Unitarian Universalism and the local congregation. These sessions should be carefully planned to involve newcomers and longer-term members in sharing personal religious views, to explore together the liberal religious heritage, and to explain the programs and organizational structure of the local congregation. In addition, as personal interests, needs, and skills of newcomers become known, the membership committee sees that they are invited to social events, special programs, interest groups, work parties, or committee meetings.

Some newcomers soon indicate an interest in becoming members. Others wait for an invitation. The membership committee should be ready to explain what is involved in joining when newcomers ask and should extend the invitation when the time seems right to newcomers who do not ask. Though we not want to pressure people to join, some people who attend fairly regularly have never become members because it was never suggested to them.

Chapter 7, "Programming for Congregational Growth," has several ideas for a membership committee.

Religious Education Committee

In many congregations the work of the religious education committee is lifespan in scope and includes programming for children, youth, and adults. Program development, teacher and leader recruitment, and publicity for programming are concerns dealt with by religious education committees.

Other congregations use a model of separate committees for adult religious education and religious education for children and youth. Sometimes the adult religious education committee is a subcommittee of the religious education committee. In either case, regular communication between committees dealing with religious education programming for children, youth, and adults is important. A joint retreat once a year is an excellent way to affirm common vision and support particular plans.

Starting a Religious Education Committee

A religious education committee, even in the smallest congregation, should be composed of at least three members to share the preparations *and* the celebrations. Start by finding out who might be interested in the religious education program. Your search need not be limited to parents. Adults without children, older teenagers, and grandparents in the congregation may also be interested. Because religious education ultimately is the responsibility of the entire congregation, be sure to invite the congregation's leadership or minister to participate.

Responsibilities of the Religious Education Committee

The work of the religious education committee generally includes setting goals, objectives, and a philosophy for the programs it establishes. Included in its responsibilities may be:

- considering the interests and needs of all members: children, youth, and adults;

- becoming familiar with the religious education materials available from the Unitarian Universalist Association and elsewhere;

- assessing the interests and skills available among members within the congregation that can be used in program development, leadership, and promotion;

- designing a program for the year that is well balanced and adapted to the needs and interests of various segments of the congregation and uses available resources;

- involving the constituents of various programs (children, parents, youth, young adults, singles, older adults, etc.) in recommending program ideas and plans;

- locating leadership for various aspects of the program and providing orientation, training, and support for this leadership;

- arranging for necessary class or meeting space and working with congregational leaders to create an appropriate learning environment in that space;

- arranging for necessary equipment and supplies;

- coordinating scheduling with other congregational events and programs;

- evaluating the program in a way that includes feedback from participants and leaders;

- planning for professional religious education leadership when feasible and covenanting with that religious educator in ways that will continually enhance the congregation's ability to meet the religious education needs of its members;

- planning programs with the congregation's leadership so that religious education programming can be an expression of the congregation's guiding vision and sense of mission, and is an outreach into the surrounding community.

The religious education committee is a very important committee in the life of a congregation. Its members need to have the vision, skills, and commitment to fulfill its important responsibilities. In the beginning, of course, not all committee functions mentioned may be necessary for your program, but as your program grows, the scope of the committee's work will evolve.

Social Justice Committee

A job description enables the members of a social justice committee to understand the tasks and functions of their group. Usually in the fall, the committee reforms and starts a new year. The fall is a good time to write or revise the job description. Writing a job description reminds longtime members of what they are supposed to accomplish and provides new committee members a chance to learn the tasks of the group.

Below are elements for a job description for your social justice committee, which you can adapt to your own congregation.

- Minimum number of members.

- Terms of office.

- Budget amount.

- Leadership structure.

- Purpose (to inform and educate congregation members and the public in areas of social concern; to find ways and means to rectify social injustices; to sponsor and support groups organized to deal with social problems; and to develop informed leaders to foster a just and peaceful world).

- Coordination (members of the committee will serve as liaisons to the board of trustees, congregation council, district, and the local Interfaith Coalition for Peace and Justice).

- Provide opportunities for members and friends of the congregation to participate in social service projects, including collecting money, donating food and clothing, and supporting senior citizen and youth programs.

- Conduct educational programs (worship services, seminars, forums) to raise the congregation's consciousness about social issues.

- Enable members and friends of the congregation to witness about social issues, including writing letters to and visiting elected officials, writing letters to the editor, participating in demonstrations, testifying at public hearings.

- Encourage members and friends of the congregation to organize to change systems of oppression and injustice.

- Research and analyze social justice issues in depth. Develop action strategies to achieve significant results.

- Develop public statements in the name of the committee or, where appropriate, in the name of the congregation.

- Publicize what is being done so that members of the congregation and the wider community know what is happening and how they can become involved.

- Use the special talents of congregation members and local citizens to implement change. Many members are gifted problem solvers, organizers, and researchers; others enjoy doing hands-on work such as typing, serving food, or staying at an overnight shelter.

- Train people in organizational and social-change skills.

- Ensure that the congregation building is used to facilitate social change: have special programs housed in the congregation; open the congregation for meetings of community groups; allow controversial groups a place to meet.

- Make sure the congregation's financial resources are used for moral ends: ethical investing of endowment funds; fundraising for community projects; purchasing supplies from organizations involved in social change; purchasing environmentally safe products; using the congregational building to support bail bonds.

- Develop links with and use the resources of denominational social change groups: the Unitarian Universalist Service Committee, Cambridge Forum, Unitarian Universalist United Nations Office, the Unitarian Universalist Peace Network, etc.

- Create alliances with community organizations; for example, the NAACP, NOW, the Rainbow Coalition, and churches and synagogues (ecumenical and interfaith groups).

- Develop a budget to allocate the financial resources of the committee. Educate members of the congregation on the use of the financial resources of the congregation to bring about social change.

Worship Committee or Sunday Service Committee

What happens on Sundays is significant to the life and well-being of the congregation. Inspiration, intellectual challenge, spiritual nourishment, community belonging, intergenerational connections, continuity with the Unitarian Universalist faith, and an expression of the living tradition of Unitarian Universalism are all possible. What happens can energize and affirm members and their families, deepening their sense of belonging and commitment. What happens gives visitors their crucial first impression of what Unitarian Universalism and a specific congregation are like, so that a return visit and a desire to know more become the norm. An overriding recommendation is to pay attention to detail, which communicates that you care enough about what you are doing to do it well.

Often, small lay-led congregations have a Sunday service committee with the significant responsibility to provide for the service every Sunday. The schedule is often coordinated by one person who uses the musical, oratorical, and other skills of committee members as needed. In such cases, the Sunday service tends to be topical, with the subject related to who has been invited. Guest speaks are often not Unitarian Universalists, so attention needs to be paid to how to create continuity and a sense of relatedness to Unitarian Universalism every Sunday.

Even the smallest congregation should deliberately and regularly schedule a visiting Unitarian Universalist minister to conduct the service. The funds to provide for this visit should be deemed as important as paying the heating bill. The Church of the Larger Fellowship's Service for Small Societies also offers, as a subscription series, a variety of Sunday services and audio-visual resources appropriate for Unitarian Universalist congregations. This do-it-yourself service provides readings, a children's story, sermon, and other resources that a lay leader can rehearse and read to plan a quality service.

Worship committees of small congregations should also maintain a library of worship resources readily available to members who are conducting services. Anthologies and other resources of inspirational readings and service components are available from the Unitarian Universalist Association Bookstore. Committee members should not be expected to pay for these resources themselves.

Larger congregations with ministers sometimes leave the Sunday morning service entirely to the minister. Others have a worship committee that provides a service monthly or on special occasions. Still others have a worship committee that works closely with the minister in planning all or some of the services.

During a minister's sabbatical leave, a worship committee can become even more active. The UUA Department of Ministry has published a *Sabbatical Leave Handbook,* available from the department. Worship committees should review the recommendations outlined in this manual, preferably a year before the Sabbatical begins.

Membership on the worship committee also varies among congregations. Most larger congregations include representatives from the music, decoration, intergenerational, public address and lighting, and dramatic committees so that the service is planned from a holistic perspective. Even highly liturgical services will be enhanced by quality music and using a variety of readers who reflect the congregation's diversity.

Many Unitarian Universalist congregations are providing space for adults and children to be together during some part of the Sunday service. An intergenerational activity may or may not include a children's story, but can include a family chalice lighting ceremony, music, and reading before the children leave for their own religious education program. Such an activity provides an opportunity for families to sit together and fosters the idea that the Sunday service is a place where people of every age are vital to the congregation's sense of community.

The worship committee may make recommendations to the congregation about the music, welcoming procedures for visitors, childcare and religious education school programming, the aesthetics of the meeting place, the coffee hour, and equipment such as a public address system. The committee should function with quality control in mind. Small matters, such as the number of spoken announcements, often require monitoring—the committee should not hesitate to make guidelines for announcements. Some committees, for example, require that a rehearsal be held for special services in which the minister(s) is not involved.

The committee should also recommend when the congregation should offer two services instead of one on Sunday. Many congregations resist the idea of having two services, because the congregation will be divided. But if the congregation wishes its growth to continue, it has to accommodate a larger number of participants. Studies show that a congregation that is more than eighty-five percent full on a Sunday morning needs to consider providing another opportunity for people to worship. Crowded church schools and a lack of parking spaces (except in urban congregations, where the situation is different) can also be symptoms that require attention, lest the congregation plateaus in membership while it grows older each year. Some congregations have alternate services on weekday evenings. A guide to holding two services is available through the UUA Department for Congregational, District, and Extension Services.

Advance planning for worship committees is essential. The larger the congregation, the longer the time frame required. Last-minute planning reduces quality. Middle-sized and larger congregations should, for example, focus on what to plan for Christmas holiday services during a meeting early in January before the next year's holidays. This allows time for obtaining special services from individuals and helps evaluate past experiences that are still fresh in the minds of the participants.

Worship committees in smaller congregations might meet quarterly. Each meeting allows time for making last-minute arrangements for services to be held within the next three months, beginning with the next Sunday, as well as advanced planning for services to be held in three to six months.

A worship committee should not be afraid to evaluate. There is always a reluctance to critique an individual's contribution. Tact is always important. But too often sloppiness or a participant's unpreparedness detract from quality and give the impression that those responsible don't really care what happens. A good exercise is to ask new members or visitors periodically how they felt about what happened on a particular Sunday in terms of quality. Sometimes even a small fine tuning of a routine can make a great difference in the overall result of the experience for everyone.

The worship committee can be one of the most exciting areas of involvement for members if it is empowered and supported by the minister(s) and leaders of the congregation. Worship is the place where so many aspects of our faith come together publicly. Opportunities for finding the right balance between innovation—to make our faith alive for younger generations—and tradition—where the tried and true still move the soul—flourish in congregations that see worship as a living, vibrant expression of Unitarian Universalism.

Committee on Ministry

The purpose of a committee on ministry is to strengthen the quality of ministry in the congregation. Such a committee serves as a support group for the minister and as a communication channel between the minister and the congregation.

In establishing the committee, the minister should submit to the governing board a list of six names, any of whom will be satisfactory. The governing board appoints three of those to the committee. Another possibility is for the minister and the board to submit six names to each other and both agree on the final three to constitute the committee. Other models for submitting names are possible.

When a minister is new, it is sometimes the practice to invite members of the ministerial search committee to fill some positions on the committee on ministry for the first six months so that the minister will have an opportunity to get to know congregation members before making nominations. However nominated and chosen, committee members must have the confidence of both minister and congregation.

The term of office for committee members should be sufficiently long to enable them to get to know the minister well and to develop effective ways of working together as a committee and with the minister. Terms should be staggered so that there is never a need to start over with an entirely new committee. To fill a vacancy on the committee, the minister may submit to the governing board a list of three names, from which to choose one.

The committee should meet monthly, with a regular agenda for each meeting so that during a year each aspect of the ministerial-congregational relationship is reviewed. Every September, for example, the committee might discuss the minister's performance expectations for the coming year; every October, the minister's compensation; every November, the minister's housing situation, etc. Reviews of the minister's performance in relation to goals should occur regularly. Various evaluation instruments are available from the UUA Department of Ministry.

Monthly meetings with a regularly scheduled review of different items avoids a crisis orientation in the work of the committee and the eyes of minister and congregation. A regular agenda helps the discussion to be focused and goal oriented. There may be a regularly scheduled meeting of the committee without the minister once a year, if it is thought desirable. However, the committee should never hold a meeting without telling the minister, and it should meet with the minister as soon as possible thereafter to share the substance of that meeting.

The most important functions of the committee on the ministry are:

- to help the minister carry on an effective ministry by being available for counsel;

- to keep the minister advised about conditions within the congregation as they affect relations between minister and members, with its main thrust being to strengthen and improve relationships;

- to continually interpret to the congregation the nature and scope of the work of the minister, including a clarification of role expectations and realistic priorities for minister and members;

- to consult with the minister and submit an annual compensation recommendation to the governing board or personnel committee;

- to work with the minister on his or her continuing education program, sabbatical planning, or other professional development and to advocate such plans to the governing board and congregation, including appropriate funding.

Young Adult Committee (YAC)

One of the best ways to oversee youth programming in a congregation is with a young adult committee. YACs remove some advance planning and decision making from the unwieldy context of the regular youth group meeting.

Ask the youth group to elect representatives to serve on the YAC. In a smaller youth group, simply invite interested members to serve on the committee. The selected youth and a few outside adults (a representative from the religious education committee, a board member, a parent, or other interested adults) meet to come up with ideas for programs and activities, to make sure that commitments are kept and projects completed, to select and supervise advisors, and to act as a forum for discussion of youth-related concerns in the congregation.

The advisors and the director of religious education would serve on the committee *ex officio*. Maintain a ratio of three youth to one adult on the committee to help foster youth leadership and engender youth ownership of the programming.

Finance Committee

Typically, the finance function includes responsibility for fundraising, budgeting, pledge record-keeping, bookkeeping, and finance. It is advisable to assign different people to these areas. The type of person who enjoys record keeping is often not the same person who enjoys fundraising, and vice versa.

In most congregations the finance committee is responsible for the management of financial resources. Occasionally this committee is also responsible for raising funds from the members each year to finance the operating budget. It is recommended that congregations separate these functions into two committees.

An effective finance committee works with all standing committees of the congregation to develop a budget, which is referred to the governing board and voted on by the membership. For information on developing a mission budget refer to Chapter 12, "Developing a Congregational Budget."

In addition to developing a budget, the finance committee monitors the congregation's income, expenses, and pledge payments, and makes regular reports to the board and the congregation.

The finance committee should arrange for an annual audit or review of the financial records by an independent accountant or financial agency.

The finance committee may also take responsibility for securing property and liability insurance for congregational facilities.

Denominational Affairs Committee

The primary responsibility of the denominational affairs committee is to provide a liaison between the congregation and the Unitarian Universalist Association and the district. The committee meets to discuss issues of denominational concern. It promotes education on Unitarian Universalist General Assembly resolutions in collaboration with other committees. It fosters an understanding of and commitment to what it means to be a responsible member of the Association of Unitarian Universalist congregations.

Through these efforts, the denominational affairs committee prepares a pool of people in the congregation to be delegates to the General Assembly and district meetings.

Every Member Canvass Committee

This committee plays a critical function in assuring the congregation's quality of life. It is responsible for providing members with an opportunity to contribute financially so that the goals of the congregation may be realized.

This committee works best when it views itself as having a year-round function. A new committee should be convened as soon as the canvass is completed. The committee has six main areas of responsibility.

Evaluation

The every member canvass committee should begin its year with a joint meeting of the retiring members and new members to conduct a canvass evaluation. The evaluation should include a review of the process: What went right? What went wrong? Did people understand their roles? Did they fulfill their responsibilities? What could be done better?

A second component of this meeting is a financial evaluation. How much was raised? How many pledges increased? stayed the same? decreased? dropped out? were new? The committee needs to look for patterns that indicate areas where the canvass needs improvement.

Planning and Coordination

The committee is responsible for developing a calendar and timetable for canvass activities and coordinating it with the congregation's master calendar. For further information on planning a successful annual canvass refer to Chapter 12, "Developing a Congregational Budget." The committee also coordinates activities with the long-range planning and finance committees and works with them to develop canvass materials.

Implementation

The committee recruits, trains, and manages canvassers. It plans and conducts canvass gatherings including campaign kickoffs, canvasser training, and postcampaign celebrations.

Communication

Communication is one of the critical functions of the committee. The congregation needs to be clear about its dreams for the coming year and what is needed from the membership for these dreams to come true. Information needs to be positive, upbeat, inspiring, and frequent, and should use a variety of formats: information sessions, pulpit testimonials, newsletter articles, brochures, and invitations. The committee should strive to ensure that every printed piece is attractive, appealing, and readable—especially the pledge card.

Celebration

The committee needs to communicate success to the congregation. Whenever possible, the congregation should celebrate its ability to fund its dreams.

Long-Range Planning Committee

The long-range planning committee develops and facilitates a process to determine a congregation's future. The result of this process, which will include contributions from the congregation's membership and special focus groups, is a long-range planning report. In this report, the committee makes recommendations to the board and probably the entire congregation based on the results of the long-range planning process.

The long-range planning committee may be a standing committee or a special issue committee. If the long-range planning committee is a standing committee of the congregation, its members should serve for staggered terms of approximately three years. Occasionally, a special long-range planning task force can be established in a congregation as a short-term committee, appointed to work on a particular critical issue a congregation is facing (e.g., whether to move to another location).

Role of the Committee

The long-range planning committee is in charge of developing a vision, gathering information, formulating crucial questions, determining critical facts to be considered, posing possible solutions, considering the congregation's reactions, shaping final recommendations, and taking those recommendations to the board and the congregation for a vote.

The long-range planning committee has to determine how to engage itself and the congregation in a long range planning process to:

- obtain the information it needs
- solicit ideas from the congregation
- involve the congregation in exploring new possibilities
- help build support for new possibilities and recommendations that come from the long-range planning process.

Chapter 4, "Congregational Planning and Goal Setting," contains a section on the long-range planning process and outlines possible steps for the committee to consider.

Composition of the Committee

Rather than attempting to develop a committee that is representative of different groups within a congregation, you should attempt to find people who can respect diverse opinions, are able to listen to others, have good communication skills, and are widely respected within the congregation.

Ongoing Work of the Committee

The long-range plan that results from the process should be subject to annual review, revision, and extension. The long-range planning committee will oversee the process of annual revisions. The committee raises questions such as, "Are we meeting our goals? If not, why not?" and "Are our vision and strategies for the future still sound? If not, what changes are needed?" to the board, congregational leadership, and the congregation.

Since implementing and monitoring the long-range plan are critical to its success, the long-range planning committee should be a standing committee.

Resources

101 Ideas for Membership Growth. A pamphlet available from the UUA Department for Congregational, District, and Extension Services.

Belletini, Mark. "Worship in UU Congregations" pamphlet. Boston, MA: Unitarian Universalist Association, 1993.

Noyce, Gaylord. *Church Meetings That Work.* Bethesda, MD: Alban Institute, 1994.

"Service for Small Societies." Boston, MA: Church of the Larger Fellowship, Unitarian Universalist.

Singing the Living Tradition. Boston, MA: Unitarian Universalist Association, 1994.

Additional Resources

REACH (Religious Education Action Clearing House) Packet, available from the UUA Department of Religious Education.

UUA Meditation Manual, published annually by Skinner House Books, available through the UUA Bookstore.

Films, slides, recordings, kits to borrow from the UUA Video Loan Library, accessed through the UUA Bookstore.

Video materials from Rocky Stegman Productions, 1715 S. Boston Ave., Tulsa, OK 74119.

Additional pamphlets on Unitarian Universalism, available through the UUA Bookstore.

Unit IV

Engaging in Mission: Programming, Ministry, Outreach, and Funding

Six

Religious Professionals

Ministry and the Services of the Unitarian Universalist Association Department of Ministry

The Department of Ministry serves the needs of congregations, ministers, and the Association by providing counsel, leadership, and resources for developing and nurturing a ministry of excellence and effectiveness, enhancing common worship, and strengthening institutional health. It develops and delivers programs ranging from credentialing and settlement to counseling in career development, ministerial-congregational relations, and financial planning.

The department is staffed and organized to provide the following services to congregations:

- The director of ministry oversees the work of the department, serves as executive secretary of the Ministerial Fellowship Committee, and provides direction and support to efforts to strengthen our ministry in congregations and community-based settings.

- The ministerial development director is responsible for administering the ministerial settlement process, which seeks to facilitate the appropriate matching of professional ministers with the needs of congregations.

- The ministerial education director is responsible for relating to all candidates for our ministry and the theological schools, administering scholarship aid to and counseling students, and working to build and support the recruitment of well-qualified candidates for our ministry.

- The church staff finances director provides resources and counseling to ministers and congregation leaders on financial issues relating to congregation staff and congregations, and coordinates the Unitarian Universalist Association insurance and pension programs.

- The ministerial development director provides counsel to ministers on career development issues and opportunities, provides information about continuing education for ministry, and develops educational programs to strengthen ministry.

Finding a New Minister

Most congregations seeking a new minister are replacing a minister who has resigned, retired, or died. Others are seeking a minister for the first time, or adding a second or third minister to the staff. Each situation is unique; a wise board of trustees will seek the advice of experienced professionals as early as possible.

It is tempting when a departing minister is present to look to him or her for counsel about the transition process. However, it is not ethical for a departing minister to suggest or recommend an interim minister or a successor, or to participate in the search process. Instead, the departing minister should refer questions about the transition process to the appropriate Unitarian Universalist Association staff members.

The staff member best able to help make basic decisions about ministry is the district executive (DE). The district executive, who may be a minister or layperson, is an experienced consultant who knows how you can benefit from the services the Unitarian Universalist Association provides to congregations. Soon after a minister's departure is made public, the district executive conducts a transition interview with your board. In some districts, a transition team assists the district executive in this work.

A decision that usually needs to be made right away is whether to employ an interim minister. A good interim minister offers a refreshing change of style, active leadership toward shared goals, and healing ministry to rebuild faith and unity. An interim minister is freed to work on these transition tasks by a firm policy that interims may not remain beyond the interim term of one or at most two years.

Information about the Unitarian Universalist Association's interim ministry program is found in *The Interim Year*, a publication of the Department of Ministry provided to all congregations in transition. Your district executive may recommend that you consider a two-year interim ministry, which may be appropriate if you have experienced a serious conflict or for other reasons need to work within the congregation before choosing your search committee.

Your board of trustees needs to decide the title, general duties, and approximate compensation of the ministry position before the search committee begins its work. It is not fair to ask a search committee to fill a position whose basic outlines are unclear. Your board should study these decisions carefully and decide which it can make itself and which should be submitted to a vote of the congregation.

Other topics the district executive may cover in the transition interview include extension ministers, ministers shared by more than one congregation, part-time and consulting ministers, assistant and associate ministers, parish ministers, ministers of religious education, and community ministers. Try not to be distracted by these numerous categories. Your job is to define your congregation's needs in simple language that makes sense locally; the district executive can help you find the appropriate Unitarian Universalist Asscoaition resource.

The Ministerial Search Process

No choice a congregation makes is more important to its future or the future of Unitarian Universalism than the selection of a minister. A thorough, fair, and dignified search process is the beginning of a partnership of lay and ministerial leaders. For both minister and congregation, the process is strenuous, exciting, and informative. It can also be frustrating and discouraging. But generations of lay leaders and ministers testify that this process, if followed well, richly repays the time and effort it requires.

The congregation places great trust in its search committee. This experienced and diverse group of Unitarian Universalists commits the time and energy to get to know ministerial prospects well. Equally important, they undertake to know each other well so that together they can make the best choice not for themselves as individuals but for the whole congregation. Indeed search committee members often become lifelong friends.

Search committees do not simply choose the best among the candidates; they engage with ministers in thoughtful exploration. For ministry to be effective, both the congregation and the minister must sense a call, a felt conviction that this match is right for both. Ministers and search committees are not adversaries in this quest, but partners.

A third partner is the Unitarian Universalist Association. Knowing the importance of effective ministry for the health of the whole movement, the Unitarian Universalist Association supports the search process through the Ministerial Settlement Office of the Department of Ministry. The Settlement Office serves both ministers and congregations by providing information, counsel, structure, and resources. Its goal is to promote excellence in ministry by helping ministers and search committees function at their best as they choose one another.

The Settlement Office consists of the settlement director and an administrative assistant. The settlement director appoints to each district one ministerial settlement representative (MSR), whose role is to help each search committee to serve its congregation effectively. The ministerial settlement representative typically meets with the settlement committee several times during the search process, providing guidance and support. Where the salary is considerably less than the recommended minimum for full-time ministers and there is little chance of competition among ministers, the district executive may serve in place of the ministerial settlement representative, recommending ministers with advice and support from the settlement director.

The procedures recommended by the Department of Ministry are described in the *Ministerial Settlement Handbook*. These procedures reflect the experience of ministers and search committee members over many years. They are intended to be fair, thorough, nondiscriminatory, and efficient. Their use provides the search committee with a wide selection of potential candidates who meet criteria of its own choosing. They enable the committee to use the department and other resources of the Unitarian Universalist Association to obtain full information about each minister's experience and qualifications. Use of this process protects ministers from violating the Code of Professional Practice of the Unitarian Universalist Ministers Association and protects congregations from committing inadvertent slights that may result in losing a candidate. Finally, the procedures lay the foundation for a happy, fruitful partnership between a united congregation and its chosen minister.

Special Ministry Programs of the Extension Staff

- **The Extension Ministry Program** is available to congregations with a commitment to and potential for growth. If accepted into the program, the congregation receives a subsidy over a three-year period, which enables it to have a full-time minister that they would have been unable to do otherwise given the size and financial capabilities of the membership. With full-time ministerial services, a mission focused on commitment to quality programs, and a long-range strategy for growth, the congregation should be able, by the end of the three years, to provide for full-time ministry without subsidies.

- **The New Congregation Ministry Program** is specialized for new congregations, usually less than three years old. The program aims to provide full-time ministry to congregations with a high energy level of commitment and the potential to have 250 members in five years. These congregations are generally graduating from the New Congregation Development Program, have a covenanting congregation, and have at least fifty members at the time of their application to this program.

- **The Minister-on-Loan Program** assists congregations with at least fifty members in a variety of ways. Congregations may have reached a plateau and need a new sense of direction; they may want to try relating to a minister without committing to calling one, or they may have lost their group self-confidence and need a new image of a minister. Settled ministers may be loaned to the congregation for a six-week or other negotiated period.

Ministerial Intern Committee and Teaching Congregations

Congregational Relationships With Persons Preparing for the Unitarian Universalist Ministry

The relationship between congregations and persons preparing for the Unitarian Universalist ministry is important to the educational and informational process of students and others who will be our future religious leaders. A congregation may be called upon to participate in a student's process in at least two ways. A student with close ties to a congregation may ask for congregational sponsorship. It also may be asked to serve as a teaching congregation for a ministerial intern.

Sponsorship

For a person to be considered a candidate for fellowship in the Unitarian Universalist Association, it is necessary to obtain sponsorship by a Unitarian Universalist congregation. The purpose of this requirement is to ensure familiarity on the part of Unitarian Universalist ministers with Unitarian Universalist congregational life and to encourage congregations to take a responsible role in the recruitment, preparation, and assessment of future ministers.

Ordinarily, a person seeking sponsorship will contact an officer of the congregation or the minister. If your congregation does not have a policy regarding sponsorship or if you want information about it, contact the Ministerial Education Office in the Department of Ministry for general information and sample policies.

Congregations may choose to sponsor a candidate in a variety of ways. Some may be able to offer financial support; others will offer encouragement; some may provide mentoring possibilities, preaching opportunities, and other leadership challenges.

Sponsorship of a candidate indicates confidence in the person's potential suitability for Unitarian Universalist ministry. The Ministerial Fellowship Committee (the credentialing body of the Unitarian Universalist Association) and the Ministerial Education Office regard sponsorship as evidence that the person seeking fellowship is actively committed to Unitarian Universalism and the institutions that uphold our liberal religious tradition.

Documentation of congregational sponsorship is provided by using a form that should be provided by the person seeking sponsorship. It should be signed by the president or chair of the congregation's governing board. In most instances, sponsorship of a candidate will be determined by vote of the congregation or its representative body. If a request for congregational sponsorship constitutes a difficulty of any kind, consult with the Ministerial Education Director at the Unitarian Universalist Association.

Becoming a Teaching Congregation

The Ministerial Fellowship Committee believes that the most effective preparation for ministry is one that combines theological understandings *about* ministry (theory) with the action and reflection experiences of *doing* ministry (praxis) in a congregational or institutional setting. Most theological schools require field education as part of a graduate school program leading to ministry, and the Unitarian

Universalist Association requires it of those whose goal is Unitarian Universalist ministry.

Congregations considering the possibility of becoming teaching sites should determine if they are ready to enter into a partnership with a theological school, a student, and the Unitarian Universalist Association to provide a student with a viable, supervised field experience. Schools look for a congregation that meet their criteria for this task; students look for opportunities that will empower them to function in roles of ministry appropriate to their goals and needs.

A good teaching site is:

- dedicated to competence and excellence in ministry
- committed to the education of theological students as part of its outreach and mission
- a place where an intern can make a significant difference
- a place where an intern can pursue his or her goals in a supportive atmosphere
- one that has a minister trained in supervisory skills who will supervise, mentor, and meet weekly with the intern
- one that provides a committee of active members that will reflect with the intern while giving support, nurturance, and honest feedback
- committed to teaching, not just filling a gap in the staff structure
- one that provides varied professional experiences to challenge and test the intern's assumptions about ministry and its practice
- willing to work closely with the theological school and the UUA
- willing to provide honest evaluations of the intern's work to the Ministerial Fellowship Committee.

A comprehensive manual about ministerial internships is available from the Ministerial Education Office. It helps you understand the process of finding an intern, setting up intern committees, deciding on contractual issues such as compensation, developing a learning/serving agreement, and how to carry out other expected responsibilities.

Hiring a Religious Educator

Congregations grow better when they include and provide for programming for persons of all ages. When planning for a new congregation it is important to include religious education needs for children, youth, and adults, even if children and youth are not initially present. Identifying and encouraging leadership in religious education is one of the earliest tasks that needs attention.

In very small congregations, religious education leadership needs are often met entirely by volunteers, usually through a committee structure, even an informal one. The majority of mid-sized congregations employ part-time religious educators who work with religious education committees to ensure that the mission and goals of the congregation in this vital area are implemented. Many congregations hire and recruit for these positions from their membership when experienced professionals are not available.

Religious education is an aspect of a congregation's ministry. Good practice suggests that when you add a new staff member it is wise to review expectations of how that person will fit with the entire staff to work cooperatively to serve the congregation. Before hiring a religious educator, it is important that you assess your congregation's needs so that whatever job description you formulate provides for the functions and coverage the congregation expects. There is no one right job description—the congregation's needs and priorities should determine the outcome. You may wish to consult with your district office or the Unitarian Universalist Association Department of Religious Education to be sure you have the latest resources to assist your congregation's effort.

Frequently a search committee is appointed by the governing board of the congregation. This search committee works closely with the religious education committee during the information-gathering phase of its work. In smaller congregations the religious education committee sometimes carries out this task. A search committee might consist of three to five persons who have the confidence of the congregation and understand the needs to be met by filling this position. The minister's input should be sought early in the process. Provisions for informing the congregation on the progress of the search should be established.

In some congregations the search committee or religious education committee makes a hiring recommendation to the governing board, which makes the appointment. In other congregations the minister or religious education committee has the final say about who is hired. In some cases a congregational vote is used to ensure full congregational support for the selection. In any case, it should be clear who has the final authority in the hiring process.

District religious education committees serve as informal networks for interested parties looking for positions. Most committees have provisions for an experienced consultant to work with you. A district field staff person may be able to provide suggestions. If the position is part time, advertising the job in your congregation's newsletter as well as through cluster and district communication channels often produces good results. In 1994 the Unitarian Universalist Association inaugurated a Registry of Religious Educators, both volunteer and paid, to acknowledge their preparation and growth and to support a placement network for congregations and religious educators. For information about search and settlement of a minister of religious education, or an associate minister with religious education responsibilities, the Department of Ministry can help.

In summary, the process of hiring a religious educator involves assessing current staffing and program provisions, consulting your constituencies and envisioning future directions, creating a realistic and satisfactory job description, deciding on processes and criteria to recruit, interview, and hire, and finally, planning and implementing how to introduce and support the new religious educator.

Whatever staffing arrangements are made, in our system of congregational polity, the responsibility for religiously educating the congregation remains with the membership. Congregations are free to choose the leadership they want to meet their goals.

Religious Education Leadership Options

The Religious Education Leadership Options Landscape Plan encourages the use of a variety of basic training, continuing education, and academic programs by religious educators. It responds to a wide spectrum of congregations' and religious educators' needs, while respecting our Association's long-held standard of graduate level or equivalent preparation for professional religious leadership.

The plan recognizes five leadership options or categories, with entry at any point:

1. Basic registry option
2. Renaissance Program with letter of recognition
3. Continuing Education Program with certificate of recognition
4. Credentialed religious educator(masters degree)
5. Minister of religious education.

The Basic Registry Option is essentially an orientation program to introduce religious educators and congregations to good practices and to identify new religious educators, ensuring that they become integrated into existing support and resource systems as early as possible. Entering the Religious Education Registry, covenanting, and connecting with district and professional resources is emphasized. Participation in district or cluster-sponsored "Consider the Basics" workshops is encouraged. In a variety of ways, early, realistic understanding of the full range of religious education leadership possibilities and the attitudes, skills, and understandings needed in religious education leadership is communicated. Emphasis is given to helping the new religious educator make a graceful transition from being a member of the congregation to being a paid religious education leader where appropriate.

The Renaissance Program With Letter of Recognition consists of eight fifteen-hour experiential training workshops on basic religious education topics. Current topics are philosophy of religious education, administration, curriculum planning, worship for all ages, Unitarian Universalist history, Unitarian Universalist identity, training teachers, and ministry with youth. The Renaissance Program also gives credit for participation in Unitarian Universalist Leadership Schools. When five of these modules have been completed, the Unitarian Universalist Association sends a letter of recognition to the participant. Many districts also give lapel pins or other means of recognition for this achievement.

Continuing Education Program With Certificate of Achievement. This category provides a "postrenaissance" component of leadership development recognition. Individual learners, as part of their covenanting process, take responsibility for developing a growth and learning action plan within general guidelines provided by the Unitarian Universalist Association. This option has been designed to appeal to a broad range of religious educators who have varied life experience, education, resources, and motivations. In all cases, choices, discretion, and mutual agreement at the level of the local congregation determine the specific plan. It is accomplished by completing seven learning experiences from at least two of the following five categories:

1. individualized independent study
2. collegial study group
3. renaissance modules
4. educational conferences and workshops
5. university or seminary courses.

Credentialed Religious Educator. This recognition option is available to individuals who hold a master of arts degree in religious education, complete a written comprehensive exam in religious education, and complete an internship or supervised experience as a religious educator in a Unitarian Universalist congregation. A person who holds a graduate degree in a field other than religious education can also be a credentialed religious educator. He or she would need to complete a specified number of graduate courses in religion and religious education comparable to the preparation needed for a master of arts degree in religious education.

Minister of Religious Education. Educational standards for ministers of religious education are established and evaluated by the Ministerial Fellowship Committee. Ministers of religious education are required to have a master of divinity degree or equivalent, completed specific graduate work in areas of education and religious education, completed a clinical pastoral education program, and fulfilled a ministerial internship or its equivalent.

Participation in covenanting, the Religious Education Registry, the Renaissance Program, and continuing education for a Unitarian Universalist Association Certificate of Recognition are forms of recognition that provide incentives for the achievement of excellence. The Credentialed Religious Educator and the Minister of Religious Education are credentialed categories. The difference between recognition and credentials is significant in that objectively recognized evaluative elements—essentially, academic degree requirements—form the basis for the credentials. Recognition is awarded, credentials are achieved. Making provisions for both provides known criteria and standards by which congregations and religious educators can make intelligent choices.

Religious Education Covenant

Covenanted relationships are a core part of our religious tradition. In 1993 the report of the Unitarian Universalist Association board's Religious Education Leadership Committee reemphasized this notion as central to relationships of honesty and integrity for congregations and religious educators. The decision was made to promote participation in the development of appropriate religious education covenants for congregations and religious educators as a key part of the Religious Education Leadership Options Plan.

Simply stated, a religious education covenant is a set of mutually agreed-upon commitments between a religious educator and representatives of a congregation, one of whom is the minister, for purposes of mutual benefit. Covenanting is a practical way to develop religious education leadership positions consistent with our congregational polity and the specific needs and desires of a given congregation at a particular time. Central to the covenanting concept are:

1. **Theological reflection** on the visions and goals of the religious education program by the congregation, the minister, and the religious educator as a prerequisite to covenant.

2. **Mutual acceptance** by the congregation, minister, and religious educator of those elements or actions that form the focus of agreement on which the covenant is based.

3. **Accountability** by the parties on commitments made.

4. **Periodic review** to assess an existing covenant or to recovenant as needs evolve and to dialogue about how to make changes in the covenant gracefully.

The goals of covenanting are to instigate a conversation between a religious educator and representatives of the congregation about their relationship and this aspect of the congregation's ministry, and to acknowledge present expectations of the congregation, the minister, and the religious educator for their religious education program. Covenanting creates the possibility for the congregation and religious educator to outline mutual hopes and to specify how they may be realized. An important part of the covenanting process is that religious educators have an opportunity to evaluate their training and experience in light of the goals for the religious education program shared by educator and congregation.

In our Association, ministerial leadership generally comes through the calling of an ordained person who has been perceived by the Ministerial Fellowship Committee to have the appropriate credentials to recommend him or her to Unitarian Universalist congregations. In contrast, most of our small and mid-size congregations secure and develop religious education leadership from within their membership. In view of this reality, covenants are especially suited for developing growth and learning between the congregation and religious educator with identified resources, mutual commitment, and support systems for the religious educator's professional growth.

For more resources on religious education leaders, contact the Religious Education Leadership Development Office at (617) 742-2100.

Congregation Administrator

The congregation administrator can function as the glue that holds things together. Every congregation, whatever its size, has communication and organizational needs. If they can be responded to effectively and efficiently, the quality of programs and interaction between people and groups will be enhanced. Congregation administrators have the opportunity and the challenge to make that happen.

In small congregations, the administrator may be the only person on the staff. It is always important to find the appropriate person to fill this position, but especially in a small congregation, where the administrator may be looked to as the person most knowledgeable about the congregation. When an administrator is approached with all kinds of questions, friendliness and tact go a long way in providing an atmosphere where people feel valued and welcomed.

In larger congregations, the administrator works with other staff, including the minister(s), music director, custodian(s), and in some cases, supervises other staff. The administrator will report to the minister or other defined supervisor. Congregations are advised to develop clearly defined channels of communication and authority for the position to avoid misunderstandings and conflict that can easily arise in so important a position.

The administrator's work varies with the size of the congregation. It can include publishing the congregation's newsletter and reports, maintaining mailing lists and other filing systems, scheduling building use, overseeing office volunteers, and making sure that messages and mail are directed to the appropriate people.

Administrators can find efficient and effective support from the right office furnishings and equipment. A computer and appropriate software, quality printer and photocopier, telephone message system, and FAX machine can help even small congregations provide the necessary support services so that committees and task forces have an easier time meeting their responsibilities.

Every administrator as well as governing boards and ministers should read the *Association of Unitarian Universalist Administrators' Guidebook*, available from the Association of Unitarian Universalist Administrators' (AUUA), c/o Gail Huggett, 12314 South 14th Street, Jenks, OK 74037.

Congregation Musicians

Congregation musicians serve a vital role in a congregation and its worship life. The Unitarian Universalist Musicians' Network (UUMN) was founded in 1982 and aims to affirm the importance of and foster the use of music in the life of Unitarian Universalist congregations throughout the Association.

The UUMN is an organization that provides mutual support, education, information, and opportunities for the professional growth of Unitarian Universalist musicians; encourages the creation of music for Unitarian Universalist use by commissioning anthems by Unitarian Universalist composers; and works to upgrade the status of musicians serving Unitarian Universalist congregations.

Membership is open to all who are involved in Unitarian Universalist music and who support the goals and purposes of the UUMN.

For more information, contact the UUMN, c/o Robert Simiele, 1517 North 67th St., Wanwatosa, WI 53213.

Finances Related to Religious Professionals and Other Congregation Staff

The Unitarian Universalist Association Office of Church Staff Finances is funded jointly by the Unitarian Universalist Association and the Council on Church Staff Finances, an umbrella group composed of the Unitarian Universalist Association, the Unitarian Universalist Ministers Association, the Liberal Religious Educators' Association, the Association of Unitarian Universalist Administrators, the New York State Convention of Universalists, the Unitarian Universalist Retired Ministers Association, the Unitarian Service Pension Society, the Society for Ministerial Relief, the Unitarian Universalist Musicians' Network, and the Unitarian Universalist Women's Federation.

The director of Church Staff Finances serves local congregations and religious professionals through a periodic newsletter, various practical resource papers, individual consultations by mail or telephone, and workshops at district meetings, professional association meetings, and the General Assembly.

The following pages cover basic financial information that should be in the hands of all Unitarian Universalist ministers, professional directors of religious education, other congregation staff, and all congregations employing them. The material is divided into four sections: employment benefits, professional expenses and allowances, determining the housing allowance, and budgeting for the services of religious professionals.

Reference is made to income tax and social security tax requirements for religious professionals and congregations within the United States. For Canadian requirements, contact the Canadian Unitarian Council at 188 Eglinton Avenue East, Suite 706, Toronto, Ontario M4P 2X7 Canada. In addition, the Office of Church Staff Finances is available for consultation with Canadian professionals and congregations.

The monetary cost of having professional religious leadership in a local congregation is composed of three elements: employment benefits, professional expenses and allowances, and salary (including housing allowances for ordained ministers). While these three elements are often lumped together in a "total package," they need to be separated. The first two elements do not constitute income to the religious professional and most importantly should be considered basic to all employees.

For several decades it has been common practice for employers of all kinds to provide their employees with various benefits and to reimburse them for expenses incurred and directly attributable to their employment. The local Unitarian Universalist society is in much the same position as any other organization that employs professional staff and should handle related costs in a similar fashion.

Employment Benefits

While many employment benefits are available, those provided by Unitarian Universalist societies to their professionals and other congregation staff tend to be of two kinds: group insurance coverage and employer contributions to the Unitarian Universalist Association Pension Plan.

The Unitarian Universalist Association operates a Group Insurance Plan available to all ministers, directors of religious education, and other congregation staff. This plan consists of three parts administered by the Office of Church Staff Finances:

- **Major Medical Insurance.** Several options are available to single, married, and same-sex partners of any age employed by Unitarian Universalist organizations. It is comprehensive, portable from one society to another, but can be expensive, so comparisons ought to be made to what is available in the community. If staff are enrolled in the Unitarian Universalist plan, local society and organizational treasurers are billed monthly. Individuals are eligible to join within the first thirty days of employment or during the yearly open enrollment period, generally in September. The current plan year for medical insurance is September 1 to August 31. The coverage is carried by Blue Cross-Blue Shield of Massachusetts, which handles and pays all claims.

- **Group Term Life Insurance** is available to those employed by Unitarian Universalist organizations and to community-based ministers, under most circumstances. The premium is based on age, offered in one basic amount only—$45,000—through age sixty-four. Availability continues beyond age sixty-four, with declining benefits. Individuals are eligible to enroll within the first thirty days of employment or at other times by showing adequate evidence of insurability. There is no open enrollment period beyond the first thirty days of employment.

- **Long-term Disability Insurance** provides income protection of approximately two-thirds of salary (and housing where appropriate), during a long-term disability up to age sixty-five, or to age seventy under certain circumstances. The cost is based on salary and is available to all employed by Unitarian Universalist organizations and to community-based ministers under most circumstances. Individuals are eligible to enroll within the first thirty days of employment with no open enrollment period after this time, but participation is possible later based on adequate evidence of insurability.

Pension Plan

The UUA administers a pension plan available to all ministers, professional religious educators, and others employed by Unitarian Universalist organizations who are employed for 1,000 hours per year and have worked at least one year. It is a multiple-employer plan, which means that the local society enters into a Retirement Trust Agreement with the Unitarian Universalist Association and enrolls the employee in the plan. Because it is an employer plan, contributions are made by the local society and credited to the account of the participant. The plan is a defined contribution plan (in contrast to a defined benefit plan) and is fully vested. The contribution recommended by the Office of Church Staff Finances is fourteen percent of salary (salary and housing for ministers).

Contributions to the pension plan are tax-deferred income to the participant and only become taxable when the account is settled, for example, when she or he retires. (The money can also be withdrawn when employment ceases, the participant becomes disabled, or when the participant dies. Under most circumstances, withdrawal prior to age fifty-nine and a half carries with it tax obligations plus a ten percent penalty. It is possible to borrow against the pension fund for medical emergencies.) Upon the retirement of ministers, the amount paid out yearly by the plan is designated as housing allowance and is not taxable income if spent for that purpose.

The recordkeeping, billing accounts receivable, etc., for the pension plan are handled by the Finance Office of the Unitarian Universalist Association, under the direction of the treasurer. Information is available from the Office of Church Staff Finances.

Please note: for all of the above items to be classified as employment benefits, the payments must be made directly by the local society employing the individual. Handling all benefits in this manner usually has a significant impact on the income tax liability of the person to whom the benefits are provided, except for long-term disability premiums.

Professional Expenses and Allowances

In most employment situations, reimbursable expenses include travel, equipment such as books and periodicals or other tools of the trade, meetings and meals with clients, conference fees and expenses, professional dues—in short, the costs of doing business. The employee is expected to pay only his or her costs of personal living, not costs connected with employment.

Religious professionals and others serving Unitarian Universalist societies are no exception. There is a correlation between performance as a religious professional and having adequate funds to do the job well. Professional expenses should be handled by including an item in the society's budget for "Professional Expenses and Allowances." This item should be listed in such a way that it will not be considered salary or confused with salary.

The professional leader should make a monthly expense report to the society's treasurer setting forth professional expenses for the month. The treasurer should write a separate check reimbursing these expenses.

Generally speaking, professional expenses are the obvious costs listed above. Three additional comments are in order.

Travel from home to congregation is considered commuting, and not a professional expense; but all other professional travel, such as to meetings, hospitals, or members' homes on call are professional expenses. Tax law requires a daily log of all auto travel to claim reimbursement.

Meals and lodging are professional expenses only when away from home overnight, but meals that are entertainment of someone connected with professional responsibilities are a professional expense. Thus entertainment of members of the congregation at home or elsewhere is a professional expense.

If a housing allowance is used to provide a home that includes an office, this office space is not a professional expense. However, the supplies and equipment used in such an office can be taken as a professional expense.

In determining the amount to budget for professional expenses, care must be taken to budget this amount as closely as possible to what will be spent. If excess budgeted funds are available at the end of the fiscal year, IRS regulations do not allow converting those funds to salary.

For more information, write or telephone the Office of Church Staff Finances.

Determining the Housing Allowance

The amount designated by the congregation as the minister's housing allowance is determined jointly by the congregation's governing board and the minister, taking into consideration both the rules of the Internal Revenue Service and the circumstances of the minister and congregation.

The amount of the housing allowance must be declared by the congregation in advance of any payments for this purpose to the minister. The amount so designated must appear in the minutes of the board of trustees, standing committee, or meeting of the congregation. A specific line item or items in the annual congregation budget clearly labeled "Minister's Housing Allowance" is ordinarily sufficient if this budget is part of the official minutes.

When a minister comes to a new congregation in mid-calendar year, the housing allowance declaration should be included in the employment agreement, but in any case must appear in the minutes of the board or congregation. The housing allowance so designated may apply only to money paid after the beginning of the minister's employment and used by the minister to "provide a home" in connection with that employment. If circumstances change mid-year, it is permissible to change the housing allowance during the year to reflect those changes, but such changes cannot be made retroactively. The declaration should be made annually following initial employment.

Three rules apply:

1. One limit on the amount of ministerial housing allowance that may be excluded from gross income is that it may include only amounts actually spent "to provide a home." These expenses may include rent or mortgage payments, utilities (including telephone and television cable), repairs, furniture and furnishings, household supplies (except food), taxes, and all other costs of providing a home, except domestic help.

2. A second limit is that the amount that may be excluded from gross income cannot exceed the amount designated in advance by the congregation as housing allowance. If actual expenses run over the amount designated in advance, nothing can be done after the fact to correct the situation. If the amount actually spent is less than the amount designated as housing allowance, this balance must be reported to the IRS as "unexpended housing allowance."

3. The third limit is that the maximum amount that the congregation may designate as housing allowance for any period is the sum of the fair rental value of the house, plus the fair rental value of furnishings, plus utilities. The best method to determine fair rental value of a home and furnishings is to contact several real estate brokers for their professional judgment. Having a letter to that effect from one in the files would serve you well in the event of an audit. Don't forget to update that amount each year.

| Example | Let us assume that the home owned by the minister is worth $80,000, with furniture and furnishings worth another $15,000. The total utility bill was $2,800 over the previous twelve months. The *maximum* amount that can be designated as housing allowance is thus: |

Rental value of house	=	$900.00 per month
Furnishings	=	200.00 per month
Utilities (5% in the last year)	=	245.00 per month
		_____
TOTAL		$1,345.00 per month

The *maximum* housing allowance can be declared is thus $1,345.00 per month, or $16,140.00 per year.

Suppose this same minister, anticipating spending $16,140, asks the congregation to declare this amount as housing allowance. The minister spends $15,700 on the actual costs of "providing a home" but then has an unexpected roof repair bill of $2,000. Expenses come to a total of $17,700, but only $16,140 has been declared in advance as housing allowance, so only the latter amount can be excluded from gross income on the tax form.

But let us assume that the minister asked to have the maximum allowable amount declared as housing allowance, in this case $16,140, but actual expenses total $14,847 for the year. The minister has then spent $1,293 *less* than the declared housing allowance and must declare this amount as income for tax purposes.

Note that it is better to have the maximum legal declaration made by the congregation to allow as much margin as possible for major and unexpected expenses. It is too late to change the housing allowance declaration after the added expenses have occurred. If the declared amount turns out to be too large, it is a simple matter to report the unexpended balance as income.

In these days of changing real estate values and increasing costs for utilities, repairs, etc., it is important to keep the fair market rental value of the house at a realistic level to permit maximum flexibility for the minister.

While there is no legal requirement that the housing allowance described above be paid to the minister with a separate check from that written for his salary, the Office of Church Staff Finances recommends using a separate check as an additional reinforcement of the declaration made by the governing body of the congregation.

Parsonages and Housing Allowance

If the congregation provides a parsonage, including furniture and utilities, or either of these items, it is still necessary to declare a housing allowance to cover expenses not paid for by the congregation, e.g., household supplies, long distance phone service, or furnishings, that are legitimate parts of housing expenses. If the minister pays *any* of the cost that may properly be included in calculating the cost of "providing a home," a housing allowance to cover these costs should be made.

Further Considerations

The tax-free money used by the minister for "providing a home" may, in the event the minister owns the home, be used for expenses that are deductible for income tax purposes, for example, the interest paid on mortgages and real estate taxes paid on the property.

The tax law provides, however, that money derived from the tax-free housing allowance, a portion of which provides an office in the home, may *not* generate an additional deduction under "business expenses" by allocation of a portion of the total housing costs. If money other than tax-free housing allowance is used to purchase office supplies, these may be treated in the usual way, as a reimbursed expense. (The *Minister's Guide for Income Tax* is provided free to each fellowshipped minister by Meadville/Lombard Theological School and the Council on Church Staff Finances.)

Budgeting for the Services of Religious Professionals

That portion of the congregation's total budget available for the services of a religious professional should be allocated and disbursed as follows:

- **Employment Benefits.** These expenses should be budgeted first and not considered available to be negotiated. Pension contributions and premiums for group health and life insurance should be paid directly by the society's treasurer to make a clear distinction between employment benefits and taxable income. Premiums for long-term disability coverage should be deducted from the employee's salary and paid by the treasurer. In this instance, the premium is paid by taxable dollars, thus making any benefits that are paid tax free.

- **Professional Expenses and Allowances.** The minister and/or professional religious educator should submit monthly vouchers or another suitable form of record for reimbursement from this account, which includes auto expenses on an agreed-on per-mile basis (not to exceed IRS limits), resource materials such as books and subscriptions, professional dues, equipment such as computers, conference fees, and expenses, nonautomobile travel, and entertainment clearly related to professional duties and functions. The amount of money allocated to the account for professional expenses and allowances (recommended at twelve percent of salary and housing), can be adjusted during the year, provided that the total amount of money allocated for professional services in the budget does not exceed the gross sum set by the congregation or other governing body. Adjustments above that gross sum usually require congregational action.

- **Housing Allowance.** There are two basic situations for housing allowances:

(a) The minister receives the rent-free use of a home and, *in addition,* part of the budget item for ministerial services is designated as housing allowance to cover such expenses as furniture, furnishings, insurance, utilities, appliances, and nonedible supplies, such as cleaning materials and paper products, for which the minister pays directly.

(b) The minister *does not* receive the rent-free use of a home, but a significant portion of the total budget item for ministerial services is designated as housing allowance to cover the total cost of providing a home. (See above on determining the amount of the housing allowance.)

In any event, the monies which the minister receives with which to provide a home and the value of the rent-free use of a parsonage are *excluded* from the minister's income as defined by the Internal Revenue Service. All such monies should be paid in the form of a separate check and not mingled with other payments. At year end, the amount paid as housing allowance should *not* be reported in any fashion on the W-2 form.

- **Cash Salary.** The amount of money actually paid to the religious professional after the above items have been disbursed.

- **Salary for Social Security Purposes.** Ministers are considered self-employed and therefore pay their own Social Security tax. For Social Security purposes, the minister's salary is considered to be the sum of the housing allowance and cash salary. For professional religious educators who are not ordained ministers and are not considered to be self-employed, the Social Security tax should be withheld from item 4, cash salary, and then matched by the society.

- **Reporting Compensation to the IRS.** The Office of Church Staff Finances recommends strongly that taxable compensation for ministers, cash salary *only,* be reported on a W-2 form, not a 1099. Both appear to be allowed by the law, but recent IRS cases have consistently treated ministers as employees for this purpose, dictating the use of the W-2. All other employees' compensation should be reported on a W-2 as a matter of course.

Example

If the steps outlined above are followed, the result might be as follows:

Total amount available in society's budget for services of a religious professional: $52,807 minus employment benefits, professional expenses and allowances.

Major Medical Insurance		$8,256
Term Life Insurance		216
Long-term disability insurance		420
	Subtotal	$8,892
UUA Pension Plan		$4,715
[a minister is limited overall to 25%		
(14% of housing allowances and cash salary)		
of taxable income]		
Professional expenses and allowances		$4,200
Total employment benefits, expenses, and allowances		$17,807
Subtracted from budget of $52,807 =		$35,000
Housing allowance (if ordained)		$16,140
Cash salary		$18,860

The society's treasurer should disburse the funds as follows:

- **Insurance premiums** are paid directly to the companies involved. For the Unitarian Universalist Association group insurance plan, there is a consolidated monthly billing for the three plans. (Reminder: long-term disability premiums are to be deducted from salary as after-tax dollars.)

- **UUA Pension Plan contributions** are paid monthly directly to the Unitarian Universalist Association Finance Office, upon receipt of bill.

- **Expenses** are reimbursed to the religious professional by separate check in the amount of the monthly voucher submitted by the professional.

- **Housing allowance and cash salary** are paid directly to the religious professional, in separate checks where there is a part of the compensation designated as housing allowance. Separate checks eliminate uncertainty in preparation of the US Income Tax return as to how much money was actually disbursed and received as housing allowance.

For more information, read *Church and Clergy Tax Guide,* 1994 edition, by Richard Hammar. Available from Christian Ministry Resources, PO Box 2301, Matthews, NC 28106 (800-222-1840) for $14.95 plus shipping. This is a very complete and well-indexed, 200+ page guide that tells how to fill out a tax return and details professional expenses, congregation reporting requirements, social security, and other tax matters.

Sabbatical

A sabbatical is a time for rest and renewal to support future growth. "Sabbatical" means every seventh year. The idea has biblical origins; it is directed in the Bible that fields should be allowed to lie fallow every seventh year to regain strength and fertility. In modern practice, college professors and others receive sabbatical leaves.

The practice of granting sabbatical leaves to Unitarian Universalist ministers is common. There is also a growing practice of granting sabbaticals to other long-term congregation staff members such as directors of religious education.

The Unitarian Universalist Ministers Association recommends the following guidelines for sabbaticals:

- The minister accrues one month of sabbatical leave each year, subject to the other conditions set forth in this section.
- No sabbatical leave is to be expected before the completion of four years of service.
- Sabbatical leave may accrue for a maximum of six months.
- The length of sabbatical is a matter of agreement between the congregation's board of trustees and the minister.
- Sabbaticals may be taken separately from or together with vacation periods.
- Sabbatical leave is to be used for professional development. The congregation's covenant may include some guidelines.
- The covenant may require the minister to continue service to the congregation following the sabbatical. This period usually will not be longer than one year.
- The congregation and the minister will jointly plan for ministerial services during the sabbatical leave.
- If a sabbatical fund is established, it should be clearly stipulated whether it is for the use of the congregation or the minister.
- The minister shall receive full salary and housing allowance as well as insurance and pension benefits during the sabbatical. The sabbatical agreement shall specify how other ministerial allowances are to be handled.
- The minister is not obligated to return to the parish during the sabbatical period. If a situation of sufficient urgency arises for which the minister and board agree that his or her presence is necessary, the congregation will provide reimbursement for the expenses.
- In the event of a minister's resignation or dismissal, accrued sabbatical leave shall not be paid in financial equivalent.
- No action on ministerial tenure shall be taken during a sabbatical period.
- The covenant should refer to these general conditions for sabbatical leave. It should be supplemented by a letter composed by the minister and board that sets forth the detailed conditions for each sabbatical.

| Two key points: | • Planning for a sabbatical needs to start early, at least one year or eighteen months before the sabbatical begins. |
| | • The congregation and staff need to evaluate and discuss the challenges and stresses that will be placed on the congregation and its leadership during the period of separation and make plans to provide the resources to meet those needs. |

A good resource available for $10.00 from the Department of Ministry is the *Handbook on Sabbatical Leaves for Ministers and Congregations* by Helen L. Cohen and David C. Pohl.

Complaint Procedures for Ministerial Misconduct

The Ministerial Fellowship Committee has established the following procedures for complaints of ministerial misconduct.

Initiation of Reviews and Investigations

Investigations of ministers for unprofessional or unbecoming conduct or other violation(s) of the rules of fellowship shall be initiated by a complaint (usually sent to the executive secretary of the Ministerial Fellowship Committee, i.e., the director of ministry at the Unitarian Universalist Association) or in unusual circumstances by a vote of the executive committee of the Ministerial Fellowship Committee.

Complaints

Complaints involving alleged unprofessional or unbecoming conduct of a minister or other violation of the rules of fellowship shall be reviewed by the Ministerial Fellowship Committee. Complaints should be from a person or persons with firsthand knowledge of the circumstances. Complaints about the general suitability of a minister should be brought by the congregational, institutional, or agency board with whom the minister works. Except in cases involving children, the committee will not generally act upon complaints by persons not directly involved in the circumstances covered by the complaint.

Complaints must be made in writing and signed by the complainant or board of trustees and shall contain a brief statement of the facts on which the complaint is based. If necessary, the executive secretary will assist the complainant in reducing the complaint to writing.

Timeliness

Complaints should be received by the committee or its executive secretary within a reasonable time period following the circumstances giving rise to the complaint. Unless the executive secretary or the committee determines otherwise for good cause, the committee will not entertain any complaint that arises out of acts or omissions occurring more than six years before the date of the complaint and when there has been no repetition of that conduct during the six years preceding the complaint. Good cause shall include, but not be limited to, complaints involving abuse of children or particularly egregious behavior.

Cooperation

At any time the committee or its designees may decide to meet with the minister to share its concern and to explore ways to deal with the problem. Failure of the minister against whom the complaint has been made to comply with the requests of the executive secretary, the committee, or its designees at any stage of the procedures, including the investigation, hearing, and resolution of the complaint may be grounds for action under Ministerial Fellowship Committee Rule 25.

Notifications

As soon as appropriate after receiving a complaint, the committee will notify the minister. With the initial notification, the committee will request a written statement of the minister's position on the allegations in the complaint. Such statement of position should be received within ten days of the minister's receiving the committee's notice of complaint, unless an extension is granted for good cause by the executive secretary.

Screening of Complaints

All complaints and the minister's written response shall be reviewed by the executive secretary in consultation with the executive committee to determine what, if any, further action should be taken. The executive secretary may determine that further proceedings are not warranted. Any determination shall be reviewed and approved by the executive committee.

Resolutions

In consultation with the executive committee, the executive secretary may explore with the minister the possibility of a voluntary resolution of the issues, including but not limited to, reprimand, suspension, counseling, or resignation, etc., at any time during the processing of the complaint. The executive committee shall recommend any such recommendation to the full committee for its action.

Investigations

The type of investigation required by a complaint will depend on the allegations and the type of additional information required.

In consultation with the executive committee, the executive secretary shall determine the type and scope of investigation required. If deemed necessary, the Ministerial Fellowship Committee chair and the executive secretary may appoint an investigative committee. The investigative committee shall be composed of one or more members of the Committee or other suitable Unitarian Universalists.

In consultation with the Ministerial Fellowship Committee chair and the executive secretary, the appointed investigators will investigate the facts and circumstances related to the alleged misconduct, including but not limited to interviews with the complainant(s) and the minister. The investigators may request any documents or written information that will assist in the investigation.

The appointed investigators will file a report and all information collected, including tape recordings, transcripts, and statements, etc., with the executive secretary promptly after the conclusion of the investigation.

If appropriate, tape recordings may be transcribed and a copy of each witness's transcript or a summary may be forwarded to the witness for review and signature.

Review of Record

The Ministerial Fellowship Committee chair and the executive secretary should review the record. If it is determined that additional information is required, the investigators and/or the executive secretary may obtain the additional information.

Determination of Probable Cause

Once the record is complete, the executive committee shall determine whether there is probable cause to believe that the minister has engaged in unprofessional or unbecoming conduct or other conduct in violation of Rule 25 of the Ministerial Fellowship Committee.

Finding of No Probable Cause

If it is determined that probable cause does not exist, the executive secretary shall so notify the minister, complainant, and other interested parties.

The determination of no probable cause made by the executive committee may be appealed by the complainant to the full committee. The appeal should be written and contain a review of the reasons why the no cause determination should be overturned. The executive committee must receive an appeal within two weeks after a complainant receives the notice of the no cause determination. As soon as an appeal is received, the executive secretary should give notice to the minister involved and the minister may file a response.

Finding of Probable Cause

If it is determined that probable cause exists, the executive secretary shall so notify the minister, complainant, and other interested parties and schedule a hearing before the committee.

Hearings

The hearing before the committee shall follow the guidelines set forth in Rule 26 of the Ministerial Fellowship Committee Rules.

Guidelines for Investigating Complaints

It is the goal of the committee to ensure the prompt investigation and resolution of complaints that allege that a minister's conduct fails to adhere to the standards required for fellowship. Because the type of investigation or resolution required will depend on the nature of the complaint and the type of additional information required, the Ministerial Fellowship Committee chair and the executive secretary are empowered under the committee's procedures to initiate an investigation and appoint an investigative committee.

The following guidelines are to be used by the investigative committee in conducting its investigation.

1. In consultation with the executive secretary and the Ministerial Fellowship Committee chair, it is the responsibility of the investigative committee to develop a full and complete record of the facts and circumstances surrounding the complaint and any rel-

evant information that may be useful to the committee in its deliberations.

2. Each person appointed to an investigative committee is expected to maintain neutrality and an open mind throughout the investigation. All information obtained through the investigation must be held in the strictest confidence. Investigators should make every effort to ensure that they conduct themselves as neutral fact-finders, mindful of the need to protect the reputation of all participants at each stage of the process.

3. In consultation with the executive secretary and the Ministerial Fellowship Committee chair, the investigative committee should determine what, if any, additional information is required to assist the committee in its deliberations and the most efficient method for obtaining that information.

4. If it is determined that personal interviews are appropriate, the appointed investigators will interview the complainant, the minister against whom the complaint has been made, and as many other witnesses with knowledge of the issues or circumstances raised by the complaint, including representatives of the congregation board, the district executive, and any other persons deemed relevant by the investigators as appropriate and necessary. Interviews may be tape-recorded and a transcript from the tape recording may be prepared.

   The investigative committee may also request the letters, position statements, materials, and other documents that might assist it and the committee and its designees in responding to the complaint and resolving the issue.

5. Tapes, notes, and any other information gathered by the investigative committee should be transmitted to the executive secretary as soon as possible after the completion of the interviews and any other investigation.

Seven

Programming for Congregational Growth

Why Congregational Growth Is Important

A congregation either grows or dies. Every congregation has a lifetime of around twenty years. Unless it renews itself by welcoming members of the next generation before the current members become too old to make that happen, the congregation will grow older and become weaker and less able to maintain itself.

If Unitarian Universalism is important enough to believe in, it is important enough to pass on to others. Many more people than those who identify with us today would benefit from our faith's perspective and welcome our values framework if they knew it existed. Just as we have been informed and, in some cases, deeply touched by our connection with a Unitarian Universalist congregation, so there are others who live within driving distance of our meeting places who would be, too.

Having more Unitarian Universalists joining with others who share our liberal religious perspectives could make our world a better place to live. World, national, and local leaders could not easily disavow the values we affirm. We need more of us around to assure this doesn't happen.

A Good Time to Grow

In 1995 there will be more five-year-old and younger children in the US than at any time since 1961. Parents of young children often seek out religious communities for their children as well as for themselves. Many in the generation of baby boomer parents share our perspectives and values (i.e., issues of individual freedom). In some communities, the schools, libraries, and other institutions may not be wholly supportive of their thinking and ways of living, so connection with similar thinking people becomes important. So too is their need to focus on the spiritual resources that our congregations can provide. Attitudes toward holistic thinking and interdependence naturally find a welcome in our circle of faith.

The realization that the younger generations have different needs than people over fifty years old is something that every congregation needs to learn if it wishes to welcome these newer generations. Here are a few identifying features of what younger generations need:

- Variety—having a variety of options, including the number of programs offered for individuals, or families, the number of times worship is possible during the week, the variety of music and formats in the service, and the number of relationships in their network into the religious community
- Quality—How well are things done in the church? How attractive are the facilities, especially for children? How are important events conveyed?
- Commitment—Are you open about what is expected, including what members need to do, how much money should be pledged, and how people should treat each other?
- Is there support for their time commitments, providing intergenerational activities and childcare for events they attend?
- Is there outreach into the community through direct, hands-on volunteer activities that make a difference?
- Is spiritual growth nurtured through reason, emotion, and community?

Significant Growth Needs Attention

Most Unitarian Universalist congregations are experiencing modest membership and church school growth. But there are certain stages in the life of a congregation in which the resistance to further growth needs to be addressed. If it is not, the congregation will experience a growth plateau or a decline in membership. Congregations of around seventy members face this wall of resistance. So do congregations at around 150 and 350 members.

When a congregation reaches a certain size, it must experience a transformation in the way it sees itself. Changes in organization, ministry, volunteer and professional staff, programs, worship service(s), and sometimes the meeting place are required. That's why a vital and growing congregation should behave as if it is larger than it really is. Growth follows from that behavior. But too often a congregation will seek the comfort of being just the size it is or begin acting smaller. This behavior leads to decline and the later necessity to downsize continually until a new vision for the future triggers a turnaround in energy and commitment and a managed strategy for vitality and growth.

Some congregation's neighborhoods have undergone population changes since the church was built. These congregations will likely decline in membership if they do not make changes in programs and staff to better meet the needs of the people who live nearby, especially in urban and other areas of racial and cultural diversity. Racial and cultural diversity are not options. Opportunities to evolve into a congregation that reflects what the demographics of North America become is an exciting challenge

Eleven Recommendations   1. **Develop a consensus among all the members of your congregation that growth is a necessary and significant objective.** Without this consensus, some individuals and groups will resist the changes that result when growth becomes a major focus. A congregational meeting to vote formally on this objective should be considered. Some congregations organize a Growth Council of representatives from each committee in the congregation, which assists in incorporating the growth agenda into every area of the religious community.

2. **Develop a mission statement, vision, or idea for your congregation's identity and purpose.** No single congregation, especially if it has less than one thousand members, can do everything. Smaller congregations particularly need to concentrate on two or three areas of church life that they can do well and promote to the community. Religious education for elementary age, young adult programs, outreach on environmental issues, a folk music coffeehouse, and connecting with the elderly are a few examples of areas in which a congregation can identify itself and be known in the community. Go with your desires and strengths and do what you do well, without being defensive about the things you are not able to do.

3. **Think and behave as if you were a little larger than you are.** Many congregations decline in membership because when growth occurs they continue thinking and behaving as if they were smaller. The reverse can also be true. When we act as if we are larger, we become larger. Thinking and behaving as if we are larger, reduces the resistance to moving in that direction.

4. **Be serious about developing specific objectives to accomplish in the next three years.** Most middle-sized congregations from 300 to 500 members should have no more than four or five objectives. Each objective should be specific enough so that everyone will know when it has been reached, yet general enough to be adapted to new learnings or changing conditions. Once the objectives have been agreed on, the committees responsible for maintaining the congregation can establish specific goals for their own areas to help meet the objectives. Opportunities for organizing task-forces that require limited time commitment can be used to assimilate newcomers in one or more networks in the congregation.

5. **Develop an intentional plan for greeting and following up visitors.** Few people return to a church after visiting once if they have not had an initial relationship to one or more individuals. Telling everyone in the congregation to be attentive to visitors rarely works. Two or three individuals need to be trained and assigned

to undertake this responsibility. Personal follow-up after a visit is equally important. Letters are passive and impersonal; the human voice or outstretched hand is far warmer and relational.

6. **Provide childcare for all important meetings.** Each family being responsible for its own childcare was once a norm. Young families of today expect the congregation to offer this service. Congregations that wish to attract younger families need to meet these basic needs.

7. **Create an organized process for assimilating new members.** Beginning with the first orientation meeting, a timeline for assimilation can be adapted to each new member. The new member ceremony in a Sunday service should convey the message that new members are important. Newcomers and new members should be asked to give impressions of their experiences with the congregation and what changes might occur to make the congregation more attractive for other newcomers. The tendency is to share the congregation's story with newcomers, but most newcomers want to know what is planned for the future rather than hear about the past.

8. **Develop a specific set of expectations for membership.** The days when "You can believe or do anything you want and still be a Unitarian Universalist" are over. The baby boomer and later generations want to know what is expected of them. Generalizations do not arouse commitment, especially when it comes to making a financial contribution. More Unitarian Universalist congregations today clearly state that a specific percentage of income is a minimum expectation. A few congregations talk seriously about five percent of one's annual income. Instead of gearing the canvass to "those who can't afford it" and not expecting too much, the expectation is higher, as is the response.

9. **Growing congregations must pay attention to their facilities.** A crowded room at coffee hour will repel those who feel uncomfortable in crowds. After a while the congregation will be made up only of people who enjoy crowds! So, too, in church school classes where only those children who are able to handle large classes will return. If a congregation can't expand its facilities, it needs to have two services and church school sessions. The rule of thumb is that no growth occurs when the meeting room is eighty-five percent filled on an average Sunday, the parking lot is full, or the church school classes are overcrowded.

10. **Quality is more important than any ingredient in a growing congregation.** Congregations that attempt to do too much usually end up doing nothing well. Burnout creates sloppiness, and the

atmosphere feels "down." Everything should be done well if you are a congregation that wants to grow. Rehearsals for Sunday services, sound systems and working lights, facilities that are well maintained and positive looking, newsletters that are crisp and attractive are important. Small matters that are overlooked or assumed to be unimportant can become the turn off that your recent visitor remembers.

11. **Diversity results from options as well as from reaching out into the wider community.** Diversity comes from options, from the visible symbols, language, colors, staff, music—everything—that you can pay attention to in recognizing differences in people's spiritual needs, schedules, lifestyles, sexual orientation, physical abilities, race, class, and culture. It is an exciting, neverending opportunity to think positively about differences rather than assuming that we are all the same and have the same needs.

The Path to Membership

Unitarian Universalism is a faith for the future. We offer people a religious home where they can find the freedom to be who they are, guidelines for living a more whole and complete life, and fellow journeyers who will challenge them to open their hearts, minds, and souls to the great gift of life.

Because our faith is important to us, we believe it should be shared with others, which has often been difficult for Unitarian Universalists. Disliking proselytizing in others, we are sometimes unclear how to reach out to those who would benefit from our religious perspective. If we believe in Unitarian Universalism, we want our congregations to grow in size and commitment.

Becoming a member of a Unitarian Universalist congregation is an important step in a person's life. How the congregation encourages, enables, and celebrates a person's journey into membership speaks volumes about the congregation's commitment to the Unitarian Universalist religious tradition. One way is to strengthen the membership programs in our congregations. In particular, we have recognized the need to develop strong membership classes that clarify what membership means and help people make the best choice about membership.

Each congregation is unique and should modify this material to fit its situation.

The Journey Into Membership

By the time most people consider membership in a Unitarian Universalist congregation, they have gone through a process of exploration and discovery that can be helped or hindered by the religious community to which they are attracted. Following is an overview of this process with step-by-step suggestions of how congregations might better serve people.

These steps are based on material from the Alban Institute, and from the Rev. Barbara Wells's own experience. Obviously, not all people on the path to membership will follow these steps in just this way. However we have found them helpful in understanding the common journey that leads people to a deeper commitment to their congregation.

Step 1. Testing the Waters

Most new people who enter the doors of a congregation are in transition. If they have been Unitarian Universalist for a while, they have probably moved recently or been through a life change that has pushed them toward a different church. If they are new to Unitarian Universalism, they are also likely to be in transition. Some interesting statistics from the Alban Institute:

- More than sixty percent of people who attend a church for the first time have not gone to church in two years.
- The average age of people returning to church is twenty-six to twenty-seven.
- Few people in the baby boom generation have strong denominational loyalty and usually attend a church for other reasons.
- Eighty percent of people attending a church for the first time do so because a friend, co-worker, or family member invited them.

When people test the waters it is important for the congregation to keep a number of things in mind.

1. How easy is your congregation to find? Is it listed in the yellow and white pages of the telephone directory? Is there good signage on the property? Is it known in the community by its activities? Does it have a good reputation? Do your members proudly share their congregation with their friends?

2. When people call the congregation, does a friendly person answer the phone? Does he or she answer questions accurately and cheerfully? If there is an answering machine, is the message professional and the information correct? Does the message answer the basic questions of who you are, where you are located, and when services are held?

3. When people come to the building can they find a place to park? Is the front entrance well marked? Is the exterior of the building well maintained?

4. When people enter the building are they greeted in a friendly fashion? Is information easily available about Unitarian Universalism and your congregation's activities? Are the religious education rooms attractive and easy to find? Are people invited but not pushed to sign the visitors' book?

5. When people sit down at a service, does the Order of Service give them enough information? Is it attractive and professionally done?

6. Are people made to feel welcome from the pulpit? Are they able to be anonymous if they want to be?

7. Following the service, is someone standing by the door to thank them for coming? If they stay for coffee hour, are people assigned to make sure they are made to feel welcome? If they ask for information, does everyone know where to find it? Do they leave the church feeling warmly welcomed?

8. If they leave their name and address are they sent a letter of welcome? Does someone call them or drop them a handwritten postcard thanking them for coming? Are they added to the mailing list if they wish to be? Are they given a semipermanent name tag so they know you want them to return?

First impressions are very important. When people seek a congregation they are often hesitant and uncomfortable. When you are intentional and genuine in your welcome, people notice and appreciate it. If someone is interested in being a part of your religious community, you want them to know up front that they are welcome. By going over these questions and shoring up any areas in which your congregation may be weak, you can ensure that people will find your congregation to be a more welcoming place.

Step 2. Making Connections

Underlying the ability of a prospective member to connect with the congregation is whether they can answer the question, "Do I belong here?" Knowing the kind of congregation you are and want to be deepens your current membership's commitment and greatly clarifies things for new people exploring congregation membership. People want to join an exciting, relevant community that speaks to their hearts, minds, and souls. If you aren't clear about who you are, people will be hesitant to join you.

Once people have found the congregation and have begun to attend regularly, they begin to move into the connecting stage. Early on their path, the connections will be tenuous. Areas to be aware of during this stage begin with the worship service and religious education programming. Questions to consider:

1. Is the worship service well thought-out and put together? Does the music suit the service and is it well performed? If the music is participatory, is someone helping to lead it? Are the speakers able to be heard? Can people see the speakers? Are children included in the service? If so, are they made to feel welcome? Does the service have a beginning, middle, and an end?

2. Is the sermon topic relevant? Is it well thought-out and well delivered? Is the minister or speaker authentic? Do all the speakers convey a sense of warmth and appreciation for the community?

3. Is the religious education curriculum clearly outlined in a brochure? Are children made to feel welcome in their classrooms? Are parents always welcome in the classroom? Is someone available during every service to answer parents' questions? Are children's names and addresses taken? Do the children communicate a sense of enjoyment about their program?

Once people begin to feel at home with the worship service and the religious education program, they look around to see how to get to know people better. Often Unitarian Universalist congregations push people into membership at this stage. In most cases, this may be too early for people to make a serious commitment. During this stage, newcomers should be encouraged to begin participating in the congregation activities that are most appealing to them. Questions to consider:

1. Are there activities such as lunches after worship service or Sunday adult classes that are easy for new people to attend? Are there occasional newcomer events to offer information about the church to which new people are personally invited?

2. Are there adult groups and classes that are spiritually enticing and easy for new people to find out about and attend? Are there classes and groups that appeal to people's real needs like parenting, dealing with sick parents, etc.?

3. Are there social events in which new people can be included and invited to be active participants (e.g., potlucks, outings)? Do active participants feel encouraged and empowered to invite newcomers?

4. Are there social justice projects to which it is easy for new people to contribute (e.g., a food bank, monthly work party)? Are new people intentionally invited to participate in these activities?

People are much more likely to join a congregation if they already feel a part of it. They will make better members if they understand the congregation's principles and see them in action. When people have friends and ties to a congregation, it becomes theirs and they want to participate and contribute. In other words, they are ready to be members.

Step 3. Making the Commitment

Often the best way to help prospective members make a commitment is to develop a new members class.

1. How often does your congregation plan to offer membership classes? Are they well publicized? Are newcomers given personal invitations? Do you have several ways to sign up for the class (e.g., at services, through the office, a tear-off sheet in the Order of Service)?

2. Do you involve a number of people in your class planning and implementation? Are they drawn from a broad spectrum of groups in your congregation (e.g., religious education, choir, social justice, board)? Are they given clear guidelines and time limits for their part of the program? Are they prepared with printed material?

3. Do you distribute membership packets? Do you go through every part of the packet during the class? Is it attractive and well put together? Does it clearly print the congregation's name, address, and phone number?

4. If members are transferring from other churches, do you offer alternative ways to join (e.g., an hour-long meeting with the minister or the board chair)?

5. Are new members welcomed in a celebrative way during the worship service? Are their names and addresses printed in the newsletter? Are they canvassed within a short period of their joining?

Joining a Unitarian Universalist congregation is a very important moment in the lives of new members. The congregation taking it seriously will make sure that new members know they are valued and that their commitment to the congregation is well worth their time, love, and money.

Step 4. Deepening the Commitment

As new members get more involved in the life of a congregation, they should be offered ample opportunities to grow in their faith and commitment to the congregation and to the Unitarian Universalist Association. It is important to offer clear guidelines on the responsibilities of membership. As you read over those responsibilities, ask yourself these questions:

1. Are committees and committee chairs open to new members? Is it clear how one joins a committee? Do committees provide spiritual nurture for their members as well as tasks to be completed? Are new committee members given clear instructions and job de-

scriptions? Are time limits clarified so people know for how long they are committing?

2. Are new members given information about the Unitarian Universalist Association? Are they promptly put on the *World* mailing list? Are they made aware of regional events they might be interested in attending?

3. Are new members given opportunities to take leadership roles as appropriate? Are they invited to work with more seasoned Unitarian Universalists on committees, religious education classes, etc.?

4. Are new members encouraged to share their congregation with others? Are they invited to be greeters or ushers, or to make coffee on Sunday?

5. Are new members sponsored by a seasoned member to make sure they are finding connections in the congregation? Are they given permission to try out a few groups and committees before making a commitment? Are they monitored for burnout?

New members are a great resource in any congregation. They are the seedbed for new leadership; they are often the most enthusiastic members of a congregation; and they are most clearly aware of issues in the congregation that longtime members (including the minister) often don't see anymore. Treat new members with love and respect and the returns will be great. Your congregation will be stronger, have less attrition, and grow in spiritual depth and commitment.

Tracking Worship and Program Attendance

Congregations use a variety of ways to gather information from their visitors and to track the participation of visitors in the life of the congregation. A visitor's book or a response card system, to be effective, must have a way to follow up those visits. There must also be clear ways to respond to and promote the participation of a visitor on the path to membership.

Greeters

Those in a greeting role in your congregation provide a significant link between a visitor and the congregation. How sensitive the greeters are to the needs of the visitor and how able they are to engage them in conversation represents your congregation's interest in being welcoming and inviting. The communication that occurs in the first four minutes of contact are crucial to whether a "stranger" feels welcome and respected within your congregation.

Greeters are often people who are naturally inclined toward this kind of role in a church. However they are chosen, greeters should be given an orientation to this role that enables them to be sensitive to its significance. The point is that more are not necessarily more effective, better trained greeters are.

Greeters should be free to focus on the needs of visitors, which means that greeters should not serve as ushers.

Visitors' Book or Response Card

A visitors' book, conveniently placed at one of the main entryways to your meetingplace and staffed by a greeter, is a helpful way to capture information about visitors. In addition to gathering a visitor's name, address, phone number, and request for information, the interaction that visitors can have with someone at the visitor table is essential to being responsive to the visitor's needs. The interaction should covey a nonintrusive but interested response to the person who visits your congregation. In particular, you could inquire about:

- what brought them to your congregation
- what interests they have
- what information they are seeking
- if they want to receive the church newsletter.

A response card is another way to gather this information, which later can be answered by someone on the membership or program committees of the congregation. A sample response card, which you can adapt for your congregation, is included in this section.

Newcomer Tracking Form

You may want to track the participation and responses of your congregation to a newcomer in a systematic way. Enclosed in this section you will find a Newcomer Tracking Form. Your congregation will have to determine the routine responses to newcomers and how you will be companions on the path to membership

Sample Response Card

Name _____

Children's names /ages _____

Address _____

Phone(s) _____

What interested you in visiting our congregation? _____

_____

I/We would like more information about:
___ the programs of the congregation
___ joining and membership requirements
___ religious education programs for children
___ nursery

___ youth programs
___ singles group
___ religious education programs for adults.

I/We would like:
___ to schedule a meeting with a minister
___ to be added to the mailing list
___ a visit from a member of the congregation
___ a call from the director of religious education.

Newcomer Tracking Form

Name(s) _____

_____

_____

Children's names and ages_____

_____

Address _____

Phone(s) _____

Want information on:
___religious education programming for children
___congregation programs
___membership
___visit from minister or congregation member.

Name of greeter _____
Entered information from response card or guest book on _____

What brought the person (s) to the congregation:

First Visit: (date)
• Welcome note.

Second Visit
• Call from member/invitation to a social program.

Third Visit
• Letter or call from minister.

Fourth Visit
• Invitation sent to adult education class.

Fifth Visit
- Invitation to orientation session.

- Orientation session.

- Invitation to membership.

- Became a member.

- Made a pledge.

- New member recognition service.

- Six-month interview on involvement in congregation.

- Twelve-month interview on participation in the congregation.

Notes:

Visitor Interviews

A team of members from your congregation could do these interviews for your congregation over a period of time (e.g., during the fall or the spring). A format for the interview, the Visitor Interview Form, is on the next page. Each team member could compile the responses to a question and summarize them on one sheet.

When the team gathers to review the results of their interviews it can use the following process to determine what it has learned from the interviews. Both positive and negative perceptions of visitors may assist your congregation in making appropriate changes.

A Process for Learning

Learn from the interview process by asking yourselves:

1. What patterns did you notice from the responses? You might respond to this question by completing the sentence, "We are a congregation that . . . " with some of the patterns you discovered in your interviews. For example, "We are a congregation that creates a good first impression."

2. What are the most complimentary things you discovered about your congregation's welcoming of newcomers?

3. What are some problematic things you discovered about your congregation's welcoming of newcomers?

4. What recommendations do you have for your congregation to strengthen and improve its welcoming of newcomers and visitors?

Visitor Interview Form

Name of visitor _____

Date of interview _____

Name of interviewer_____

1. How many times have you visited this congregation?

2. When was the last time you visited this congregation
   for a Sunday service? _____
   for a program? _____
   for another event? _____

3. Why did you decide to visit the first time?

4. What expectations did you have about your first visit?

5. Can you describe your first impressions of the congregation as you approached and entered on your first visit?

6. What were some of your feelings about your first visit?

7. Did anything happen of particular significance during your first visit?

8. What did you find interesting or attractive about this congregation during any visits?

9. Was there anything that the members might have done that would have improved your experience?

10. Can you tell me why you haven't returned since your last visit?

11. Are you still looking for a connection with this congregation?

Other comments:

Resources

District Executive/Consultant
Arrange a staff visit to discuss options for growth, including ministry and staffing for growth, long-range planning strategies, special district programs on growth, and finances.

District Extension Committee
Some district extension committees offer consultants and other resources to congregations in their district.

Publications available from the UUA Office of Extension Services on membership growth:

101 Ideas for Membership Growth
New Congregation Development Packet
Resource Packet for Unitarian Universalist Congregations
    Considering Two Services
Decisions for Growth Packet
Extension Ministry Packet
Minister-on-Loan Packet
Sample Bylaws Packet

UUA Extension Services staff offer many resources for different size congregations. Below are some of these programs and services.

FOR SMALL CONGREGATIONS Up to 150 Members	FOR MID-SIZE CONGREGATIONS 150-600 Members	FOR LARGE CONGREGATIONS 600 Members or More
Weekend "Workshops on Growth for Small Congregations" Extension Ministry Internship Minister-on-Loan Program Extension Training for Ministers of Small Congregations Metro Extension Ministry Program Building Loans Fundraising Consultants Young Adult Ministries Extension Ministry Program	Weekend "Workshop on Growth for Middle Sized Churches" Decisions-for-Growth Program Mid-Size Church Continental Conferences Covenanting Congregation for New Congregations Metro Extension Ministry Program Building Loans Fundraising and Capital Campaign Consultants Young Adult Ministries	Specially Designed Consultation for Individual Large Churches Large Church Continental Conferences Covenanting Congregation for New Congregations Metro Extension Ministry Program Building Loans Fundraising and Capital Campaign Consultants Young Adult Ministries

Self-Study and Profile of Your Congregation

This Self-Study and Profile of Your Congregation Form is provided as a way for a congregation to gather important data about itself for planning purposes. It may also be used as a mechanism to give a profile of your congregation to your leadership, the district office, Unitarian Universalist Association staff, and others who may work with your congregation.

Current Membership

A. Total number of current legal members _____

This figure should be available from your congregation's clerk, membership chair, secretary, or administrator.

B. Five-Year Adult Membership Analysis

Year	Members Joining	Members Lost	Net Gain (or loss)	Total Members at End of Year
5 Year Totals				

C. Children and Youth

Total number of children (under 12 years old) _____

Total number of youth (ages 12 to 18) = _____

Include here all the children and youth in your church school and youth programs. Youth who have become legal members of the congregation should not be included here, but in the total number of legal members.

D. Total number of adult nonmembers affiliated with your congregation _____

This number should include those who have not officially joined but who participate in the life of your congregation and its programs. They are referred to as friends in some congregations and associate members in others.

E. Total current constituency _____

This is the sum of adult legal members (Item A), total number of children and youth (items C-1 and C-2), and total number of adults affiliated (Item D).

F. Age Groupings of the Total Congregation

For the following table estimate the number of members, affiliated adult members, children, and youth in the following age groups. If exact ages are not known, make an estimate.

AGE GROUP	MALE	FEMALE	TOTALS
0-4 YEARS			
5-11 YEARS			
12-17 YEARS			
18-21 YEARS			
22-29 YEARS			
30-35 YEARS			
36-44 YEARS			
45-54 YEARS			
55-64 YEARS			
65-74 YEARS			
75 OR MORE			
TOTAL			

G. Active Households

An active household is defined as those living at a particular address who are considered active members of your congregation. At least one person from this household should be involved in regular activity of the congregation to be considered active.

Single persons without children   _____

Single persons with children   _____

Couples without children at home   _____

Couples with children at home   _____

Other household type   _____

Total number of households   _____

H. Describe the approximate racial/ethnic composition of your membership.

African	____ %	Latino	____ %
Asian	____ %	Native American	____ %
European	____ %	Other _____

Program and Participation

A. Number of worship services your congregation has: _____
Day(s) and time(s) of worship service(s): _____

B. Average attendance at worship services in the past year. What is the percentage of total membership attending this service?

- First or only service   _____   _____%
- Second service   _____   _____%
- Third service   _____   _____%
- Weekday service   _____   _____%

C. Worship attendance in weekly worship service(s) for the last five years.

If your congregation takes worship attendance, these figures should be available. If your congregation does not take worship attendance you might do so to determine trends in active participation.

	Average	High	Low
Year:			
Year:			
Year:			
Year:			
Year:			

D. Church School and Youth Programs Attendance and Enrollment

What are the trends in enrollment and attendance in your church school and youth programs over the last five years?

1. Church School

	Enrollment	Average	High	Low
Year:				
Year:				
Year:				
Year:				
Year:				

2. Youth Programs

	Enrollment	Average	High	Low
Year:				
Year:				
Year:				
Year:				
Year:				

Community Demographics

A. What is the total population and the area from which your members come?

_____

B. Is there another Unitarian Universalist congregation in this demographic area?

Yes _____   No _____

If yes, please give the name of the congregation and the distance from your site.

_____

C. What is the expected population of this area? (Check with your local chamber of commerce or government planning office.)

       In five years? _____

       In ten years? _____

       In fifteen years? _____

D. Has the population of this area increased or decreased over the past ten years?_____

By how much? _____

E. Has the membership of your congregation kept pace with the population increase or decrease?

F. Household Distribution Map

A study of the geographical distribution of households in the congregation, both member and nonmember, may be plotted on a large wall map of the community where the congregation exists. Indicate each household by a map pin or 1/4-inch adhesive dot, using different colors for member and nonmember households or for those who have become involved in your congregation over the last two years (or after a major transition in your congregation, e.g., new minister, new building, move to second worship service).

Religious Education Programs for Adults and Youth

A. How many religious education programs for children and youth are in your congregation on Sunday? _____.

B. Are some religious education programs for children and youth more popular? What are they?

C. If there is more than one Sunday service for adults, is there more than one religious education session? _____

If there is more than one RE session, when did they begin?

_____

If you have more than one session of children's religious education programs are they the same and serve the same ages? If not, how do they differ?

D. How many adult religious education programs do you offer each church year? _____

E. What are the most popular adult religious education programs?

F. What percent of adults participate annually in:

One program _____

Two programs _____

Three or more programs _____

G. What method is used to discover individual needs for programming? Check all that apply:

One-on-one conversations _____

Congregational survey _____

Small-group meetings _____

Congregational planning session_____

Welcoming Visitors

A. Do you have a visitors' book in plain view every week?
Yes ____ No ____

B. How many local visitors signed your visitors' book last year? _____

C. How may new members joined last year? _____

D. Are there adequate interior and exterior signs around the church? _____

E. Are there greeters at your worship services? _____

F. Are greeters at your worship services trained? _____

G. Are there registration cards for visitors? _____

H. Are there convenient parking spaces designated for visitors? _____

I. Is there a class for new members? _____

J. If so, how many times a year is it held? _____

K. Do you provide information packets for visitors? _____

L. What percent of your congregation wears name tags during coffee hour? _____

M. Do you educate new members about the congregation's finances? _____

N. Are new members contacted for a pledge within one month of joining? _____

O. Do you conduct all canvassing in face-to-face meetings? _____

Social Activities and Programs

A. What social activities have been offered within your congregation during the last twelve months (include activities targeted at distinct populations including singles, religious education teacher recognition, new member socials, etc.) The list includes circle suppers, canoe or bicycle trips, family retreats, potluck suppers, picnics, or dances.

Activity   Focus Population

_____   _____

_____   _____

_____   _____

_____   _____

_____   _____

_____   _____

_____   _____

_____   _____

_____   _____

_____   _____

_____   _____

_____   _____

_____   _____

_____   _____

B. Describe special efforts to include new members or integrate them into social, educational, and leadership activities.

Level of Activity of Members	Number	Percentage of Total Membership
Very active		
Moderately active		
Slightly active		
Inactive		
TOTAL		

Your Congregation's Vision

A. Does your congregation have a vision statement?
Yes____ No ____

Does your congregation have a mission statement?
Yes____ No ____

If yes, how were they developed?

B. What is your vision statement?

C. What is your mission statement?

D. Does your congregation have a long-range planning committee?

Yes ____   No ____

If yes, has the plan been circulated among members of the congregation and committees?

Yes ____   No ____

Is your long-range plan reviewed and revised annually?

Membership Growth Plans

A. Current official or legal membership _____   One year ago ____   Two years ago ____   Five years ago ____

B. Expected membership   In one year ____   In two years ____   In five years ____

C. Child & youth participation in RE programs   One year ago ____   Two years ago ____   Five years ago ____

D. Expected RE participation   In one year ____   In two years ____   In five years ____

E. Does your long-range plan include membership growth goals and objectives? Yes ___ No ___

If yes, what are they?

F. Is your congregation seeking to increase membership?
Yes ____   No ____

If no, please explain.

G. Do you have plans for increasing the racial or cultural diversity of your membership? If yes, please describe.

H. Does your congregation plan to be a "Welcoming Congregation" for gay, lesbian, and bisexual people? If yes, please describe.

I. What are challenges to your congregation's membership growth?

Cash Flow Projections	Previous Year	Current Year	Next Year	Next Year	Next Year
Income					
Pledges	_____	_____	_____	_____	_____
Gifts and endowments	_____	_____	_____	_____	_____
Fundraising	_____	_____	_____	_____	_____
Rental income	_____	_____	_____	_____	_____
Plate collections	_____	_____	_____	_____	_____
Other sources	_____	_____	_____	_____	_____
Total Income	_____	_____	_____	_____	_____
Expenses					
Personnel	_____	_____	_____	_____	_____
Administration	_____	_____	_____	_____	_____
Programming	_____	_____	_____	_____	_____
Contributions	_____	_____	_____	_____	_____
Building maintenance	_____	_____	_____	_____	_____
Debt service	_____	_____	_____	_____	_____

Other   _____ _____ _____ _____ _____

Total Expenses   _____ _____ _____ _____ _____

Current Finances

	Current	Three years ago	Five years ago
A. Number of contributing units	_____	_____	_____
B. Average pledge	$_____	$_____	$ _____

C. Total restricted & unrestricted funds $ _____
(endowment)

E. Denominational support
(fiscal year)   19 ___ - 19 ___

F. Amount contributed to
UUA Annual Program Fund $ _____

G. Annual Program Fund suggested share $ _____

H. Amount contributed to district (dues paid) $ _____

I. District dues suggested share $ _____

Information on Meeting Place

A. Existing Space

   1. Do you own _____ or rent _____ your space?

   2. How long have you been meeting there?_____

   3. Adult seating capacity _____

   4. Number of rooms for religious education _____

   5. Number of off-street parking spaces _____

B. New Facility Plans

   1. Describe the grounds (size, visibility of the building from street, location in relation to local population concentrations).

   2. Describe the building (age of building, adult seating capacity, number and capacity of rooms for religious education classes (youth and adult), space for fellowship gathering).

C. Is your building generally clean and presentable?

D. Is your building handicapped accessible?

E. Are your restrooms clean?

F. Are your restrooms handicapped accessible?

Eight

Religious Education Programming

The Role of Religious Education

The greatest gift we can give our children, it is said, is "roots and wings." Unitarian Universalist religious education seeks to give us all, no matter what age, roots of connection and wings of possibility and hope. Our religious education is lifespan in scope, progressive in theory, experiential in method, and liberal in theological and ethical perspectives. The role of religious education in Unitarian Universalist congregations is to help individuals of all ages experience connections, compassion, and creativity.

We need to understand our connection with our liberal religious heritage: the Jewish and Christian roots from which we spring; the Eastern religious traditions that have nurtured us; the insights of philosophy and science that have expanded our knowledge; and our mystical sense of union with one another, our planet, and the universe. Such connections occur in the curricula we offer, the presentations we sponsor, the opportunities we create for our rich heritage to ennoble us as we move into the future in transforming ways.

We need to feel compassion and act on it; to empathize with the struggles and joys that are a part of every life journey; to transform oppression into justice; to persevere on behalf of what we believe is right. We need to encourage such compassion through caring for one another, support groups, and outreach and action in the larger community.

We need to encourage and unlock the creativity in each of us to use fully our individual gifts and in so doing to find solutions to complex problems. Tapping our creative spark happens in church school classes with hands-on learning, in youth groups with special activities that focus on the creative arts, in classes and groups for adults where new skills can be learned and new talents tapped, and in intergenerational events where laughter, learning, and creativity combine for all ages.

Lifespan religious education, programming for all ages, is critical to a healthy congregation. Lifespan religious education is vital for the growth of our liberal religious movement. Our congregations are truly learning communities where interactions model our values and community actions cause our visions to spring into living form.

As you consider your congregation's religious education program, look at its mission statement. How does religious education fit into this statement directly? How does lifespan religious education fit into this statement indirectly?

Included is an overview of ways to look at where you are and where you want to go with your lifespan religious education programming.

Developing a Religious Education Program

There are several steps to developing a healthy and thriving religious education program. All of the steps involve commitment to reflection, honesty, and congruence.

Step 1. Your Mission Statement and Religious Education Goals
A healthy religious education program is based on a firm and honest foundation. Your congregation's mission statement is the baseline. What does this statement have to say about ministry to children, youth, young adults, adults? What does it say about the role of education in your congregational life? How does your mission statement speak to the needs of the larger community you serve? Who do you hope will find and join your congregation? Who are you trying to exclude, if anyone?

The use of such materials as *Philosophy Making: A Process Guide* by Elizabeth Anastos and David Marshak can help your congregation find answers to these questions: What does our congregation believe religious education should concern? Who do we want to include? What do we hope they will gain from our religious education programming? If someone entered our program as an infant, what do we hope she or he would gain by the time he or she finished high school?

Step 2. Evaluating Age Groups
A crucial second step is to evaluate carefully the age groups your congregation would like to serve. What are these groups? What is the estimated number in each group? What groups would you like to add next year? in five years? in ten years? How far do folks have to come to reach your congregation? Driving distance often affects the type and frequency of programs you will find successful.

Step 3. Determining Available Resources
What meeting space does your congregation have? Prioritizing the groups you would like to serve helps your congregation match up available space with potential program groups.

Volunteer resources are most crucial. What size of pool will you be able to draw on for childcare helpers, church school teachers, youth group leaders, and adult program leaders? Does your congregation have the resources to employ someone to coordinate the religious education program in conjunction with your committee? What special skills in the areas of teaching, education, and curriculum do members of the congregation have? What fiscal resources are available to purchase curricula and equipment? How adequate are the furnishings for learning areas—are chairs too big or too small? Are there enough tables and chairs?

Step 4. Choosing Curricula

Given your mission statement, religious education goals, desired target groups, and availability of resources, what types of curricula does your program need? *Curriculum Mapping,* edited by Elizabeth Anastos, is a wonderful aid. It describes and critiques the many curricular resources available from the Unitarian Universalist Association and independent Unitarian Universalist authors. You can match your goals and age groups with curriculum choices.

Step 5. Recruitment and Publicity

Your first requirement is teachers, advisors, and leaders. Who might be good in the available positions? What kind of training can you offer? Your district religious education committee and district office may offer useful resources. How long will you ask each person to teach? A written job description for volunteer positions is extremely helpful. As you create such descriptions, reflect again on the goals your congregation has for the program and the commitment you are asking for.

The second recruitment is for participants. Publicity that is inviting but not overwhelming is the key. Your method of sharing the exciting news of your congregation's program needs to reflect creativity and warmth. Newsletter articles, religious education prospectus, individual flyers, sign-up or registration tables on Sunday mornings, a special information meeting (with refreshments) are a few ideas. Publicity outside your congregation is important, too—in the local newspaper, on bulletin boards in interesting bookstores or community centers. Such publicity is often a way new members are introduced to Unitarian Universalism.

Step 6. Maintaining and Encouraging

As your congregation's programming begins each semester, it is important that physical and emotional aspects are attended to. Are the classrooms clean and ready? What set up is needed and who will do it? Are resources and supplies on hand and easy to locate? Are attendance lists and registration forms provided? If an emergency occurs, who should be contacted?

Religious education committees need to make the nurture and appreciation of teachers and group leaders as a top priority. This appreciation means formal and informal words of thanks as well as checking in to see how classes and groups are progressing. Teacher breakfasts, lunches, picnics, and banquets are great for building a sense of community among the religious education workers. Formal recognition in teacher dedications at the beginning of the year, or teacher appreciation times at the end of the semesters, are important. Newsletter columns, words and pictures on prominent bulletin boards, and listing names in the Sunday program are additional ways to nurture religious education programming and its hardworking volunteers.

Step 7. Evaluating and Planning

Evaluation is an important step in any programming. It is usually done at the end of the class or semester. What worked? What did not work? What did the students gain from the experience? What did the teachers gain? What needs to be changed for next time?

Each year's evaluation should include revisiting the congregation's mission statement and the religious education goals. Are they providing our theory-in-use or have we strayed from the pathway they indicated? Do we need to reconceptualize our religious education goals? What groups did we successfully serve? Who do we need to reach? What are the needs of the adult congregation? What support do parents need? What are the concerns of children and youth?

Questionnaires can be used as well as friendly feedback sessions (again with refreshments). Evaluation forms from teachers can offer a great deal of insight about particular curricula and resources. What is our vision for next year? for two years? for ten years? The representation of these visions in a creative art form as well as in words is helpful and enlightening. A celebration of the hard work of the committee is a must for the whole process. Fellowship and fun along with hard work help strengthen bonds, visions, and commitments.

Recruiting for Religious Education Programs

Whether we call them religious education teachers or religious education leaders, people are the program's most important resource. Identifying, recruiting, and giving attention, support, and nurture to volunteers is essential to a successful religious education program.

How do you recruit them? The first step is to arrange a small meeting of the congregation's key leaders who have the best knowledge of the membership. Ask not "Who has time?" or "Who would be most likely to say yes?" but "Who would we most like to see influencing our children?"

Approach those members in person. Sit down with them when there is plenty of time to talk. Let them know that you would like them to participate because you value them as people who have much to contribute to the growth and nurture of young people in the congregation. Be specific about the commitment you are asking them to make. How many Sundays? Will they plan sessions or use ones that are already planned? Ask them to think it over and to let you know in a few days.

While it is natural to look to parents of children to provide leadership in the religious education program, newcomers need to affiliate with the congregation. They are often new to Unitarian Universalism and they need time to absorb its spirit. It is important for them initially to be free to participate in the adult community's programs and worship, while someone else leads the children's group. In time, they will be ready to take their turn.

Recruiting leaders is sometimes problematic. In many cases, members of the congregation are reluctant to miss the shared experience of the Sunday worship or program. *Starting from Scratch*, published by the Unitarian Universalist Association, lists several strategies to provide partial compensation. Check to make sure that your process for enlisting and nurturing teachers has the following qualities:

- **Affirmation.** Tell the prospective leader why he or she is being invited to teach. For example, "I've noticed how friendly you are to the children."

- **Enthusiasm.** Become familiar with the curricular materials to be used so that you can describe them in an inviting way to the prospective leader.

- **Flexibility.** Find out if the prospective leader would enjoy working with a co-leader, and if so, with whom. Often people find being part of a team easier and more fun than working alone. (It is not necessarily twice as hard to recruit two.) On the other hand, some people prefer to teach alone.

- **Help.** Offer your own or someone else's help with clean up, at the end of sessions. That way the leader can enjoy mingling at the coffee hour. (Be sure to recruit the someone else.)

- **Specificity.** Be specific about the time commitment: "Would you teach for half of the Sundays this fall?"

- **Acceptance.** Listen well to the response and see what you can learn from it. Accept a "No" graciously and the next time you may hear a "Yes."

- **Support.** Make sure the supply closet is kept stocked and the religious education area kept clean. Ask the leaders what would be helpful; they may need something you haven't anticipated.

- **Appreciation.** Publish news about the children's program in your congregation's newsletter, and express gratitude to the leaders. Hold an occasional teacher appreciation coffee hour.

Religious Education Programming

Religious education for the twenty-first century reflects an evolution in the Unitarian Universalist vision and mission. At the core of our religious journey is our ministry—the interactive, interconnected ministry with adults, youth, *and* children. The model of our religious communities engages congregations as learning communities as well as worshipping communities.

The creative tension of our religious growth and learning is inherent in the words "religious" and "education". Our twofold purpose is to care enough to draw forth or educate the greatness within each person and to pursue the binding together or the religious experience of persons into wholeness and community. The methods and messages of Unitarian Universalist religious education are the expanding and deepening of the relationships of life to self, others, the earth, and the universe. The spiral model of education for religion as relationship encompasses our religious ways of being and our educational ways of becoming.

Growing into relationships is essential to becoming a person. We all exist within an interacting web of relationships. As we grow we become aware of their enormous variety and complexity. We begin with these qualities and experiences in the process of becoming a self. We start with our own bodies and move to experiences with other persons, building relationships with parents, siblings, extended family members, friends, and acquaintances. Equally important in our growing are relationships beyond other individuals—communities, institutions and ideologies, networks and systems, history and time. We discover our relationships with the earth and all living things as well as our emergent relationship to the universe and the *mysterium tremendum*. The spiral is our model (see next page) associating our values with evolving relationships.

Religious education is a lifelong adventure shared with a community of seekers. Along our religious journey we ask the abiding questions: Who am I? Who are you? Where have we come from? Where are we going? We explore and integrate many different possibilities and we act on our examined choices.

Unitarian Universalist religious education strives to give children, youth, and adults opportunities that enable them to develop their own religious philosophy and theology, thus freeing them to be their own best selves and to become kind, fair, and responsible persons. Our goal is to provide participants with the most compelling and vivid experiences of the power of Unitarian Universalism and to help them develop life-enhancing relationships.

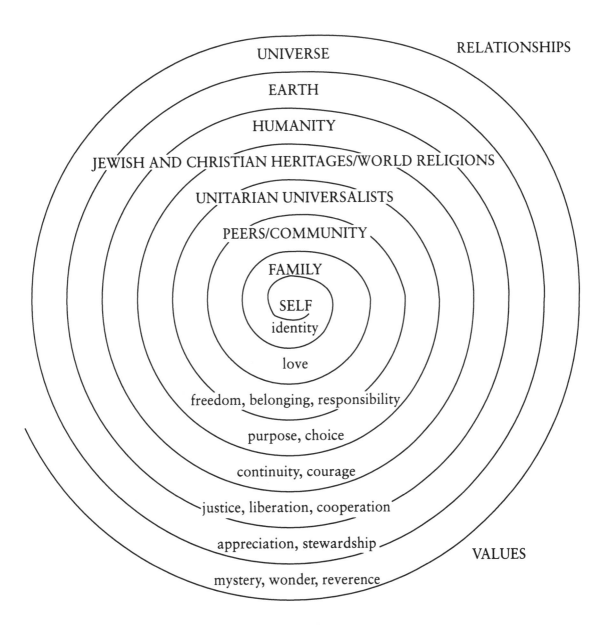

RELATIONSHIPS

UNIVERSE

EARTH

HUMANITY

JEWISH AND CHRISTIAN HERITAGES/WORLD RELIGIONS

UNITARIAN UNIVERSALISTS

PEERS/COMMUNITY

FAMILY

SELF

identity

love

freedom, belonging, responsibility

purpose, choice

continuity, courage

justice, liberation, cooperation

appreciation, stewardship

VALUES

mystery, wonder, reverence

These experiences are the diverse paths of the religious journey in our community life and the goals of our curricular efforts. Our curricular themes are both timeless and timely. Our programs are committed to the timeless themes of our living tradition as Unitarian Universalists, our Jewish and Christian heritages, the teachings of world religions, and the insights of prophetic visions and actions. We strive to respond effectively to contemporary issues such as AIDS, violence, and abuse. We seek a balance in pursuing our purposes. Our guiding principles are to enhance our spiritual dimensions, to further pluralism, and to empower ethical action. The following chart offers curricula examples that relate values and concerns along the spiral of religious relationships to various curricula goals.

CURRICULA EXAMPLES

Relating me to:	VALUES	CONCERNS	GOALS	UUA PROGRAMS	AGE RANGE

SELF	identity
	authenticity
		Who am I?
		Where did I
		  come from?
		Where am I going?
			I'm okay
			self-respect
				Celebrating Me and
				  My World
				Growing Times
				In Our Hands
				About Your Sexuality
				L.I.F.T.
				About Sexual Abuse
				BYOT I & II
				Life Tapestry
					preschool
					
					preschool
					all ages
					junior-senior high
					senior high
					junior-senior high
					adult
					adult

FAMILY	love
	sharing
	helpful
	forgiveness
		belonging
		responsibilities
			security
			responsibility
			interdependence
				Growing Times
				About Your Sexuality
				Parents as Resident
				  Theologians
				Parents as Social
				  Justice Educators
				Being a UU Parent
					preschool
					junior high
					adult
					
					adult
					
					adult

PEERS/ COMMUNITY	belonging independence interdependence	autonomy vs. community	friendship self-confidence integrity	Rainbow Children Race to Justice In Our Hands Beyond Pink and Blue About Your Sexuality L.I.F.T. About Sexual Abuse	elementary junior high all ages junior high junior high senior high junior-senior high

UUs	identity
	choice
	truth
	doubt
	faith
		values
		philosophy
		history
			knowledge
			freedom
			self-chosen
			commitments
				Around the Church,
				  Around the Year
				Stepping-Stone Year
				Travel in Time
				Messages in Music
				Religion in Life
				We Believe
				BYOT I & II
				Being a UU Parent
				Our Chosen Faith
				Prophetic Imperative
				Prophetic Sisterhood
				Prophethood of
				  All Believers
				The New UU
				Welcoming Congregation
					elementary
					
					elementary
					elementary
					junior high
					junior-senior high
					intergenerational
					adult
					adult
					adult
					adult
					adult
					adult
					
					adult
					adult

JEWISH &
CHRISTIAN
HERITAGES/
WORLD
RELIGIONS
	past
	interdependence
	courage
	gratitude
		roots
		differences
		similarities
		comparative
		  religions
			you're okay
			tolerance
			knowledge
			respect
				Special Times
				Timeless Themes
				Growing-Up Year
				World Religions
				Understanding the
				  Bible
				Conversations With
				  the Bible
					elementary
					elementary
					elementary
					junior high
					adult
					
					adult

HUMANITY	caring
	inclusiveness
	cooperation
		origins
		ethics
		universals
			we're okay
			acceptance
			understanding
			respect
			justice
				Stepping-Stone Year
				In Our Hands
				New Men—
				  Deeper Hungers
				Parents as Social
				  Justice Educators
				BYOT III
					elementary
					all ages
					adult
					
					adult
					
					adult

EARTH	awareness responsibility	living things ecology ethics	appreciation stewardship	In Our Hands	all ages
UNIVERSE	wonder uncertainty humility imagination	curiosity meanings	awe reverence meaning belonging	L.I.F.T. On the Path	junior high junior-senior high

Youth Programming

In the many and varied Unitarian Universalist congregations throughout the continent, there exists a broad spectrum of youth programming. Many congregations claim that they have no youth, and their religious education programming stops at the sixth or eighth grade. Other congregations have youth programming during the Sunday morning service as part of the general religious education program with adult teachers leading a curriculum. Still others have a youth group, often called YRUU (Young Religious Unitarian Universalists), that meets Sunday evenings or at a time other than Sunday morning that has adult advisors and fosters youth leadership.

Many congregations have a combination of the above. There is no one right way to design youth. What works perfectly for one congregation may not be possible for another. The most important thing is to be flexible and develop a program that meets the needs and interests of the youth in the congregation.

Not Enough Youth for a Youth Group

Youth don't just vanish at age twelve or fourteen. If you have a religious education program that only goes up to the sixth or eighth grade, you have youth members even if you don't see them at the congregation. Youth will not come when there is no programming, so the fact that you have no youth may reflect a lack of programming that meets their needs or interests.

If you have only a few youth (one to four), you may not have enough for a youth group, but they should still have a place in your congregation. Meet with them to find out what their interests are. Perhaps one would love to teach in the religious education program with younger kids, one may want to work in the bookstore during coffee hour, or one may be interested in working with the social action committee. Make sure they know that they are as wanted and cared for as the other members of your congregation, and that you hope they won't vanish.

With only a few youth, you can sponsor an individualized coming-of-age program, which allows them to explore their Unitarian Universalist identity and to connect with their congregation. Contact the UUA Youth Office for a list of coming-of-age resources.

Youth crave the opportunity to socialize with peers who share their values (as adults do). So even if you only have a few youth in your congregation, give them the opportunity to socialize and bond together. Have an event just for them every month or so. Invite them to the minister's house for a pizza dinner, go to a local amusement park together, or participate in a district YRUU youth conference so they can see that they are not the only Unitarian Universalist teenagers.

Components of Balanced Youth Programming

Whether your youth group meets as a class Sunday morning, as a group in the evening, or as an adaptation or combination of the two, it is important to address the needs and interests of youth members.

Look at the five components of balanced youth programming and see what areas your congregation is addressing.

1. Learning. Youth, like all people of any age, hunger to gain new knowledge and skills. Youth programming should offer opportunities to explore new horizons in ways that look and feel different than the rest of their academic life. Many curricula exist to meet this need (call the UUA Youth Office for ideas), but don't limit yourself to published curricula. Youth are very capable of directing their own learning. For example, if they want to learn more about photography, invite a congregation member who is a photo buff to come and lead several sessions with the youth group. They could do a photo study of the congregation and have a photo show culminating their project. Look at the resources your congregation has to offer and suggest them to the youth group.

2. Social Action. Part of being Unitarian Universalists is expressing our values through our work in the world. Youth are developing their identity as Unitarian Universalists and have an incredible amount of energy and passion to express their new values. Serving at a homeless shelter, working with Habitat for Humanity, or volunteering at a children's center are great projects for a youth group.

3. Socializing. Like adults who attend the congregation and enjoy meeting people at coffee hour, chatting with friends at pot lucks, or connecting with Unitarian Universalists with similar interests on committees, youth also desire the opportunity to hang out with friends who share their values. Because so many youth don't go to the same school or live in the same neighborhood as their congregation mates, they often feel like the youth group is the only place they can be themselves. Don't be afraid to incorporate a lot of socializing time into your youth programming. Giving youth the opportunity to be with peers who share their values and support them for who they are is one of the greatest gifts your congregation can give.

4. Worship. The youth group provides an excellent place for youth to explore their spirituality and figure out what it means to be a Unitarian Universalist. Youth worship does not look like adult worship, though, and youth should not be forced to attend Sunday services that are not addressed to their needs and concerns and do not involve them. Encourage youth to lead their own worship within the youth group. This alternative may involve more music, personal sharing, and creative rituals than in adult worship. Youth groups can plan a worship service for the entire congregation one Sunday morning.

5. Leadership Development. One of the unique aspects of Unitarian Universalist youth programming is the respect for the inherent worth and dignity of youth and its encouragement for each individual's spiritual journey. To accomplish this, we don't have adults create programming *for* youth, but provide a model where adults work *with* youth to enable them to create their own programming. We encourage youth to take responsibility for their own programming while giving them the support and resources they need to be successful— youth empowerment. It does not mean that adults abdicate their power, but rather share it with youth to enable them to grow into mature and responsible Unitarian Universalist adults.

Advisors

To provide quality youth programming, a congregation needs committed adults to serve as advisors. Finding adults who are committed to youth empowerment, who have the time and interest to share, and who are not intimidated by teenagers is not always easy. To make the job more manageable, always have at least two advisors working with the group. If you have a team of three or four advisors, every advisor need not be at every meeting and the job will be less overwhelming.

When recruiting adults, be specific about your expectations of them and of the position. A useful tool is to develop a contract with your advisors that spell out how many youth group meetings a month they will attend; how many weekend events a year; who will pay for snacks, transportation, and phone calls; what kind of training and support they will be given; who will supervise them; and how often they will meet with their supervisor. If adults realize the boundaries of their commitment, they are much more likely to volunteer. Also make sure that you check the background and references of individuals you do not know well. (Call the UUA Department of Religious Education for their Sexual Abuse Clearing House for more information about creating safe churches for young people.)

Young Adult Programming

If you are asking "How can we attract young adults (18 to 35 year olds) to our congregation?", you are more than half way there. In fact, *intention* is ninety percent of a successful young adult ministry. If you believe that we have an obligation to minister to young people and that they have much to give to the denomination, the work has already begun.

Ten Tips

1. **Educate.** Ask your minister or worship leader to preach a sermon on young adult ministry.

2. **Investigate.** Find out if any young adults are associated with the congregation. Ask the religious education staff about the young people who came through the church school.

3. **Be hospitable.** Have a young adult greeter on Sunday morning who pays particular attention to the young adults attending the worship service.

4. **Awareness.** Ask a young adult to share with you what he or she sees when they walk through the door on a Sunday morning.

5. **Worship.** Ask a young adult to view the worship service through their eyes. Is the service participatory? What is the pace of the service, the music? Who are the visible people in leadership?

6. **Ask.** If you have a few young adults in your congregation, gather them together and ask them what they need—worship, discussion, social time, service opportunities, etc.

7. **Publicize.** Hold well-publicized, regularly scheduled meetings in a public space, preferably at the congregation's building.

8. **Support.** Give them staff support but let them provide the leadership.

9. **Brunch.** Set up a table at coffee hour, staffed by young adults, and have any young adults, both new people and first timers, go out for brunch after services.

10. **Young Adult Ministry Office (YAMs).** Contact the coordinator for young adult ministries, in the Department for Congregational, District, and Extension Services for resources, suggestions, and ideas for your congregation.

Developing Adult Religious Education Programming

Review the adult activities and courses that are being offered or have been offered in the last year:

Activity/course	Date/time offered	Average attendance

- From your review of current and past activities/courses, do particular topics, themes, and events seem especially popular?

- Do particular time slots work better than others?

- Clarify and prioritize your goals for adult education programming. Why do you want to begin or to expand adult programming?

Your goals may be broad, such as finding your sense of religious identity as Unitarian Universalists or promoting compassion, respect, and sensitivity for each other. Or, your goals may be more specific, such as learning about Unitarian Universalist theologies, exploring world religions, deepening your spiritual life, discovering how the arts can express your sense of the religious, studying a social action concern in depth and building bonds of support between members.

Determine the wants and needs of the members of your congregation.

- Hold an open half-hour meeting on Sunday morning after coffee hour for folks to share their interests and needs.

- Have an adult education table set up during coffee hour where folks can come and offer ideas.

- Send out or hand out on a Sunday a simple adult education questionnaire offering a variety of ideas and asking for additional ideas for courses, activities, teachers, and leaders.

- Have your adult education committee review the list of needs and interests generated. Revise your goals as needed and create a tentative list of two to four courses or activities with which to begin.

Determine the topics and possible formats for these offerings.

- **Discussion group**—for example, a book discussion group where different members of the group act as facilitators of the discussion.

- **Support group**—people facing similar life challenges who meet on a regular basis. Often support groups may be closed after the first several meetings to promote confidentiality and increase a sense of bonding; if such a group is to be closed after a certain time, make sure this policy is announced publicly.

- **Class or course**—to be lead by a teacher or facilitator (usually a member of the congregation or staff, sometimes an outside professional) to focus on a particular topic or body of material.

- **Seminar**—a series of presentations on aspects of one topic, for example, ecology, coordinated by a congregation member but often utilizing experts from the community. Sometimes such a seminar can help begin a social action project.

- **Workshop or retreat**—an intensive one-day or weekend experience led by a teacher or facilitator (often an outside professional) with a particular focus and specific goals.

- **Forum or lecture**—a one-time event offered by one or more individuals, often with time for questions and discussion.

- **Activity**—a one-time or regularly scheduled event such as hiking or birdwatching, coordinated by one or more knowledgeable persons.

Plan your program.

- Review adult education materials available from the UUA Bookstore. Consult with your minister and religious educator. Contact the Department of Religious Education at the Unitarian Universalist Association for consultation.

- Recruit teachers and leaders. Be clear and specific about your expectations. Write guidelines for adult education teachers. Samples are available from the Department of Religious Education.

- Publicize your new or expended program in inviting ways. Write up brief and interesting course descriptions to be included in your congregation's newsletter or prospectus, or as an individual mailing.

- Develop simple adult education registration forms that include a line for people to indicate if they would be willing to help with the adult education committee or in teaching or leading a course. (This volunteer recruitment tool is very effective.) Include the registration form with the list of courses.

- Develop simple evaluation forms that teachers and leaders can hand out at the end of each course. Include a question asking for ideas and suggestions for other course topics and leaders.

- Review the evaluations received to help plan for future semesters. The adult education committee should be working one semester ahead (i.e., working in the spring on fall semester offerings and in the fall on winter and spring offerings).

A Safe Congregation

Violence and sexual abuse are two very troubling issues in society today. They represent frightening violations of trust and intimacy. These problems cross all socio-economic levels and all racial, cultural, and religious groups. Unitarian Universalist congregations have a special responsibility to be responsive and sensitive to these issues. Our congregations need to be places of safety for children, parents, and all adults, and need to provide opportunities and resources to address the issues of sexual abuse and violence in open and honest ways.

Most Unitarian Universalists are fortunate to be part of a caring religious community that is proactive about religious and social issues. Many initiatives are underway in our congregations. Some of the compassionate and constructive ways Unitarian Universalists have chosen to respond include *breaking the silence* through preaching and teaching; offering *healing services* for survivors, *support groups* for congregation and community members, and *education and training programs* with safety policies formulated; screening and supervising defined procedures, and reporting identified procedures; and *prevention programs* for adults, parents, and children. The Religious Education Department has a Clearing House Safety/Abuse Packet with samples of the above mentioned responses and resources.

Unitarian Universalist congregations and Unitarian Universalist Association of Congregations are united by a covenant. We covenant—our free and voluntary pledge of mutuality—to affirm and promote the dignity of every person, the importance of personal responsibility, and the basic interdependence of all people. Our covenanting includes the codes of professional practice of the Unitarian Universalist Ministers Association and of the Liberal Religious Educators' Association, as well as the Unitarian Universalist Association Code of Ethics for Leaders of Children and Youth.

The UUA Department of Religious Education and the Department of Congregational, District, and Extension Services are working to produce *Safe Congregations,* a Unitarian Universalist Association curriculum designed to address issues of safety and abuse in congregational relationship: minister to congregation, adult to adult, and adult to child. The primary goal of this curriculum is for participants and congregations to increase their knowledge, skills, and resources in addressing and responding to the dehumanizing experience of sexual abuse. The curriculum helps Unitarian Universalists—participants of all ages and congregations throughout the Association—gain knowledge, expand understanding of our core values, and augment skills and resources needed to express safety, integrity, and responsibility in sexual ethics in life-enhancing ways.

A Code of Ethics for Adults Working with Children and Youth

Adults working with children and youth in the context of the Unitarian Universalist faith have a crucial and privileged role, one that can carry a great deal of power and influence. Whether acting as a youth advisor, chaperone, childcare worker, teacher, minister, registrant at a youth-adult conference, or in any role, adults have a special opportunity to interact with young people in ways that are affirming and inspiring to young people and adults.

Adults can be mentors, role models for, and trusted friends of children and youth. They can be teachers, counselors, and ministers. To help our children grow up to be caring and responsible adults can be a meaningful and joyful experience for the adult and a lifetime benefit to the young person.

While it is important that adults be capable of meaningful friendships with the young people with whom they work, adults must exercise good judgment and mature wisdom in using their influence with children and young adults and refrain from using young people to fulfill their own needs. Young people are in a vulnerable position when dealing with adults and may find it difficult to speak out about inappropriate behavior by adults.

Adult leaders need to posses a special dedication to working with young people in ways that affirm the Unitarian Universalist Association Principles. Good communication skills, self awareness and understanding of others, sensitivity, problem-solving and decision-making skills, and a positive attitude are important attributes. Additionally, adult religious leaders need to be people who:

- have a social network outside of their religious education responsibility in which to meet their own needs for friendship, affirmation, and self-esteem

- are willing and able to seek assistance from colleagues and religious professionals when they become aware of a situation that requires expert help or intervention.

It is ultimately the responsibility of the entire congregation or conference community, *not just those in leadership positions*, to create and maintain a climate that supports the growth and welfare of children and youth.

With the aforementioned in mind, the following statement is a Code of Ethics for adults working with children and youth.

Code of Ethics

Adults and older youth in leadership roles are in a position of stewardship and play a key role in fostering the spiritual development of individuals and the community. It is, therefore, especially important that those in leadership positions be well qualified to provide the special nurture, care, and support that will enable children and youth to develop a positive sense of self and a spirit of independence and responsibility. The relationship between young people and their leaders must be one of mutual respect if the positive potential of their relationship is to be realized.

There are no more important areas of growth than those of self-worth and the development of a healthy identity as a sexual being. Adults play a key role in assisting children and youth in these areas of growth. Wisdom dictates that children, youth, and adults suffer damaging effects when leaders become sexually involved with young persons in their care; therefore, leaders will refrain from engaging in sexual, seductive, or erotic behavior with children and youth. Neither shall they sexually harass or engage in behavior with children and youth which constitutes verbal, emotional, or physical abuse.

Leaders shall be informed of this code of ethics and agree to it before assuming their role. In cases of violating of this code, appropriate action will be taken.

Resources

The Religious Education Department offers consultation on programming for children, youth, and adults, curriculum planning, worship and diversity resources, and religious education leadership development.

Liberal Religious Educators' Association. This professional organization publishes a journal and newsletter, and offers support and professional development opportunities for religious educators.

REACH Packet. A collection of religious education resources compiled by the Religious Education Department is sent free to every congregation three times a year, in September, January, and April, addressed to the RE Coordinator.

Curriculum Loan Library. Programs may be borrowed free from the Curriculum Office for a two-week review. Many districts also maintain loan libraries. Contact your district office.

Video Loan Library. A free service of the UUA, the Video Loan Library includes many video materials for all ages. Videos are borrowed through the UUA Bookstore.

Catalogs. Mailed to every congregation and available from the UUA Bookstore: UUA Bookstore Catalog, Video Loan Library Catalog (updated regularly in the REACH Packet), Beacon Press Catalog, Skinner House Books Catalog

For Religious Education Administration

Starting from Scratch: How to Begin Your Own RE Program. A little bit of everything about establishing and building a religious education program.

Search Manual for DREs and Congregations. Suggestions for establishing a successful professional relationship between congregations and religious educators, including hiring, evaluation, compensation, and job descriptions.

Curriculum Mapping. Descriptions of all major Unitarian Universalist curricula and suggestions for building a workable curriculum plan.

For Youth Groups

Local Youth Group Programming Handbook. A resource for local youth groups that covers such topics as organization, fundraising, games, and worship. Available from the UUA Bookstore.

Youth Advisor's Handbook. A guide for advisors that addresses the many facets of the adult's unique role in working with youth. Out of print, but it may be in your congregation's or district's religious education library. The UUA Youth Office is working on a new handbook.

How to Be a Con Artist: Conference Planning Handbook. A resource for local youth groups and district youth organizations produced by the UUA Youth Office. It discusses the steps involved in planning any youth conference, from the preplanning stages to cleaning up the facilities. An invaluable tool for any youth organization, available from the UUA Bookstore.

From YACs to SACs: District Youth Programming Handbook. Covers everything you need to know about developing and supporting district youth programming. Available from the UUA Bookstore.

Synapse. The continental biannual YRUU newspaper, written by youth and advisors from across the continent and edited and published by the UUA Youth Office. Subscription is free and may be obtained by sending the Youth Office your name, address, phone number, and (for youth) date of birth.

Youth Advisory. A free newsletter for advisors written by advisors and published by the UUA Youth Office. Send to the Youth Office your name, address, congregation, and district, and whether you are a junior or senior high advisor.

Coming of Age Programs. The UUA Youth Office has compiled several programs from various congregations. Contact the Youth Office for samples.

District Resources   A number of resources are available on the district level. Contact your district office for information about the district religious education committee, curriculum loan library, and consulting services.

<u>Nine</u>

Social Justice Programming

Characteristics of an Effective Social Justice Program

Many Unitarian Universalist congregations have vital, energetic social justice programs that focus on social concerns, responsibility, action, or justice. The variety of ways that congregations do justice is enormous. The style of a congregation's efforts varies with context, energies, issues, trust levels, established decision-making guidelines, leadership, finances, and the willingness to make a difference.

Below are some of the qualities essential to developing a successful social justice program in a local congregation.

- **Identity.** The members of your congregation are committed to having the congregation involved in social justice issues. The congregation has a mission statement that articulates its role in the community. (See Chapter 2, "The Guiding Vision and Mission of a Congregation," for ways to develop a mission statement.)

- **History.** The members of your congregation know the story of how their congregation has been involved in social change ministry. They are informed through sermons, brochures, and new member orientation sessions about actions the congregation has taken. People are aware of the history of social justice work in the Unitarian Universalist movement.

- **Committed members.** A significant number of the members of the congregation are involved in its social justice program. In addition, a number of members may work in social change professions or be active in social change groups. These members are skilled, knowledgeable, and hardworking.

- **The social justice program is integrated into the life of the congregation.** Social justice ministry is seen as an integral part of the overall life of the congregation, as are worship, religious education, and the creation of a caring community. But social justice activities can be integrated into the worship, religious education, caring community, and social programs of the congregation. Worship services can focus on social issues. Education programs can be held on social justice topics.

- **The congregation has structures for making decisions about social justice issues.** Some congregations use surveys or have special meetings so members of the congregation have opportunities to set priorities for issues to be worked on. Members of the congregation can vote to make commitments to key projects, to take a stand on a controversial issue, to determine policies for socially responsible investing, and to provide funds for the congregation's social justice program.

- **The congregation's social justice program is organized around action groups.** Social justice committees are not effective ways of organizing social justice programs in congregations of more than 100 people, because it is difficult for a social justice committee to manage several projects at once. Congregations with attendance of fewer than 100 people are most effective when they pick one issue. In congregations of more than 100 people, the most effective way to organize is to form action groups and then create a way to coordinate the action groups. This coordinating vehicle might be a steering committee of action group leaders or a meeting time when all the action groups meet and share information.

  The best way to start action groups is to identify issues about which people are deeply concerned. Unitarian Universalists are successfully organizing people around women's issues, environmental issues, and peace issues because people care deeply about them.

- **The social justice program is well balanced.** The overall program has a good balance of different styles for doing social justice ministry: service, education, witnessing, advocacy, and community organizing. Service involves hands-on involvement. Education means raising awareness. Witnessing includes making one's views known through demonstrations or picket lines. Advocacy consists of working in the legislative process. And community organizing entails helping oppressed people organize themselves.

- **People doing social justice ministry are intentional about what they do.** Action groups establish program priorities and set clear goals and objectives for projects. They carefully develop strategies and tactics to meet their goals, rather than jumping into action quickly. People make a careful analysis of the problems they are trying to solve and they develop concrete, specific, manageable projects.

- **Social justice program leaders use the financial resources of the congregation.** Social justice leaders make use of the financial resources of the congregation by establishing a line item in the budget. They get financial support from the members of the congregation by special fundraising events and collections at Sunday services. They know how to apply for funding from the Unitarian Universalist Funding Program. (See Resources at the end of this chapter.)

- **Publicity.** Social justice leaders publicize what is going on so that members of the congregation and the wider community know what is happening and how they can become involved.

- **Recruitment.** Social justice leaders are intentional about recruiting members of the congregation to be involved in programs. They attempt to use the special talents of members.

- **Denominational links.** Social justice leaders make use of the resources provided by the Unitarian Universalist Association departments and affiliated groups involved in social justice programming.

- **Alliances with community organizations and interfaith groups.** Often our congregations or social change groups are small. We can increase our effectiveness by working with community organizations (NAACP, NOW, Rainbow Coalition, Sierra Club, etc.) and interfaith groups.

- **Ministerial leadership.** The minister (or ministers) supports social justice activism in the congregation. The minister informs people about important issues, connects the congregation with the wider community and the Unitarian Universalist Association, assists the social responsibility committee and action groups in defining issues and setting goals, and provides leadership training.

- **Inclusivity.** The members of the congregation make a special effort to develop a faith community that includes people from different racial and cultural backgrounds and with different lifestyles, such as gays, bisexuals, lesbians, and the physically challenged.

- **Deal effectively with conflict.** The members of the congregation know how to deal creatively with controversial social issues and how to resolve the inevitable conflicts that arise in doing social justice ministry.

- **Training.** Social justice leaders train people in organizational and social change skills.

- **Evaluation.** Social justice leaders are continually evaluating their program.

Creating a Caring Community for Those Involved in Social Justice

Participants in your congregation's social justice programs want to feel that they are part of a caring, trusting community. Part of caring for the world is caring for one another as persons. A caring community can be fostered by running effective meetings, attending to the spiritual needs of the participants, enjoying social time together, and celebrating accomplishments.

The committee or action groups should meet on a regular basis. The important thing is to get the meeting date on everyone's schedule. A meeting notice with an agenda should be sent to committee members in advance.

Here are some suggestions for how to structure task group or committee meetings.

Social Time

People participate in social justice programs to meet important personal needs as well as to work on social issues. Such needs include being part of a group, making a difference in the world, and having a chance to live out one's faith. Moreover, each of us needs a sense that we are part of a community that cares for us as a person.

For these reasons it's important to build social time into the meetings, a time for people to get to know one another, to share what is going on in their lives, and to enjoy one another's company.

Social justice organizations help people meet these needs in different ways. Some have potluck suppers before the meeting or send out for pizza. Others have social time for a half hour before the meeting. A group member is assigned to provide beverages and refreshments. At this time the group can write letters to political leaders on pending legislation.

Worship

Some people are concerned about how to make a stronger connection between living a spiritual life and doing social justice work. One way is to have a brief worship experience as part of the meeting. Some groups begin or end their meetings with worship.

A member of the group volunteers to lead the worship. That person may read literature, lead singing, or guide a meditation. Such experiences provide a spiritual grounding for the actions we take in the world.

Agenda Setting

It's good to mail a meeting notice and a copy of the agenda before the meeting. At the beginning of the meeting review the agenda. See if there are additional items to add.

Structuring Social Justice for Small Congregations

The size of a congregation has a lot to do with how to structure a program. There is a difference between structuring a program in a small congregation and a middle-sized or large congregation. A small congregation organizes through a social justice committee. In a middle-sized or large congregation, the ideal way to work is through action groups and a coordinating committee. Of the total number of Unitarian Universalist congregations (1,120), 780 congregations have fewer than 150 members.

Small congregations do not have a large number of people or a sizable budget for their program. But they have strengths on which they can build effective social justice ministry, including a strong feeling of family and community, and a short chain of command. It's easier for people to communicate in a small congregation than in a large, complex institution. These congregations are often located in communities where they can provide important leadership.

Small congregations also have particular challenges for their social justice programs:

- Often there is no social justice committee or the committee is small.

- Because there are few people on the committee, members burn out easily.

- Personality clashes in the committee or in the congregation can be particularly harmful.

- The congregation's budget often contains no money for the social justice program.

- Members of the congregation may provide leadership to social change groups in the community and thus not have time for congregation projects.

- Sometimes groups exist in conservative communities where it is difficult to take a stand on controversial issues.

- Often there is no building to help provide a community identity.

In spite of these obstacles, small congregations have been able to do some significant programming. Here are some examples:

Unitarian Universalist Society of the Palisades in Englewood, New Jersey
This congregation has approximately thirty members, who sponsored a fundraising event for a project to end hunger. The members of the

congregation joined with other Unitarian Universalist congregations in New Jersey. They reserved a large hall at a school and invited the Jubilee Singers, a gospel group from All Souls Church in Washington, DC. The event was so successful that they raised $10,000.

First Universalist Church of Yarmouth, Maine
This congregation has a membership of approximately 150. Members of the congregation's social justice committee approached the board of trustees about choosing a unifying issue to work on. Together they agreed to focus on the environment.

As a result, some Sunday services during the year focused on environmental themes. The social justice committee worked with members of the religious education committee to develop curriculum materials for children on environmentalism. All members of the congregation had a chance to participate in a recycling project.

Blue Hills Unitarian Universalist Fellowship in Rice Lake, Wisconsin
The religious education director uses the UUA General Resolutions Study Guides as a way of generating reflection and action.

Harrisonburg Unitarian Universalists in Harrisonburg, Virginia
This congregation of sixty-two members takes the third Sunday of the month and creates an intergenerational program on a social issue. For example, all of the adults and children might participate in a park clean-up project.

To develop a social justice program in a small congregation, involve the whole congregation. Pick one or two focus areas. Small groups can't support a whole network of action groups like a larger congregation can. But they can select one or two issues that can receive broad support from the members of the group.

Structuring Social Justice for Middle-sized and Large Congregations

Middle-sized and large congregations that have strong social justice programs carry out their programs through action groups. By using action groups a congregation can engage in a number of substantial ongoing projects.

Action groups are necessary because it's difficult for a social justice committee to manage several projects at once. There isn't enough time in a monthly meeting to do all the committee business and develop in-depth projects. A typical pattern is that ten people come to the meeting with ten issues. During the meeting each person tries to persuade others to work on their issue, but the group never achieves consensus. At the end of the meeting everyone goes home frustrated. At the next meeting they repeat the cycle.

The best way to start action groups is to identify those issues people are deeply concerned about and want to act on. Unitarian Universalists have successfully organized people around women's issues, environmental issues, and peace issues because people care deeply about them.

Coordinating Action Groups

Once members of a congregation have set up action groups they must develop a way to coordinate these groups and an overall social justice program. They set up a coordinating group or a council to do so.

Some action groups meet together once a month. Such is the case with the Unitarian Universalist Community Church in Park Forest, Illinois. This congregation has action groups called Hunger and Homeless Housing, Peace and World Affairs, Women's Issues, and Ecology. The action groups have a joint meeting the last Sunday of each month at an adult forum at 9:30 a.m. They share news of their activities and host speakers on other social justice issues. During this meeting people are also encouraged to write letters to legislators.

Other congregations structure their coordination so that the task group leaders meet only four or five times a year. For example, the First Unitarian Society in Chicago has a social justice council that consists of a regular liaison from each task force, denominational groups, larger community groups, and three at-large representatives. The council meets at least quarterly. The council proposes policies and action groups to the trustees; establishes priorities and goals for social justice; and initiates, facilitates, and coordinates activities consistent with its goals.

Another way to coordinate the action groups is to have them meet every month or two. One evening of the month all the action groups come together. For the first twenty minutes the group discusses issues such as funding, recruiting, and developing publicity. Each month they select one focus issue to discuss. Then each action group meets separatly for an hour and a half to work on its issue. At the end of the meeting the action group members come back to share with the others what they discussed and suggest ways that others can help with their projects. The advantages of this model are that all members of the action groups meet together instead of only the leaders of each action group. Participants still can focus on their projects because they break into separate groups and members of action groups have a face to face opportunity to stay informed about what other action groups are doing.

There is no best way to coordinate action groups. Experiment with what works for you in your congregation, if you want the coordinating group to meet monthly, every other month, or three or four times a year. You will need to determine if all the task group members should meet or just the leaders of the task groups.

Your congregation's board of trustees also has a role in providing leadership for the congregation's social justice program.

The board and the minister(s) are responsibile for the total life of the congregation. They should make sure that social justice concerns are integrated into the overall program, which involves infusing social justice concerns into the education, worship, and community-building aspects of the congregation's life. It means creating a healthy balance among all of the congregation's programs.

The board also provides leadership by ensuring that the congregation is a moral community that exemplifies the values its members believe are important, including nondiscriminatory hiring practices, socially responsible investing policies for endowment funds, and purchasing congregation supplies with environmental values in mind.

The board should make sure that a viable structure—including action groups and a coordinating mechanism—exists for the social justice program.

The board can also ensure that the social justice program has enough financial resources to carry out its program, including adequate funding in the congregation's budget and provisions for special fundraising events.

Resources

Adams, James Luther. *The Prophethood of All Believers.* Edited by George K. Beach. Boston: Beacon Press, 1986.

Dudley, Carl S. *Basic Steps Toward Community Ministry.* Washington, DC: The Alban Institute, 1991.

Ethics and Action. Periodical about social justice work in Unitarian Universalism, published three times a year by the UUA Department for Social Justice.

Gilbert, Richard. *The Prophetic Imperative: UU Foundations for a New Social Gospel.* Boston: Unitarian Universalist Association, 1982.

Resolutions and Resources Handbook. Contains resolutions passed by the Unitarian Universalist Association General Assembly since 1961. Available from the UUA Bookstore.

UUA Departments With Social Concerns

Department for Social Justice
Keeps information on social issues, networks with more than thirty-five affiliated organizations working on social justice issues, and provides training for districts, congregations, and theological schools. As of June 1994, the department had trained twenty-seven social justice facilitators to conduct social justice empowerment workshops. Contact the department to find out about the availability of this program for your congregation.

Office for Racial and Cultural Diversity
Provides information and training resources to enable Unitarian Universalists to address issues of diversity and antiracism in their congregations and communities.

Office of Lesbian, Bisexual, and Gay Concerns
Provides the Welcoming Congregation program for the inclusion of gays, lesbians, and bisexuals in the Unitarian Universalist movement; works with groups countering the radical religious right.

Department of Religious Education
Provides a variety of curricula, such as *In Our Hands*, that focus on social justice issues.

Commission on General Resolutions
Facilitates the process by which General Resolutions dealing with social issues are brought before the General Assembly.

Unitarian Universalist Women's Federation
Concerned with prochoice, violence against women, and other issues affecting women.

Washington Office for Social Justice
100 Maryland Ave., NE, Washington, DC, 20002, (202) 547-0254. Following the General Resolutions, advocates for Unitarian Universalists with the federal government. Provides training in advocacy methods for districts and congregations.

Unitarian Universalist United Nations Office
777 UN Plaza, Room 7D, New York, NY, 10017, (212) 986-5165. Focuses on international issues.

Unitarian Universalist Service Committee
130 Prospect St., Cambridge, MA, 02139-1813, (617) 868-6600. The Service Committee carries out international development projects, human rights activities, and programs to empower children.

In addition to the organizations listed above, affiliated organizations involved in social change projects are listed in the Unitarian Universalist Association Directory.

Funding Resources

For information about these funds, contact the Unitarian Universalist Funding Program, Unitarian Universalist Association, 25 Beacon St., Boston, MA 02108.

Unitarian Universalist Fund for Social Responsibility
Provides funds for congregations involved in social change projects.

Fund for a Just Society
Makes grants to community organizations addressing social issues.

Ten

Developing a Diverse Congregation

Age Diversity

The UUA Office of Young Adult Ministries (YAMs) was created to address the needs of Unitarian Universalists between the ages of eighteen and thirty-five. The office, staffed by a YAMs coordinator and support personnel, recognizes that young adults are a vital link in the Unitarian Universalist chain. It focuses on promoting this underrepresented population.

Working from the premise that we are spiritually and morally obligated to minister to Unitarian Universalist young adults and that young adults will lead the denomination into the twenty-first century, we recognize the need to lay new groundwork and build communities that reach out to young adults. Unitarian Universalism is challenged with the task of creating an atmosphere that accommodates and facilitates the personal and spiritual growth of persons from diverse cultures, backgrounds, and eras. Congregations that include and encourage diverse, intergenerationally active membership ensure that the Unitarian Universalist movement will remain a vital and growing tradition.

Unitarian Universalist ideals and values fit the lifestyle and profiles of today's young adults. Although young adults tend to be less involved than older adults in a congregational setting, "this group has demonstrated the greatest openness to change, and showed the lowest need for unchanging structure, the least generalized prejudice, the least acceptance of middle-class norms, and the least desire for distance from differing social and religious groups." (Gribbon, 1990, from Strommen, 1972). These findings suggest that young adults are a population in accord with Unitarian Universalist ideas, and that now is a fertile time for innovative programming that will engage young adults in developing their faith.

The Office of Young Adult Ministries acknowledges a threefold mission. The office works to train and empower young adult leadership throughout the continent. It strives to foster and encourage a variety of projects in congregations, regional areas, and on college campuses, with the help of supporting grants. It advocates for young adults in the Unitarian Universalist Association administrative structure and within the Unitarian Universalist Association.

The office operates in conjunction with the Young Adult Ministries Working Group. The Working Group is a five-member committee appointed by the Unitarian Universalist Association Board of Trustees. Their combined efforts provide a framework for continued growth and support of young adult ministry so that ministry to, by, and for young adults remains an integral part of the Unitarian Universalist Association mission.

The role of the coordinator is to monitor and address the issues in young adult ministry with an eye toward developing resources, spiritual growth, empowerment, consciousness raising, and issues of justice.

In collaboration with the Young Adult Working Group, the office provides the following services.

Grants

Grants of up to $500 are available to assist young adult groups with start-up expenses or special projects that benefit young adults. Information on grant criteria, guidelines, and applications can be obtained by contacting the office.

Leadership Training and Educational Workshops

The office conducts yearly leadership training events to organize and empower young adults across the continent. The office is available to conduct workshops at conferences and district events.

General Assembly Programming

The office sponsors young adult activities at General Assembly. It offers at least two workshops, one on the basics of starting a young adult group and one on campus ministry.

Campus Connection

In an attempt to ease the transition from youth status to young adult status, the office compiles a list of Unitarian Universalist Campus Connections. It identifies schools with full service campus ministry programs, student-led groups, or other Unitarian Universalists, either faculty, administrators, or students. The office can give the name of a contact person on those campuses and asks people to help by contacting the YAMs office with additional connections.

Consultation

The coordinator of the Office of Young Adult Ministries is available to conduct site visits to infuse enthusiasm, confidence, and vision. The coordinator is also available to explore options, possibilities, and creative ideas to enhance YAM projects, whether programmatically, structurally, or financially.

Continental Unitarian Universalist Young Adult Network (C-UUYAN)

The Continental Unitarian Universalist Young Adult Network is a grassroots organization whose ministry is geared to enhancing and empowering young adults. C-UUYAN has an annual week-long summer conference called OPUS, which gathers to do business and annual planning and to have fun. Information about OPUS can be obtained through the Young Adult Ministries Office. Members of C-UUYAN are also available to consult on issues pertaining to young adults.

For More Information

The Office of Young Adult Ministries in the Department for Congregational, District, and Extension Services has gathered information on resources that enhance the effectiveness and scope of young adult ministry projects. Included are bibliographies, monographs, manuals, videotapes, project ideas, and events for young adults. Other resources are being produced on an ongoing basis. The monographs are practical guides for establishing and maintaining ministry with young adults. (See below.) The office staff is also a source of information and is eager to help with brainstorming and problem solving.

Through its ongoing efforts to educate and sensitize people to the unique gifts and needs of young adults, the office hopes to assist people in providing meaningful ministry through programming, social events, spiritual deepening, social outreach, and pastoral care.

For Further Reading

Macklin, Mary Ann. *A Unitarian Universalist Campus Ministry Manual*. Available from the Young Adult Ministry Office.

ten Hove, Jaco B..*UU Youth and Young Adult Leadership School Handbook*. Available from the Young Adult Ministry Office.

Young Adult Information Packet. Available from the Young Adult Ministry Office.

Monographs
Lynch, Suzelle. *How To Start A Young Adult Group*.
Lynch, Suzelle. *Worship*.
Winner, Alice. *A Social Action Guide for Unitarian Universalist Young Adults*.

Racial and Ethnic Diversity

Why We Need a Racial and Cultural Diversity Initiative

Essential ingredients in creating a racially inclusive culture are the concepts of justice and equality, where all people have approximately equal power and privilege. We are nowhere near reaching this circumstance in North America and our predominantly white Unitarian Universalist congregations reflect this inequality. Nevertheless, we have a long Unitarian Universalist history of justice seeking and have made significant contributions in terms of race relations and desegregation efforts. That is why Unitarian Universalist congregations need to be committed to dismantling racism in Unitarian Universalism and equipping members to create a truly antiracist, multicultural society.

The Unitarian Universalist Association Racial and Cultural Diversity Initiative does not intend to rearrange the demographics of each community where there is a Unitarian Universalist congregation. We are growing, but we need to expand more and at the same time mirror our communities. Statistically, the majority of all people, of whatever color, are unchurched. We have a wonderful religion to share and a tremendous opportunity and responsibility to share it more widely with people of all racial and cultural groups.

Homogeneity is limiting; there is racial imbalance in most communities. Our tendency to sameness in an increasingly racially and culturally diverse society is disturbing. We need to prepare ourselves and our children to function in the real world—the larger community—and the reality of the human community is racial and cultural diversity. By nurturing a climate of racial and cultural diversity and justice in appropriate ways in local communities, we can better live out our Unitarian Universalist principles. If we are not part of the solution to inequality, are we not part of the problem? We can all address issues of injustice and powerlessness and grow in knowledge and appreciation of other people and cultures.

Unitarian Universalists and Racial Justice

The UUA Racial and Cultural Diversity Initiative has many roots. The history of Unitarians and Universalists is intertwined with the abolitionist, freedom, and civil rights movements. Following the activism of the 1960s and 1970s, Unitarian Universalists began to sharpen our understanding about the "new racism" of the 1980s and to acknowledge and recognize institutional racism within Unitarian Universalism.

In 1981 the Unitarian Universalist Association board of trustees commissioned an Institutional Racism Audit that identified the need to address racial justice issues in our Association. In 1985 the General Assembly passed a resolution recognizing the presence of racism within our denomination, as identified by the 1981 Institutional Racism Audit, and called for the establishment of a Black Concerns Working Group to assist congregations in addressing racism.

In 1992 the General Assembly passed a Resolution on Racial and Cultural Diversity in Unitarian Universalism. The resolution called on Unitarian Universalists to support a vision of a Unitarian Universalist faith that reflects the reality of a racially diverse and multicultural global village. The resolution was sponsored by a broad grassroots coalition that included African American, women's, gay/lesbian, urban, youth, and district committees and organizations.

Following the passage of the resolution, the Unitarian Universalist Association board of trustees appointed a Racial and Cultural Diversity Task Force composed of representatives of various Unitarian Universalist groups to develop and implement a process involving a broad representation of congregations, organizations, and staff to realize our vision of a racially and culturally diverse Unitarian Universalist Association.

The Office for Racial and Cultural Diversity was established in 1992 with the primary responsibility of implementing the 1992 Resolution on Racial and Cultural Diversity. The director for racial and cultural diversity (formerly the advocate for racial inclusiveness) develops and coordinates the process of designing and implementing a long-term strategy for racial and cultural diversity, working with the Racial and Cultural Diversity Task Force, Unitarian Universalist Association staff, the Black Concerns Working Group, the districts, and other Unitarian Universalist organizations, on various levels, to dismantle racism and to increase our racial and cultural diversity.

The Unitarian Universalist Association is moving forward on the commitment made in 1992 to increase racial and cultural diversity in Unitarian Universalism and to create an antiracist Unitarian Universalist Association and society. The Racial and Cultural Diversity Task Force is coordinating a series of General Assembly programs on racial justice and racism.

At the 1993 General Assembly our Association focused one full day on "Racial Justice: For Such a Time as This." Unitarian Universalists examined our efforts for racial justice and reflected on our sometimes proud and sometimes painful history. There was a "More Racial Justice" Special Focus Session at the 1994 General Assembly where Unitarian Universalists explored antiracist models for institutional change. The 1995 General Assembly racial justice programming focuses on spirit building, including theological and philosophical foundations and worship, as well as activities for dismantling institutional racism.

For More Information

The UUA Office for Racial and Cultural Diversity is responsible for implementing the 1992 Resolution for Racial and Cultural Diversity. The director develops and coordinates education and training, programming, models for change, assessment procedures, and resources for creating antiracist institutions, policies, and practices. Consultation, support, information, and resources are provided by racial and cultural diversity staff to congregations, districts, and organizations working on racial justice and diversity issues and projects. The racial and cultural diversity staff also coordinate the work of the Task Force for Racial and Cultural Diversity and the Black Concerns Working Group.

The Office for Racial and Cultural Diversity is leading and coordinating efforts to develop resources for the Association. Available from the office are guidelines for becoming a multicultural congregation; bibliographies and resource lists of publications, videos, programs, training organizations, and consultants; and reports and models. Call or write the Office for Racial and Cultural Diversity for an information packet.

The UUA Racial and Cultural Diversity Task Force is composed of representatives from various Unitarian Universalist organizations and provides leadership for the Unitarian Universalist Association's long-term initiative for racial and cultural diversity. The Task Force sponsors racial justice sessions at General Assembly and presents annual reports to the assembly. The Task Force also sponsors antiracism training for groups in the Association. To receive the Task Force's reports, write or call the Office for Racial and Cultural Diversity.

The Racial and Cultural Diversity Research Group was appointed as a subcommittee of the Racial and Cultural Diversity Task Force to design a multiphase research effort. The purpose of the research is to build a foundation for understanding what the racial and cultural diversity initiative means to Unitarian Universalists in our congregations and to identify both within Unitarian Universalism and the larger faith community what models exists for implementing it. The research program is to create a comprehensive information base on which to build a strategic plan to achieve realistic levels of racial and cultural diversity in the Unitarian Universalist movement. To be effective the research is divided into two phases: exploratory (qualitative) initial research and quantitative data gathering. Qualitative and quantitative research reports are available from the Office for Racial and Cultural Diversity.

The Black Concerns Working Group promotes racial inclusivity at all levels and conducts a variety of workshops, including the antiracism workshops "To Be Equal—Beyond Racism" and "Creating a Jubilee World" 1 and 2 for congregations and at General Assembly. The workshops help participants examine personal and institutional racism and advise congregations on how they can work to free the world of racism. The workshops are scheduled for Saturdays and held on area, regional, and district bases. Workshop leaders also participate in the congregation's Sunday service.

The working group also develops partnerships with districts, encouraging the formation of district black concerns working groups that coordinate and support efforts at the local level. The Black Concerns Working Group is developing a new antiracism resource notebook as a follow-up to its successful *We Have No Problem . . . Again* publication. The Black Concerns Working Group can be contacted through the Office for Racial and Cultural Diversity.

The Whitney M. Young, Jr., Urban Ministry Fund, administered by the Office for Racial and Cultural Diversity, provides grants of up to $3,000 for Unitarian Universalist congregations and Unitarian Universalist-sponsored groups doing urban ministry, racial justice, and multicultural urban-suburban projects. The fund is supported by congregations that hold Urban Ministry Sundays during January for Martin Luther King, Jr., Day; in February for Black History Month, or in March to honor James Reeb. Donations to the fund have totaled between $10,000 to $15,000 annually, with an increased number of grants anticipated because of growing awareness of and support for the program. To contact the fund for information, grant applications, or more about Urban Ministry Sundays, write or call the Office for Racial and Cultural Diversity.

The Office of Worship and Diversity Resources helps congregations plan racially inclusive worship services and provides programs and curricula for diversity efforts. The office is working on a new curriculum, *Weaving the Fabric of Diversity*, that allows participants to explore the deep connections that link us beyond our categories of race, ethnicity, class, gender, sexual orientation, and physical condition. The office conducts the Beyond Categorical Thinking Program, which encourages congregations to consider racially and culturally diverse candidates as ministers, religious education professionals, and other church staff positions. The program, which typically takes place on a weekend, includes a two-and-a-half hour workshop and a Sunday morning service and is provided at no cost.

The UUA Department for Social Justice assists congregations working on racial-justice issues in their communities and is creating a national Racial Justice Task Force. *Ethics and Action*, published by the Department for Social Justice three times a year, covers diversity efforts inside and outside the Unitarian Universalist Association and is sent to congregational social action chairs and other interested Unitarian Universalists.

The UUA Department of Religious Education offers a variety of racial and cultural diversity materials and curricula including *How Open the Door*, an eight-session, multimedia adult education curriculum focusing on African Americans' experience in the denomination; the *In Our Hands* peace and justice curricula for students from grade one through high school, components of which deal with racial justice; and three new curricula on diversity—one each for elementary, junior high, and high school students. The Religious Education Department also includes diversity-related resources and bibliographies in the REACH packets it mails to congregations three times a year, and assists in locating specific pieces as needed.

For Further Reading

Barndt, Joseph. *Dismantling Racism: The Continuing Challenge to White America*. Minneapolis, MN: Augsburg Press, 1991.

Morrison-Reed, Mark. *Black Pioneers in a White Denomination*. 2nd edition. Boston: Skinner House Books, 1994.

Whittemore, Katherine and Gerald Marzorati, editors. *Voices in Black and White* (an anthology of essays on race from *Harper's*). New York: Franklin Square Press, 1993.

West, Cornel. *Race Matters*. Boston: Beacon Press, 1993.

Wade-Gayles, Gloria. *Pushed Back to Strength: A Black Woman's Journey Home*. Boston: Beacon Press, 1993.

Feagin, Joe R. and Melvin P. Sikes. *Living with Racism: The Black Middle Class Experience*. Boston: Beacon Press, 1994.

Hopson, Darlene Powell and Derek. *Raising the Rainbow Generation: Teaching Your Children to be Successful in a Multicultural Society*. New York: Simon and Schuster, 1993.

Duvall, Lynn. *Respecting Our Differences: A Guide to Getting Along in a Changing World*. Minneapolis, MN: Free Spirit Press, 1994.

Fiffer, Steve and Sharon Sloan Fiffer. *Fifty Ways to Help Your Community: A Handbook for Change*. New York: Doubleday, 1994.

"Soulful Journeys," a pamphlet sold in packs of 25. Riveting and diverse African American voices that narrate their religious journey toward Unitarian Universalism. Boston: Unitarian Universalist Association, 1994.

Singing the Living Tradition, the Unitarian Universalist Association hymnbook provides inclusive hymns and readings. Boston: Beacon Press, 1994.

Videotapes and cassettes on racial and social justice issues, including the 1994 General Assembly Racial Justice Day, are available through the Unitarian Universalist Association Video Loan Library at the UUA Bookstore.

Office of Lesbian, Bisexual, and Gay Concerns

The Office of Lesbian, Bisexual, and Gay Concerns fosters acceptance, understanding, and equality for gay, lesbian, and bisexual persons in the Unitarian Universalist Association and in society at large.

The office serves as an educational resource center, promotes advocacy of gay, lesbian, and bisexual issues, and encourages networking among Unitarian Universalists, member congregations, and interfaith allies. It provides information, advice, and support to communities facing antigay, antidemocratic initiatives from the religious right.

The Welcoming Congregation Program

The creation of the Welcoming Congregation Program was mandated by the 1989 General Assembly. Congregations choose to use it, and each congregation does it differently. Congregations who successfully welcome lesbian, gay, and bisexual people have the following qualities.

- Includes and addresses the needs of gay, lesbian, and bisexual persons at every level of congregational life—in worship, programs, social occasions, and rites of passage (including union services, memorial services, and child dedications—welcoming not only their presence but the gifts and particularities of their lives as well.

- Assumes the presence of lesbian, gay, and bisexual people. (Worship celebrates this diversity by having inclusive language and content.)

- Fully incorporates the experience of lesbian, gay, and bisexual persons throughout all programs, including religious education.

- Includes an affirmation and nondiscrimination clause in the bylaws and other official documents affecting all dimensions of congregational life, including membership, hiring practices, and the calling of religious professionals.

- Engages in outreach into the gay, lesbian, and bisexual communities by advertising to and by actively supporting lesbian, gay, and bisexual affirmative groups.

- Offers congregational and ministerial support for services of union and memorial services for gay, lesbian, and bisexual persons, and celebrations of evolving family definitions.

- Celebrates the lives of all people and welcomes same-sex couples, recognizing their committed relationships, and equally affirms displays of caring and affection without regard to sexual orientation.

- Seeks to nurture ongoing dialogue between gay, lesbian, bisexual, and heterosexual persons and to create deeper trust and sharing.

- Encourages the presence of a chapter of Interweave (Unitarian Universalists for Lesbian, Gay, Bisexual, and Transgender Concerns).

- Affirms and celebrates gay, lesbian, and bisexual issues and history during the congregational year (possibly including a gay pride celebration, usually in June).

- Attends to legislative developments and works to promote justice, freedom, and equality in the larger society. Speaks out when the rights and dignity of lesbian, gay, and bisexual people are at stake.

How to Set Up a Welcoming Congregation Committee

A welcoming congregation committee may be an autonomous task force in the congregation, or may include liaisons or representatives from other groups, such as religious education, worship, membership, music, social action, youth, adult education, the board of directors, and the program council. All professional staff should be brought into the process.

Each congregation will adapt the process most appropriate for creating a committee. However, good communication between the welcoming congregation committee and related groups improves the effectiveness of the program and reduces the stress of change.

Celebrating After the Program

Congregations that want to mark a successful welcoming congregation process may receive a free poster declaring them a welcoming congregation by writing the UUA Office of Lesbian, Bisexual, and Gay Concerns, 25 Beacon St., Boston, MA 02108. See guidelines in *The Welcoming Congregation: Resources for Affirming Gay, Lesbian and Bisexual Persons.*

Interweave (Unitarian Universalists for Lesbian, Gay, Bisexual, and Transgender Concerns)

Interweave is a Unitarian Universalist membership organization open to all interested persons, with a membership of approximately 1,000. It has chapters in many Unitarian Universalist congregations and in districts throughout the United States and Canada. Its two primary goals are the creation of local groups for gay, lesbian, and bisexual Unitarian Universalists for support, socializing, and sharing of life issues, and outreach to the larger gay, lesbian, and bisexual communities to publicize the religious alternative offered by Unitarian Universalism. Annual membership dues enable one to vote at general membership meetings and receive the Interweave newsletter. No members are turned away for an inability to pay dues. Membership and subscription information are available by writing Interweave, c/o the UUA Office of Lesbian, Bisexual, and Gay Concerns, 25 Beacon St., Boston, MA 02108.

Mission Statement

Interweave is a membership organization affiliated with the Unitarian Universalist Association. It is dedicated to the spiritual, political, and social well-being of Unitarian Universalists who are confronting oppression as lesbians, gay men, bisexuals, transgender persons and their heterosexual allies. It celebrates the culture and lives of its members.

Interweave World

The Interweave membership newsletter appears three to four times a year and chronicles upcoming social events, chapter updates, gay, lesbian, and bisexual politics and political organizing, and serves as a general reference guide for members.

Events

Convocation is Interweave's major programmatic and social convention, held each year Valentine's Day weekend. The site for convocation rotates annually. Convocation features speakers, panels, a business meeting, and social events.

A second general membership meeting is held each year at the General Assembly. Among many of the events offered are panels, an Interweave worship service, and a membership business meeting. An information table and an Interweave hospitality suite are also available.

How to Form a Local Chapter

Local chapters may be organized around any model in a given congregation community: regular monthly evening meetings, Sunday morning meetings before the service, social events held in the congregation building. A local group might begin with a well-publicized, well-planned service and program or may start with an informal planning dinner announced to the general congregation at a Sunday service.

Often it is important to begin with a smaller gathering, announced in advance in the district and congregation newsletters of nearby Unitarian Universalist congregations. After a core group has come together, a public event should be planned to announce the existence of Interweave to the community as well as to attract additional members.

Consider turning to local congregations and districts for help—including financial help. A successful Interweave group probably means newcomers to nearby Unitarian Universalist congregations. Capitalize on the group's official existence as an Interweave chapter for publicity purposes. List in the local gay press and national guides, such as *The Gay Yellow Pages*, under "Religious Groups."

Finally, get in touch with the Interweave Coordinating Committee and/or the Office of Lesbian, Bisexual, and Gay Concerns to add the new chapter name to the Interweave *World* mailing list.

For Further Reading

The Welcoming Congregation: Resources for Affirming Gay, Lesbian and Bisexual Persons. Contains specific guidelines and action steps, including an eight- to ten-week workshop program, designed to facilitate the creation of Welcoming Congregations, guidelines for enhancing religious education classes and youth groups, helpful discussion questions, and readings for participants to study. Also contains plans for shorter programs, an annotated bibliography, and a section on Christian worship. Available from the UUA Bookstore.

Unitarian Universalism: A Serious Spiritual Alternative for the Gay and Lesbian Community. Available from the UUA Office of Lesbian, Bisexual, and Gay Concerns.

Unitarian Universalism: A Welcoming Place for Gay, Lesbian, and Bisexual People pamphlet. Pack of 25 available from the UUA Bookstore.

Unitarian Universalism: A Religious Home for Gay, Lesbian, and Bisexual People pamphlet. Pack of 25 available from the UUA Bookstore.

Welcoming Lesbian, Gay, and Bisexual Youth Into Young Religious Unitarian Universalists (YRUU). Available from the UUA Office of Lesbian, Bisexual, and Gay Concerns.

Where Love Is: Affirming Lesbian and Gay Ceremonies of Union pamphlet. Pack of 25 available from the UUA Bookstore.

Planning Guide for Same-Gender Services of Union. Available from the UUA Office of Lesbian, Bisexual, and Gay Concerns.

Certificates of Holy Union. Pack of 12 certificates available from the UUA Bookstore.

Gay and Lesbian Worship Services. Available from the UUA Office of Lesbian, Bisexual, and Gay Concerns.

The Murder of Charlie O. Howard. Available from the UUA Office of Lesbian, Bisexual, and Gay Concerns. Unitarian Universalist responses to a gay bashing of a Unitarian Universalist that occurred in Bangor, Maine, in 1984.

Unitarian Universalist Association Resolutions on Gay and Lesbian Issues (1970-1991). Available from the UUA Office of Lesbian, Bisexual, and Gay Concerns.

Timeline of Unitarian Universalist Involvement in and Support of Lesbian, Bisexual, and Gay Issues. Available from the UUA Office of Lesbian, Bisexual, and Gay Concerns.

Homophobia: How We All Pay the Price, edited by Warren Blumenfeld. Boston: Beacon Press, 1993. Anti-homophobia workshops included in appendix. Available from the UUA Bookstore.

Bibliography for Children and Youth: Diverse Families Inclusive of Gay and Lesbian Family Members by Jean Durgin-Clinchard. Available from the UUA Office of Lesbian, Bisexual, and Gay Concerns.

Religious Liberals Respond to the Religious Right. A resource packet. Includes media tips, programming ideas, sample services. Emphasis on grassroots activism. Available from the UUA Office of Lesbian, Bisexual, and Gay Concerns.

The UUA Video Loan Library has videos on lesbian, gay, and bisexual issues.

Copies of sermons, articles, and monographs about inclusivity of lesbian, bisexual and gays are available through the UUA Office of Lesbian, Bisexual, and Gay Concerns. Write for a complete listing.

AIDS Action and Information Program

The AIDS Action and Information Program (AAIP) provides educational and program materials, information and referral services, and consultations for local AIDS ministries. AAIP particularly seeks to educate congregations about advocacy needs and opportunities for marginalized groups suffering from AIDS: people of color, homosexuals, poor people, and women.

For Further Reading

AIDS and Your Religious Community: A Hands-On Guide for Local Programs. Provides models for everything from personal to pastoral support, housing and hospice care, legal and medical assistance, food shopping and "meals on wheels." Available from the UUA Bookstore.

Information Packets

AIDS Resource Packet. Available from the UUA Department for Social Justice.

AIDS Memorial Services. Available from the UUA Department for Social Justice.

The Family and AIDS: How to Talk About AIDS With Your Children (Ages 3-16). Available from the UUA Department for Social Justice.

A Brief Bibliography for Children About AIDS by Jean Durgin-Clinchard. Available from the UUA Department for Social Justice.

Articles, sermons, and monographs dealing with HIV and AIDS are available from the UUA Department for Social Justice. Write for a complete listing.

A Sexism Audit for Congregations

Cleansing Our Temple is an instrument of change. Developed by the Women and Religion Committee of the Unitarian Universalist Association, this program enables a congregation to look systematically at the practices in its group that perpetuate old myths and assumptions about gender and the roles of women and men in the congregation's community.

The program helps a congregation monitor its progress in eliminating sexism. *Cleansing Our Temple* features an overview of the study process, a two-hour training session for survey leaders, a sample worship service for evaluation, six easy-to-follow questionnaires, six resources for discussion and reference, and a feedback form for sharing findings.

An organizational strategy is presented, involving the formation of a core group of three or four people. This group familiarizes itself with the materials and challenges itself to identify the leadership whose support will be needed. Potential participants are approached and encouraged to learn more about the program and to participate in the training session.

Sample readings and worship materials are included as well as a series of questionnaires about worship services, meetings, leadership, and religious education programs and resources. Especially valuable are the guidelines for using inclusive language, with examples of alternative wording to avoid using sexist language. They list all women's rights resolutions passed by the General Assembly and the Unitarian Universalist Association board from the time of the merger of the Unitarians and the Universalists until 1987.

Beyond the Sexism Assessment

In addition to *Cleansing Our Temple*, the Unitarian Universalist Association offers other materials for ensuring that congregations are safe and caring communities. The curriculum, *About Sexual Abuse*, developed by the Department of Religious Education, is available through the UUA Bookstore. The department has also published a "Code of Ethics for Persons Working with Children and Youth in Unitarian Universalist Association Sponsored Programs" (see Chapter 8, "Religious Education Programming").

Sexual ethics guidelines as well as the procedures for reporting instances of abuse are available from the Unitarian Universalist Ministers Association. Congregations across the continent are beginning to develop materials that deal with the issue of abuse and harassment in all aspects of society.

Eleven

Public Relations and Communication

Why Public Relations and Communication Are Important

How can we understand our constituencies, let the wider world know of our good work, and establish our congregation as having a real impact in our community? Through public relations. But where must the work start? And should we engage in "PR" if our congregation is not serious about growth and extension?

Congregational Readiness

At the most basic level, a good congregation public relations effort begins at home. Congregations cannot successfully reach out to the larger world to promote services or activities if the membership is not enthusiastically engaged in the life of the congregation. So before taking your congregation's wares to market, consider whether your first—and perhaps biggest—public relations hurdle needs to be waged at home. Consider these questions:

- Does the congregation know how to have fun together?
- Are members warm and welcoming to visitors?
- Do members enthusiastically participate in programs and activities?
- Do members tell others about what the congregation is doing, so that visitors hear about the congregation's good work from its members?
- Do members feel good about being Unitarian Universalists and know how to talk about what Unitarian Universalism means to others in plain language?

If you answer "yes" to these questions, then, your congregation is probably ready to begin reaching out to the community in a full-scale public relations effort. If, on the other hand, you respond negatively to some of the questions, you should remember that good public relations begins at home, which is where you should begin.

Public Relations on Your Own Turf

If your congregation has a newsletter, take a look at it first. See "Writing a Congregation Newsletter" on page 217 and consider the following:

- Does the newsletter tell the story of your congregation's good work?
- Is there an inspiring piece by your minister or a member?
- Would newcomers know how to join the Hiking and Muffin Club if they wanted to participate?

These basic questions and others provide members and newcomers with a picture of your congregation. If the picture is blurred or negative, your efforts to interest more people in the congregation may falter.

Other things can be done within your own congregation to make all of you feel good about who you are before you go out to tell the world.

- Purchase the UUA Print Ad Packet, available from the UUA Bookstore. These camera-ready ads, which use the faces and words of real Unitarian Universalists, talk about their commitment and connection to a vital, living faith. You can use the ads for print advertising or for worship services (the questions our children ask about God and religion, the search of young adults for meaningful religion, the needs of families, etc.), for order of service covers for themed services, as posters, as Wayside Pulpits, or as flyers to promote the congregation before a "Bring a Friend" Sunday.

- Hold several continuing education events for members of the congregation to talk about how to witness their Unitarian Universalist values or how to become more at ease with the idea of being Unitarian Universalist evangelists.

- Work with your congregation's membership coordinator or volunteer coordinator to see if there are interests on the part of the congregation's new or long-time members that are not being met, but which, if addressed, would involve your congregation more in the larger community. If this is the case, work with a group to establish links that help raise your congregation's visibility and provide fulfillment and meaning to members.

Developing a Public Relations Campaign

Once you have addressed the climate within the congregation (assuming that it welcomes newcomers), you are ready to work outside the congregation, typically called "PR." Examine several elements of your congregation's life as you craft your PR campaign:

- What elements of your congregation's life do you want to take to market. That is, what do you do well that should be shared with others?

- What new programs or initiatives are coming up that might be interesting PR features?

- What about your congregation's mission can promoted to the larger community as attractive and desirable?

Work to get the word out about your program through flyers to the community, letters to new homeowners in the area, print and radio ads (if you can afford them), or notices attractively laid out on a personal computer or desktop publishing system and displayed in the local childcare facilities. Once you have promoted your program, be ready for new arrivals.

If you develop your public relations program from the inside out, your congregation will be both more willing to welcome the new-comers you attract (because many members are invested in the program) and better able to promote the strengths of your congregation.

Developing a Public Relations Program

There are various ways to develop the public relations campaign of a congregation.

Press releases are used to announce a major event or activity, the appointment of a staff person, a capital campaign, or a program with community impact.

1. Use the **inverted pyramid format** (most important information at the *top* of the article). Include who, what, where, when, why, how.

2. Use a **crisp format**. Use the heading "press release," and give a contact name and phone number, date for releasing the information, and a headline. Note if the article is continued on a second page. Begin the second page with a condensed repeat of the headline and the notation, "page two."

3. Make sure the release is directed to the **right person**. If the story is important, follow it up with phone calls.

4. Make sure you allow **adequate time** for the information to get to the people who need to receive it: releases should be mailed two weeks in advance for most activities.

Calendar listings publicize a specific activity or event in the calendar section of a newspaper or magazine.

1. Include **essential information** first (see item 1 above).

2. **Be concise.** A one- or two-line description of your event is sufficient.

3. Make sure the listing is directed to the right people: find out who the listings editor is.

4. **Observe deadlines.** Calendar listings are often required four to six weeks in advance; magazine deadlines can be up to ten weeks in advance.

5. Make sure you **include a name and contact number** for someone to call if there are questions. This is not necessarily the same name and number that might be included in the listing for publication.

Public Service Announcements are delivered on radio or television and provide basic information about an activity or event to encourage the public to participate.

1. **For radio,** preproduced recorded spots are most useful. Provide reel-to-reel tape, tails out, clearly marked with subject and spot length. Use a good voice for the announcer and have a clear and inviting message.

2. Preproduced cassettes are second-best. Clearly mark subject and spot length. You can include more than one spot on a tape, if you send a cover sheet to explain the contents.

3. **For radio and TV,** if your public service announcement is not preproduced, write a thirty- and fifteen-second version of the announcement. Include essential information and a brief "color" descriptive (i.e., "the work of seventy-five of the area's finest artists will be on display").

4. Include a name and contact number (see item 5 above).

5. **Add "start date" and "kill date"** at the top of the announcement sheet or on the cover sheet. These are the dates during which the announcement should be aired.

6. **Follow up** with the public service director of the station to make sure your message has been received and to see if it can be logged for use. If the answer is "no," try (not defensively) to find out why. Was it the content or the production?

Paid advertising is used to promote a specific activity or an institution in general on radio, television, or in print media.

In all of our advertising, we need to make Unitarian Universalism a large public presence. We need to be clear and comfortable about the fact that our denomination is not a secret, that we have something important to say in the life of our community and society. As Unitarian Universalists we must not be embarrassed to say that we are a liberal religious community that supports what we believe in. If we are clear in our presence and outlook, we have the best opportunity to connect with people in the larger community and to provide a warm welcome that will encourage others to join us.

1. **Make space reservations at least a week in advance of placement.** If you are advertising in a special section, check deadlines for space reservations and receipt of advertising.

2. **Check your newspaper's circulation figures** and what you know of readership practices for your area: many newspapers have a larger Friday weekend edition or a Wednesday midweek edition that may be best bets for placement.

3. Find out if you are able to **negotiate a reduced rate** because of nonprofit status as a congregation or because of the frequency with which you will run your advertising. It may require signing a minimum-line contract, but can save dollars.

4. **Find out about combination rates** if there is more than one daily newspaper and both are owned by the same company.

5. If there is more than one newspaper in the city and they are competitive (i.e., owned by different companies), make sure you **conduct a readership survey** of your congregation to determine what newspapers they tend to read. Use this information to determine where to place ads.

Local talk shows, news features, and supportive PR are used to support other public relations efforts that will make the public aware of an event, activity, program, or issue your congregation is sponsoring or supporting.

Support paid advertising and regular press releases by organizing a **campaign that uses all available resources** in your community. Try to get guests placed on local talk shows (radio and TV) on topics of importance, particularly to the local community. (For example, if your congregation is taking the lead in trying to get a mandatory recycling law passed, play on it as an issue that will position your congregation well in the community.)

1. Make sure you know the names of the *producers* of local talk shows. Don't try to contact the host of the program, who in most

cases will be too busy; most of them don't do their own bookings. The producers are the people that need to be approached and sold on your idea.

2. Provide an appropriate amount of background to make your best case to the producer. Again, focused press materials and supporting articles on the subject will help.

3. Be prepared to set a date and time when you talk with a producer: know whether your potential guests can handle an hour or half-hour.

4. Know whether the people you are trying to place are going to do well on a live versus pretaped show. Don't set up your people to do publicity that they will not be good at or comfortable with.

5. Make sure that your people know directions to the station and understand the format of the program. Do research on the host. Find out if she or he is known for pulling questions out of left field that might confuse your people.

6. Follow up with the producer—say thank you, find out what topics might be of interest in the future.

Photographs provide visual interest, usually in conjunction with a story about an event or program or a new appointment or initiative. Photographs are important and can help to tell a story or add a dimension to an article. If you have photographs available and don't have to rely on a press outlet to take them, so much the better. But remember the following.

1. 8 x 10" or 5 x 7" are the best sizes.

2. Photos should be **well-focused, crisp, of high-contrast,** and "tight" (i.e., not a distance shot with a crowd of people). If you're working with "community" newspapers, black and white is best. High-tech papers can reproduce color.

3. If you're using a group photo, three to five people is the maximum number. More will clutter the photo and make the photograph lose its focus.

4. Make sure the photo is **captioned** on the back with a typed label that lists the people in the shot (from left to right) and their titles (if applicable), why they're being photographed, the time, date, and place of event, the sponsor, etc. Make sure you give a "for more information, contact" telephone number.

Special events and tie-in promotions focus additional public attention on your activity or event, and should be used only to support primary public relations efforts (i.e., press releases, media advisories, etc.).

It is one of the best ways to support paid advertising and a basic PR campaign. Perhaps during the active portion of your outreach, your congregation could advertise a "Sundays at Four" concert series or a special speaker presentation that you're sponsoring. These are opportunities for you to get your congregation's name out to the public, to obtain feature coverage in print, radio, or television (interviews or pretaped features). Don't overlook this potential angle for receiving coverage.

In-house pieces promoting life in your congregation provide information about the strong points of your congregation (or specific programs) to members, friends, and interested newcomers.

Make sure that they're concise, well-printed, and that anyone who picks one up knows which congregation is being discussed, plus where to find you, your phone number, who the paid staff members are, and when your Sunday services and congregation school are held. This sounds basic, but you'd be amazed at how many pieces don't have the basics covered! Photos help, but follow the rules above to make sure that your photo tells the story in a way that will support your congregation.

Don't forget your newsletter. Your newsletter is the best in-house promotional piece available. Make sure that it's clear, effective, and good at conveying your congregation's unique personality.

Direct mail promotes your congregation and its activities to the outside—that is, to people who have not become friends of the congregation, and invites them to participate.

Direct mail pieces should **emphasize warmth and clarity**: A letter that's two pages long is one page too long. Make your invitation to join the congregation friendly and pleasant, but don't give too much information in the letter. Remember that if people are interested in what they read, they will do something to follow up. As refined as your direct mailing piece may be (keyed to particular zip codes or groups of individuals new to the area), it is still in essence a "cold" solicitation. A two percent return on a direct-mail solicitation is considered excellent, so construct the best piece that you can, and monitor carefully the mailing's return.

Indirect Public Relations Methods

What makes people feel connected to what you have to offer? One congregation made a point of having a member "drop by" with a homemade pie within a week of a person or family's first visit to a congregation. That also gave the newcomer an entry to ask questions. Most of all, it made them feel welcomed and important. Whether it's pie, a loaf of homemade bread, or a personal note followed by a phone call and an invitation to a circle supper, a hands-on approach will increase your return rate with a greater chance for involving committed people in your congregation.

Media Purchase/ Paid Advertising

Often when we think of doing public relations, we mean purchasing paid advertising. To effectively purchase paid advertising that will yield the best return for the money, consider both the climate in which to place ads (i.e., the current culture, what approaches to product sales seem to be most effective), and the media that people who might become Unitarian Universalists find most appealing.

Don't think that just because the local radio station or cable television company offers you a terrific bargain that it necessarily presents the best buy. Do not purchase advertising until you have thoroughly investigated whether the media you are buying really reaches the audience you want to attract.

Television

Television is the quintessential example of the term *mass media*. TV advertising is bought in relationship to two measurements. One is *reach* (that is, how many people will see it); the other is *frequency*. Frequency is the average nuber of times that a viewer will see your commercial. So when you buy television advertising, it's less a matter of how many stations you buy, as it is the reach and frequency.

While the growing number of cable stations allows for much greater market segmentation, it remains a very large market that is hard to reach through a small-budget advertising campaign. It is also expensive and does not represent the best buy for the average congregation's dollar.

Radio

There are a large number of radio stations that can be weeded out to get the exact demographic profile we are looking for. If we decide, for instance, that our primary market is ages 35 to 49, with incomes of over $40,000, young children, etc., it is possible to find stations that reach these people. For this reason, radio is a very efficient way to buy media.

Radio is also an intrusive media. When someone has the radio on and a commercial comes up, it's the only thing there: it's not like a newspaper, with other announcments on the page. When your ad is on the radio, it's the only show in town. And people are very loyal to radio stations. TV is viewed program by program, but people are station loyal to radio. Most people listen to only two or three radio stations, which increases the likelihood of reaching the optimum audience.

Radio is purchased in *flights*, each running a minimum of two but preferably three weeks. For example, a thirteen-week schedule could be three weeks on, one week off, two on, one off, and so on.

The cumulative effect of this schedule is that people *think* they're hearing your message all the time. You want to reach at least fifty percent of your target market on the radio. To accomplish this, you want a frequency of at least four to five times per person. Thus you run a minimum of twelve spots a week as bare bones, but eighteen is better.

Print

Print advertising is ideal for our market because we know that despite national trends to the contrary, people who match the profile of typical Unitarian Universalists tend to read. Our best print buy is the newspaper, although it is worth carefully examining city and regional magazines (i.e., *Washingtonian, Pacific Northwest, Milwaukee*). You don't want to advertise in trendy publications, but you want reach. Magazines should know a lot about their audiences, so ask for demographics before you buy. Get samples of the publication to review.

In newspapers, see if there is a religion editor or religion section. But don't restrict advertising to the religion page, which is read just by those who know they want to go to church. Look for the education page or a special supplement on the environment or social justice, which might accept advertising that ties in with a theme.

Newspaper advertising isn't worth running if you can't run an ad at least four times in six weeks. The frequency of the newspaper ad run has a lot to do with its size. There is more impact if the ad is large enough to catch the eye.

Writing a Congregation Newsletter

Setting a Newsletter Policy

The most important public relations piece your congregation has is its newsletter. To create an effective newsletter, you need a newsletter policy.

- If news is to be included, what news goes in and what doesn't?
- If opinions are to be publicized, whose opinions?
- Who makes policy decisions?
- If a decision is challenged, what happens?

First, a congregation must empower an editor to edit. An editor must have the authority to assign, improve, edit, and cut articles. The editor may also oversee design and production of the newsletter. Second, the editor, the board of the congregation, and staff should agree on guidelines to help make the newsletter be what the group's leadership wants it to be.

The newsletter should be a free forum, but not an unrestricted one. The interests of the congregation as a whole must be paramount, thus the power to edit should be delegated to someone who will use it carefully.

The Three Functions of a Newsletter

Calendar. The most obvious function of the newsletter is that of a calendar. Even if notices of upcoming services, events, and meetings are described in detail in individual articles, a capsule summary of all activities (in a list or month-at-a-glance format) provides a quick overview. Listings can be cumbersome, one easy solution is to insert a calendar page (often on the back cover) with all upcoming events. The calendar can be detached easily and retained for reference.

Messenger. Newsletters are a direct link from the religious professionals and volunteers of the congregation to members and friends. In regular columns, ministers, lay leaders, and directors of religious education communicate with those who do not come to the congregation regularly. This function is especially important for the religious educator, who may rarely speak to the congregation as a whole but who has the important function of promoting all educational programming.

News Source. The newsletter should help build communication among everyone participating in the life of the congregation. It should summarize important agenda items from meetings of the congregation's governing board, describe past events (social gatherings, community service projects, potluck dinners) and thank those who helped; welcome visitors and new members; and inspire members and visitors to attend future events.

Sources for news are numerous: professional and lay leadership, committee chairpersons, youth groups, community organizations, district executives, national and international denominational representatives, Unitarian Universalist Association affiliated groups, and newsletters from other congregations.

In short, the editor must know the congregation and be attuned to its news. It is useful to have boxes around the congregation for receiving news items. The editor may also announce specific hours during which he or she is willing to be called.

Projecting a Welcoming Voice

Good newsletter writing is journalistic writing. The most important information comes first in each article. The five w's—who, what, when, where, why (and how)—should be answered in the first paragraph or sentence. Paragraphs should be short and articles should be specific. They should include dates, times, and locations along with the name and phone number of a contact person.

Editors should show at least one other person the newsletter copy before it goes to print. Others may pick up grammatical and spelling errors. Don't rely on spell-checker programs!

Putting It All Together

Identity. The most striking part of your newsletter should be your **nameplate** on the top of the first page. It features the newsletter's name, the congregation's name and logo, the date of publication, and the congregation's complete address and phone number.

Other elements are reserved for a **masthead**, or roster of key contacts, which appears in the same location in each issue. These include the names of congregation staff and minister(s), a listing of other important offices with their phone numbers, and office hours.

Paper and Ink. White paper with black ink is the easiest to read and recycle and is the least expensive. Paper can be a light color, but it must be good quality. Sixty-pound offset paper is most appropriate.

Graphics. Graphic art makes pages less dense, more appealing, and thus more likely to be read. Used sparingly, drawings, inexpensive clip art, photos, lines, and boxes around articles will enhance the copy. Volunteers can often provide artwork.

Type Size and Style. Be consistent. Use one type style and size (preferably a typeface with serifs) for the text throughout the newsletter. Make the point size large enough for all ages to read—twelve point is standard. Use strings of capital or italic letters sparingly since they are hard to read.

Grids. Two- and three-column formats make the copy appear less dense and more digestible than one-column formats, whose line lengths are often too long.

Resources

Beach, Mark. *Editing Your Newsletter*. Portland, OR: Coast to Coast Books, 1988.

Heesch, Kristi. *Creating Successful Church Newsletters*. Boston, MA: Unitarian Universalist Association, 1993. Available from the UUA Office of Public Relations, Marketing, and Information.

The NEWSLETTER Newsletter. A newsletter for church newsletter editors from Communication Resources, PO Box 2625, N. Canton, OH 44720.

Sample Survey of Media Trends and Membership. Available from the UUA Office of Public Relations, Marketing, and Information.

Using Pamphlets as Membership and Outreach Tools

One of the best ways to get the good news about Unitarian Universalism to the public (while building membership in your congregation) is to use the Unitarian Universalist Association's pamphlets to provide information to newcomers, visitors, and those seeking specific information on a variety of topics. The list offers ways pamphlets can be used.

Place a Pamphlet Rack In an Obvious Location
If you do not already have a pamphlet rack or cannot obtain one from a stationery store, consider building one with plexiglass panels to attractively display the pamphlets. Make a variety of pamphlets available, emphasizing what newcomers would want to know about Unitarian Universalism.

Send Pamphlets to Prospective Visitors
Some congregations offer at least one "Bring a Friend" Sunday a year, which is promoted by a flyer or letter, often accompanied by a pamphlet on Unitarian Universalism. You may also send a welcoming letter to people new to the residential area of your congregation, inviting them to visit. Include a brochure about your local congregation and several Unitarian Universalist introductory pamphlets ("We Are Unitarian Universalists" and "Should I Send My Child to Sunday School?" are particularly valuable). To support this effort, the Unitarian Universalist Association produces two popular introductory products (the "We Are . . ." pamphlet and "What Do UUs Believe . . ." wallet card), available in packs of 100 from the UUA Bookstore.

Send Pamphlets With a Welcoming Letter to Visitors
After people have visited your congregation, it is important to recognize their visit with a follow up letter and phone call. Unitarian Universalist Association pamphlets are particularly valuable if a visitor has experienced your congregation's service and hospitality and is interested in finding out more.

Encourage Members to Give Pamphlets to Friends
The "We Are . . ." pamphlet as well as "Meet the Unitarian Universalists" are well suited to offer friends who might be interested in Unitarian Universalism. One Unitarian Universalist family places pamphlets in its guest bathroom so that visitors will take them home.

Use Bookmarks or Pamphlets as Inserts in Orders of Service
The Principles and Purposes Bookmark is a useful and concise statement of our faith. Pamphlets inserted in an order of service, particularly for services designated as "Bring a Friend" Sundays, can also be an attractive information tool.

Use Pamphlets as the Text for Introductory Classes
"Meet the UUs" by Jack Mendelsohn provides a good introduction to our liberal faith and can be used in conjunction with the "New U" class or other classes. The book-length *Unitarian Universalist Pocket Guide* is also ideal for this purpose, as is the pamphlet *Five Smooth Stones of Religious Liberalism* by James Luther Adams. They suggest several topics useful for discussion by an adult education class.

Use Pamphlets as the Text for Special Focus Classes

Congregations can use Unitarian Universalist Association brochures as the starting point for a valuable discussion group on a variety of topics. While people interested in adult education may be reluctant to commit their time to reading books, they are often willing to read a brochure. Pamphlets that may provide springboards for further discussion are "Soulful Journeys: The Faith of African American Unitarian Universalists," "Unitarian Universalism: A Welcoming Place for Gay, Lesbian, and Bisexual People," "Universalism: For Such a Time as This," and "Religions of the World."

Supplement Sunday Service Presentations With Pamphlets

If a sermon is about the significance of the flaming chalice, for example, make sure that copies of the pamphlet "The Flaming Chalice," by Daniel D. Hotchkiss, is available to provide further information.

Pamphlets Can Supplement Newsletter Stories

Pamphlets are an excellent source of information to provide amplifying quotes for newsletters, orders of service, or information sheets. A newsletter article on the Welcoming Congregation Program, for instance, becomes more interesting with a quote from the pamphlet by Barbara Pescan, "Unitarian Universalism: A Religious Home for Gay, Lesbian, and Bisexual People."

Offer Pamphlets to Individuals With Special Questions or Interests

If an individual in the congregation has expressed a particular interest in how child dedications are performed in our faith, offer the pamphlet "How We Welcome Our Children." Similarly, those who are thinking of membership would be interested in "Becoming a Member" to provide more information and background on the expectations and rewards of Unitarian Universalism.

Provide Pamphlets to Individuals With a Particular Need or Concern.

People come to Unitarian Universalist congregations for a variety of reasons and sometimes with particular complications in their lives. Useful pamphlets include "Welcome to Unitarian Universalism: A Community of Truth, Service, Holiness and Love," "Affirming Interfaith Marriages," "All Our Losses," or "Can I Believe Anything I Want?"

Send Pamphlets With an Invitation to Join the Congregation

Not everyone decides to join a congregation out of their own initiative—some are waiting to be asked. If your congregation sends out a letter to friends who have not yet joined, include appropriate Unitarian Universalist Association pamphlets: "Becoming a Member," or the Unitarian Universalist Association Principles and Purposes bookmark.

When Speaking to Children, Youth, and Young Adults

The concerns of children and young adults about their religion are particularly compelling and often cause articulate leaders to become speechless. While the response, "Here—read this," cannot address all concerns it is important to use all our resources to reach out to our children, youth, and young adults. You may find such pamphlets as "UU Kids Say . . . Church Is," "UU Kids Say . . . God Is," "Should I Send My Child to Sunday School?" and "Can I Believe Anything I Want?" particularly helpful in speaking to some of the important concerns of young people. The pamphlet, "On a Quest for Meaning," by Suzelle Lynch, is keyed to the experience of young adult Unitarian Universalists.

Use Pamphlets in Developing Worship Services.

UUA pamphlets make excellent readings for use in worship services for adults and children. Our pamphlets include thoughts on important issues such as membership, worship, the Bible (and Unitarian Universalists), the flaming chalice, and more.

Use Pamphlets for Visitor's Packets.

If a congregation is particularly intentional in welcoming newcomers, it often will have a visitor's packet ready for newcomers. The packet may contain a brochure about the local congregation, a copy of its most recent newsletter, a copy of the UUA *World* magazine, a Principles and Purposes bookmark, and basic brochures like "We Are Unitarian Universalists," "Meet the UUs," "Welcome to Unitarian Universalism," or "Should I Send My Child to Sunday School?" These packets are a clear and attractive way of expressing welcome and interest in prospective members.

For More Information

For more information on UUA pamphlets or to suggest a pamphlet topic, contact the UUA Office of Public Relations, Marketing, and Information, 25 Beacon Street, Boston, MA 02108.

Twelve

Developing a Congregational Budget

How to Develop a Congregational Budget

There are generally three types of congregational budgets: a cost budget, an organizational budget, and a mission budget. The mission budget is the best method, as detailed below.

Cost Budget

This is the line item budget or incremental budgeting generally developed by a finance committee. Line item budgets tend to focus on past performance, reasonable projected increase in expenses, and projected income. This approach to budgeting uses this year's budget as the basis for the next year's budget, by making adjustments for expected increases in costs. Line item budgets tend to be focused on the bottom line and elicit the least enthusiasm and support from members of the congregation.

Organizational Budget

A second approach to budgeting is the organizational budget, which invites various committees to submit to the congregation's finance committee proposals or requests for the next year's budget. In some congregations this elaborate process includes projecting program plans, cost analysis, and zero-based budgeting. Typically in small congregations, committees are told what they spent last year, given a general percentage increase to work with and asked to submit their requests to the finance committee. The finance committee tries to juggle all requests and rework the budget after the canvass.

The organizational budget opens up the financial process by involving more committees. However, committees often become competitive and after real dollars are pledged the finance committee has to cut proposals. In other words, the congregation is back to bottom line thinking and planning. The organizational budget has a broader base of support but does not truly inspire members to pledge.

Mission Budget

The mission-based budget is founded on the vision the congregation has declared for itself and on its mission statement and the mission objectives it has set for the year. The mission budget is based on the congregation's dream about itself and its future. The foundation of the budget and its process is the mission statement. The major pillars of the budget are the mission objectives (See Chapter 2, "The Guiding Vision and Mission of a Congregation".) Ordinarily, these objectives are specific, achievable, and measurable goals that the congregation can achieve within five years.

A mission budget does not eliminate a cost budget or organizational budget from consideration, but places them within the context of an overall mission budget for the congregation. Line items in the budget are correlated to these major objectives. Some of these are obvious; some will cause existing programs or committees to reorient themselves. For example, what would it be like for the worship committee to think of itself as an aspect of outreach? Other items in the budget are simply arbitrary.

It is possible to restructure the organization of the congregation around these mission objectives.

Stages of a Mission Budget Approach

1. Clarify and cultivate your congregation's overall vision. Articulate your mission statement and the mission objectives that follow from this mission statement (see Chapter 2).

2. Ask, "How well are we furthering this overall vision, mission, and mission objectives in our current programs and activities?"
   - What are the ways we can point to our effectiveness?
   - What are the gaps between where we want to be and where we are now?
   - What adjustments to our programs do we need to make?
   - What other programs are needed to fulfill our mission and bring us closer to our vision?
   - What resources are required to adjust our current programs and/or add new programs?

Every Member Canvass

The Every Member Canvass can be driven by the vision of the mission statement and objectives. Each canvasser takes to every home a presentation chart that expands the objectives as they represent the dream of the congregation. This plan allows the Every Member Canvass another opportunity to affirm its mission for the next five years. After the canvass the committee sits down with the Finance Committee to lock in specific numbers. Its function at this point is not to cut requests but to appropriate commitment.

Giving Development

The mission budget process is the foundation step toward an overall giving development plan in a congregation. Together a mission budget and a giving development plan help to move a congregation toward an effective method of connecting the financial dimension to the other vital aspects of a congregation.

Giving Development in Your Congregation

The focus for many Unitarian Universalist congregations might best be expressed as "giving development" rather than "fundraising." Ultimately, the task is more than developing funds for the congregation's budget. The task also includes developing the givers and volunteer leaders who will advance the giving. Another word for this development of the giving level and the giver is "stewardship."

Kennon Callahan, in *Effective Church Finances: Fund-Raising and Budgeting for Church Leaders*, offers insightful perspectives on giving development in a congregation.

Long-Range Goals

To develop giving in your congregation, you have to create a long-range giving development plan for a four-year period. If the aim is to "grow the giving of your congregation in solid ways," it is essential and realistic to consider how you get there over a period of four years. Consequently, you need to ask, "What do we want to accomplish that will grow the giving in our congregation?"

Your response will help you articulate a sequential strategy to advance you toward your long-range goal. For example, Callahan outlines these sequential strategy objectives with the eventual aim of advancing the congregation's giving by a quantum leap:

Year one: Increase the number of new giving and pledging
  households.
Year two: Advance the number of workers and leaders who
  participate.
Year three: Increase the giving of specific households who currently
  give and pledge.
Year four: Advance the congregation's giving by a quantum leap.

Each year's strategy sequentially builds toward the fourth year strategy. This approach is wiser than a strategy that tries to produce a quantum leap every year.

A Campaign Method for Each Strategy Objective

Once you have articulated your strategy objective for each year, determine what campaign method will best help your congregation achieve that goal. Many congregations that have difficulty raising money reverse this by putting their focus solely on a campaign method. Moreover, some congregations use the same campaign method year after year. Instead, a strategy objective should determine which campaign methods you use.

Giving Campaign Stages

The next stages of a giving campaign build on these strategies:

1. The Education Stage
Your giving campaign should include a definitive education stage that can be accomplished by personal visits, small and large group gatherings, worship services, phone calls, videotapes, personal notes, let-

ters, brochures, and direct mail. The aim of this stage is to deliver information on the mission of your congregation:

- who will be helped
- what help is needed in order to pursue this mission.

2. The Motivation Stage

During this stage, build motivation in people to increase the generosity of their giving. We often assume that by educating, we are motivating. However, during this stage you help people to see what an increase in their generosity to the congregation and its mission will bring.

3. The Invitation Stage

Often, the motivation stage is followed by the invitation stage. The invitation stage is when you confidently and assuredly invite people to give generously to the mission of the congregation during the coming year.

Making a confident invitation to your membership is the stage when many congregations become nervous or feel awkward. The important thing to remember is to give people a significant amount of time to make a genuine decision.

4. Follow-up Stage

Sometimes after all the pledges, estimates of giving, and other resources are assessed the total projected giving for the coming year falls short of what you *must have* for your mission budget.

If a congregation has not raised the amount it needs to pursue its mission budget, then it may require a second chance to advance its giving. The purpose of the follow-up stage is giving development, not budget raising.

A Long-Range Giving Development Plan

A long-range giving development plan should be outlined over a four-year period with strategies for each year that build cumulatively on the previous year's strategy. For example:

Strategy	Year 1	Year 2	Year 3	Year 4
Objective				
Education				
Motivation				
Invitation				
Follow Up				

A Mission Budget and Giving Development

This approach to developing both a budget and the giving is a radical departure for many congregations. However, it fits wholeheartedly in the approach to congregational development espoused in this *Handbook*.

Kennon Callahan's observation is a good rationale to consider when breaking a pattern of giving prevalent in some congregations:

> Some congregations suffer from budget stress. They become stressed out over whether the budget is raised. They develop high anxiety over raising the funds and developing the budget. They push inordinately hard to raise that last three percent. They create more ill will than goodwill. They do not look to the long haul. They do not look four years ahead. They press for quick closure, immediate satisfaction, and short term results. What does it profit a congregation to raise its budget but lose it mission? What does it profit a congregation to raise its budget but lose its goodwill?

The practices of mission budget and giving development are challenges that some Unitarian Universalist congregations have decided to accept for their overall development.

The Annual Canvass

Before you begin planning the next annual canvass, ask the congregational leadership these four important questions:

- What dreams do we hold for the congregation?
- What is holding us back from achieving these dreams?
- Would it help if we could raise more money?
- What is holding us back from asking for it?

In a survey published in *Newsweek*, Unitarian Universalists were revealed as having the highest average incomes of twenty major denominations, but their average pledge to their congregation was the lowest of all groups studied. The implication is that the major fundraising challenge facing most congregations is not the capacity of members to give, but their willingness.

Unitarian Universalists love their congregations just as much as their friends and neighbors do. When the mission and the goals of the congregation are clear and actively shared by the membership, the financial needs clearly communicated, and the budget "owned" by the congregation, Unitarian Universalists give just as generously as their neighbors. This is most clearly seen in our new congregations, filled with members who pledge between $1,000 and $1,200 annually.

Evaluation

Every Unitarian Universalist congregation is full of skeptics who believe that their congregation doesn't fit traditional models. To help them and the leadership feel confident about setting a higher canvass goal, conduct an income evaluation of the congregation. Here is one simple method of conducting an assessment.

1. Convene 4 or 5 members of the congregation who know most of the congregation well. Consider inviting the treasurer, a past president, the chairs of the religious education and the membership committees, and the minister.

2. Provide this group with a stack of file cards that have the names of the members who comprise a pledge unit written on each one. (One simple way to do this is to apply labels from the congregational mailing list.)

3. Ask the group to take no more than thirty seconds to place each card into one of six piles that they guess represents that household's total annual income. Suggested pile categories are:

Less than $20,000 per year
$20,000-35,000 per year
$35,000-50,000 per year
$50,000-75,000 per year
$75,000-100,000 per year
more than $100,000 per year

Count the number of cards in each pile, multiply that number by the median income for that category, and add the incomes for all categories. You now have an estimate of the total household income in your congregation. You can guess how much money your congregation could raise if everyone gave a modest two percent of their income.

For example the Unitarian Universalist Fellowship of Greater Jonesville is composed of one hundred households or pledge units, with an average household income of $50,000. Total household income is approximately $5,000,000. If all the families pledge at 2%, the congregation could raise $100,000 per year.

Now that they know it is possible, how does the leadership of the Jonesville fellowship develop an increased level of commitment from the membership?

The Mission Budget

Some congregations delegate budget preparation to a small group that creates a budget based on the question, "How little can we spend to keep the doors open on Sunday?" Not unsurprisingly, these congregations usually find themselves struggling to accomplish just that. Successful congregations develop a mission statement that answers the question, "What is the work of this congregation?" They use this mission statement to develop goals that are voted on by the congregation. Working with each committee, the congregational leadership develops a budget that reflects the vision of the congregation. This mission budget is the basis for the canvass goal. Developing a mission budget takes time and requires widespread participation. But successful congregations gain stakeholders in the budget by opening up the process and empowering their membership.

Conducting the Canvass

The most effective method of conducting a canvass is face to face, which works well for a number of reasons: members are encouraged to discuss their hopes and dreams for their congregation; feedback can be collected; the goals for the coming year are clearly communicated; and most importantly, members are personally asked and thanked for their support.

The difficulty with face-to-face canvasses is that they require members to talk openly about money and they require a lot of organization. Many UU congregations that pride themselves on their open-mindedness and ability to talk about difficult subjects still find deep resistance to discussing money. Changing such traditions isn't easy, but the benefits go beyond increased funding for congregational programs. A congregation that believes in its ability to accomplish its goals is a force to be reckoned with.

Following is an outline of the four parts of a face-to-face canvass. For more detailed information the UUA Annual Program Fund Office provides a manual, *The Green Book*.

Canvass responsibilities can be divided into five committees: leadership gifts, general gifts, communications, kickoff, and follow-up. Their work should be coordinated by a canvass chair or co-chairs.

The Leadership Gifts Committee is responsible for recruiting and training canvassers to conduct the first phase of the pledge drive. This committee is responsible for asking the minister, the canvass leadership, the members of the board, committee chairs, and the top contributors to the congregation for their pledges before the canvass kick-off event.

This step allows the leadership to demonstrate their commitment to the pledge drive goal through example. It thus gives the campaign credibility and integrity.

The General Gifts Committee is responsible for recruiting and training canvassers who will ask the remaining friends and members of the congregation for a pledge. A good rule of thumb is to recruit enough canvassers so that no one person need canvass more than three or four others. It is especially important that each canvasser be asked personally for a pledge before he or she makes calls.

The Follow-up Committee is responsible for monitoring the pledge results to make certain that everyone gets asked for a pledge. They should take over responsibility for the pledge drive approximately one month after the kickoff event.

The Communications Committee is responsible for publicity, developing a canvass brochure and pledge card, holding information sessions, and promoting the message of the canvass in a variety of ways. A good communications committee can make an enormous difference in the way a congregation responds to the canvass. It is also responsible for organizing ways to report the results of the campaign. Too often there is no clear end date and celebration of success.

The Kickoff Committee is responsible for organizing an event to which everyone is invited and which inspires and encourages everyone to pledge as generously as they can. Members should not pay to attend, nor should the committee or the membership be expected to provide the food. It is also important that there be no requests for pledges at this event. This is an ideal time, however, to recognize and honor the canvassers. They play a critical role in the congregation and they should be thanked for making the commitment.

The kickoff committee should also work with the communications committee in preparing a simple celebration to mark the successful completion of the end of the canvass. This celebration, which could be held after worship services, should involve an announcement of the results, recognition, and thanks of the canvass leadership.

Planned Giving

A wide range of giving opportunities fit under the planned giving umbrella, including charitable bequests, life income gift arrangements (charitable trusts, gift annuities, and pooled income funds), as well as gifts of real estate and gifts that use retirement and insurance plans.

Most planned gifts are deferred, that is, the congregation will enjoy the financial benefits after the donor dies. Often a planned gift is the largest single gift the donor will ever make, and careful thought and estate planning may be called for. For these and other reasons, planned giving programs and the volunteers who manage them must be patient.

The best prospects for planned gifts are people over the age of fifty-five who have fulfilled their family obligations (or are single or have no heirs). They have a history of making gifts to good causes and they are dedicated and committed to your congregation and to Unitarian Universalism.

A planned giving program promotes contributions to the congregation's permanent endowment fund, making it possible for members to contribute in perpetuity to the future of Unitarian Universalism. Every congregation should have a planned giving program and be prepared for gifts to its endowment. Congregation volunteers need not be experts in financial planning, but they should have a general knowledge of the possible kinds of gifts and who to contact for help. The UUA Office of Planned Giving has resources to help.

How to Organize Planned Giving

You may organize your planned giving volunteer(s) any number of ways. You may want to establish several committees (canvass, endowment, investment, planned giving) that report to the board or finance committee. You may add a few people to your canvass committee or form one committee that manages the endowment, its investments, and fundraising. In some congregations one person manages the whole program.

In any case, planned giving volunteers should be linked to other congregation committees with financial responsibilities for reporting and planning purposes. In addition, wherever possible, identify trustworthy tax and estate planning professionals who can review gift plans on behalf of the congregation or as a personal adviser to individual members. The UUA Office of Planned Giving is available for consultation on complicated gift arrangements, but its assistance should not substitute for independent legal counsel.

An Endowment Fund   If your congregation does not have an endowment fund, the first step should be to establish one, at least on paper. It is usually easier and healthier for a congregation to do so before gifts arrive, rather than in reaction to an unexpected bequest. Doing it in advance allows you room to include the endowment in the mission and long-range plans of your congregation.

Using the same basic principles described earlier, a committee should initiate a congregation-wide discussion about how an endowment fund will be used to fulfill its mission as a congregation and its outreach to the community. Once you have established the purpose and management systems for the endowment, use every possible opportunity to tell people about the fund and how they can make it grow.

Types of Gifts   **Testamentary gifts** are by far the most popular, reliable, and inexpensive deferred gift. Bequests will be made during the leanest and the best of times. Promote bequests in the congregation newsletter, an estate planning seminar open to the community, a bulletin board, a brochure. Consider forming a bequest recognition society to honor members who have included a charitable bequest in their wills or estate plans. Publish their names. Ask them to tell others that the congregation is in their will and why. Feature one of these people in your congregation newsletter.

Life income gift arrangements are another popular form of deferred giving. Simply stated, a donor makes a gift of $5,000 or more, enjoys an immediate income tax deduction for a portion of the gift, and receives a quarterly check for the rest of her or his life. After the donor dies, the gift distributes to charity according to the donor's wishes. Charitable trusts are appropriate for gifts above $100,000; the Pooled Income Fund and charitable gift annuities generally start with a minimum of $5,000.

The **UUA Pooled Income Fund** (PIF) offers an easy way for congregations to build their endowments. It is ideal for gifts of low-yield, highly appreciated securities. Donors generally owe no capital gains taxes and can increase their annual income. The income amount varies with the performance of the fund, and is taxable as ordinary income. Income is payable to two people for life (donors' suggested minimum age is 65); the donor may specify the congregation as the ultimate beneficiary. The minimum gift is $5,000 and $1,000 for additional gifts.

The Office of Planned Giving   Planned giving isn't only for the very rich; everyone can get involved. To learn more about the Pooled Income Fund and other gift arrangements, contact the UUA Office of Planned Giving. Call (617) 742-2100, ext. 509 or 511 for a telephone consultation or to request a Congregation Kit of tips, sample brochures, detailed descriptions of particular gift arrangements, and which assets work best in which arrangements. There are articles on fundraising to grow an endowment fund, suggested newsletter inserts, instructions on how to organize an estate planning seminar, and more.

Resources

Kennon L. Callahan. *Effective Church Finances: Fund-Raising and Budgeting for Church Leaders*. New York: HarperCollins Publishers, 1992.

Vargo, Richard. *Effective Church Accounting: Planning, Budgeting, Cash Control, Accounting Systems, Computers, Bookkeeping, Financial Reports*. New York: HarperCollins, 1989.

Software programs are available to congregations for accounting and bookkeeping procedures. Contact the UUA Computer Services Department for recommendations.

The *Church Bytes Software Guide* is a comprehensive survey of available church management software. Obtain this guide and their newsletter by contacting Church Bytes, Inc., 562 Brightleaf Square, #9, 905 West Main St., Durham, NC 27701, (919) 490-8727.

Thirteen

Your Congregation's Building and Facilities Program

New Building

Perhaps your congregation owns property and has held for years the dream of building when size and financial resources permitted. Now that dream is in reach. Before you call in the architect, consider alternatives:

- you already own a building, perhaps you should remodel rather than build anew
- perhaps you could buy an existing building.

After you have carefully examined all alternatives, review your decision openly and thoughtfully before you proceed. Do *not* base a decision to build solely on the expectation that a new or enlarged building will attract new members in sufficient numbers to fill and pay for the structure. While membership growth often follows a building program, so many other factors are involved, making such an assumption dangerous.

Gathering Information

Whether you build a new building, renovate your existing space, or buy an existing facility you will need complete knowledge of your congregation's situation and as clear a projection as you can make of its future needs.

The decisions about your congregation's permanent home are expensive and long-lasting. It is crucial to have a good fit between spirit and space. Equally crucial is that such decisions be made openly, including as many members as possible.

The Architect

An architect's advice may prove helpful when considering alternatives to building. Certainly an architect could help you explore remodeling possibilities and assess the advisability of purchasing a pre-existing building. He or she may have professional and knowledgeable suggestions about a building site that may not be obvious to the average person.

It can be useful to have a professional architect who is a member of the congregation serve on a task force. However, do not use a volunteer for design or engineering work. Hire a professional who is not a member of the congregation to assume this responsibility.

If, after careful consideration, you decide to build, an architect should be chosen with great care. The Guild of Religious Architecture publishes a leaflet (see Resources at the end of this chapter) with guidelines for selecting and working with an architect. It points out that architects who are members of the American Institute of Architects have a code of professional ethics and that members of the Guild of Religious Architecture, an AIA affiliate, indicate a special interest in religious buildings.

In choosing an architect, consider skill, experience, individual style, and personality. You'll be working closely with this person, sharing the congregation's needs, dreams, and ideas, and together spending a good deal of the congregation's money and shaping its future. Find out as much as you can about the architect you are considering by looking at previous work and talking with previous clients. Do not expect architects to submit sketches as part of your selection process unless you are prepared to set up and pay for a professional competition. Besides, it is easy to be misled by quick, impressionistic sketches when what you really want and what an architect wants as well is to work together step by step from programs and purposes to plans that are uniquely yours.

Where to Build

Factors that enter into the selection of a building site are:

- Where do most of your members live?
- In which direction is your community growing?
- Would your building be easy to find?
- Is public transportation available?
- What about highway access, parking, traffic?
- What are the zoning laws and other local regulations that affect building?
- Are water and sewer lines and other utilities available?
- Is fire and police protection available?
- Are there special drainage problems or other potential construction difficulties?
- Does the site lend itself to energy conservation in building placement (protection from winds, optimal exposure to sun, existing trees for shelter and shade)?
- Is there room for expansion?
- Is the site aesthetically pleasing or able to be shielded successfully?
- How will the site affect the design of your building?

Help is at hand in the form of local community planning agencies, consulting engineers, and your architect. Find out as much as you can about a prospective site before making a decision to purchase. If you own a site that proves unsatisfactory when you are ready to build, consider selling it and buying another rather than investing a great deal of time, energy, and money in a poor location.

Design Considerations

To facilitate discussions about the design of your building with an architect, consider the following:

- planning for future expansion, building in stages
- optimal energy efficiency and environmental impact
- formality or informality—designing to fit the style of the congregation
- flexibility versus single-purpose and multipurpose space
- appropriate, attractive activity areas for children and adults
- easy access for people with disabilities
- space for works of art
- types of construction materials for easy maintenance
- doing some or all of the construction yourselves
- incorporating outdoor areas (parking, courtyard, playground, garden, pool, fountain, natural features) in the overall design while staying within your budget
- telling the world who you are by means of your building.

The information you gathered about the purpose, spirit, program, size, style, and financial resources of your congregation should be at hand during these discussions. Your architect should be invited to "live in" for a week or two, attending various programs, watching the flow, and talking with people in addition to studying all data and written materials you can provide. Finally, as the architect becomes acquainted with the congregation, it is important to listen to his or her ideas with an open mind. A fresh viewpoint and professional expertise may teach you things you didn't know about yourselves.

Organizing to Get the Job Done

There are at least two organizing principles for a building committee:

- organize around the tasks of building
- organize around the program of the congregation.

Either option, or a combination of the two, may be used. Consider the following organizational structure.

A **steering committee** for the overall building program is composed of a representative of each of the following task forces:

- survey
- location and landscape
- design and furnishings
- construction
- finance
- communications

Additional members of the steering committee should be representatives of the governing board, plus any professional staff members of your congregation (minister, religious educator, music director). The architect should meet with the steering committee as needed.

The **Survey Task Force** is responsible for gathering the preliminary data about the congregation, its membership, programs, and goals. Appropriate committees of the congregation should be represented (religious education, adult programs, membership) as well as members with special know-how about information gathering. As work progresses, this task force ensures that decisions are made on the basis of the data collected.

The **Location Task Force** is responsible for checking out possible sites and making recommendations for purchase to the congregation. It will thus be involved in information gathering from the architect, engineers, local planners, transportation services, utility companies, and others.

The **Design and Furnishings Task Force** works closely with the architect in the design stage and is responsible for the selection of furnishings, fabrics, colors, and special equipment. It will need the services of artists, designers, and decorators among your membership as well as representatives of the religious education, worship, hospitality, adult activities, and house and grounds committees.

The **Construction Task Force** keeps close tabs on the progress of the building from groundbreaking to dedication. It serves as the liaison between the architect and contractor and is responsible for bringing to the steering committee all questions about construction that need broad-based decisions. If members are doing some construction work themselves the task force will coordinate these efforts. Members who are engineers or skilled with tools or familiar with building construction are particularly valuable.

The **Finance Task Force** is responsible for the financial side of the building program, from drawing up a preliminary budget to paying the last bills. It explores various options for financing the building and makes recommendations to the steering committee. This task force also handles the details of special fundraising efforts for the building. It submits regular financial reports to the steering committee. The congregation's finance and canvass committees should be represented here and the treasurer of the congregation should work closely with this task force.

The **Communication Task Force** is responsible for getting the word out about the building program from start to finish. It is impossible to overestimate the importance of this committee. A successful move to a new building is only possible when the will of the entire congregation—not just the leadership—is united. Clear communication about all phases of the building process is critical, including frequent open meetings, regular newsletter articles, posters, banners, and cottage meetings.

If your congregation is small, this structure may seem overwhelmingly large with too many roles. Even though you'll want to involve as many members as possible, you may streamline the plan considerably. Perhaps a single building committee, corresponding to the steering committee suggested above, will suffice. In this case, each building committee member will carry the responsibility suggested for one of the task forces described above and should involve others as appropriate.

Financing a Building Program

Any congregation undertaking a building program should be in sound financial shape. It is not required that all the necessary money be in the bank before the architect is engaged. However, according to the best possible projection, the congregation should be capable of carrying the immediate expense of undertaking a building program as well as future mortgage payments. Beware of assuming that new members who may be attracted by the building will pledge generously enough to carry a mortgage that is too large for your current membership.

Most congregations can raise two and a half to threee times their annual canvass in capital campaign with pledges paid over three years. The UUA's fundraising consultants can help advise a congregation. Over the past ten years, they have helped nearly 100 congregations raise millions of dollars.

The question often arises as to whether a special building capital fund drive will have a negative effect on the Every Member Canvass that supports the ongoing program of the congregation. In general, the experience of congregations indicates that if a building fund has any effect on the regular canvass, it is positive. People seem inclined to raise their regular pledge at the same time they make an additional pledge to the building fund.

Obviously, for this happy turn of events to come about, preliminary work must be done carefully. People willing to share the extra expense and work of building are those who feel optimistic about the future of the congregation; they heartily support the decision to build; they feel that they have had a say in that decision; they have confidence in the leadership of the congregation; they share the sense of excitement. This kind of attitude is the result of clear and honest communication, inclusive decision making, and excellent ongoing programming before and during the building effort.

In *Effective Use of Church Space,* Ralph Belknap suggests financial guidelines for building programs. It is best if a building loan has an amortization period of twenty years or less. The amount of money committed to debt retirement should not exceed twenty-five percent of the congregation's total annual budget. Beyond this proportion, the building expense seriously limits resources available for program and professional salaries. In such a case, the congregation exists to serve the building rather than the other way around.

To determine the amount of debt service a congregation can carry, a small task force should develop a ten-year cash flow projection. Two or three forecasts should be developed based on different assumptions. For example, in reviewing changes in pledging and membership over the previous five years, a congregation might develop one forecast based on modest membership and pledge growth; a second forecast might assume higher membership growth with modest pledge increases. Leaders can use these forecasts in developing the project budget.

It is important to draw up a construction budget early in the process and to include it with the architect's contract in written form. Early estimates are often misleadingly low, with the result that congregations are dismayed with true cost figures. A net amount is commonly given, sometimes without the understanding that an additional twenty to twenty-five percent in related expenses can be anticipated.

To draw up a construction budget is to determine accurately what the congregation can afford as well as what it will cost to build. First, itemize the resources your congregation can draw on:

- current building funds (monies set aside for building)
- additional building funds to come in before construction is completed (current building funds plus income from a capital fund campaign)
- maximum borrowing potential (see above)
- income from sale of property
- other.

Next, itemize the expenses of construction, estimated as accurately as possible:

- fees for professional services (architect, attorney, consultant, appraiser, realtor, etc.)
- furnishings and equipment
- property expenses (including demolition if necessary, surveying, soil testing, access roads, utility connections, landscaping)
- miscellaneous expenses (interest, insurance)
- contingencies (inflation factor, items overlooked)
- cost of construction.

If a congregation is unable to obtain adequate financing through regular lending institutions, it should call the Unitarian Universalist Association for information about loan guarantees. Details of the Building Loan and Guarantee and Grants Program and application forms are available from the Building Programs staff in the Department for

Congregational, District, and Extension Services, 25 Beacon St., Boston MA 02108. Other sources of financial help may be available. Check with your district office and interdistrict representative for information.

Undertaking a building program can build a congregation as well as a meetinghouse. Through information gathering and shared decision making, a new sense of your congregation's identity emerges and a stronger sense of community develops. The joint enterprise of expressing this identity and community in a concrete, visible form for all to see and for the congregation to use and to share for years is exciting and challenging. The adventure of building, and the building itself can be as Unitarian Universalist as anything else.

Property Insurance

Some congregations have learned the hard way about insurance, especially in cases of fire. Only after suffering a major loss does the congregation discover the inadequacies of its insurance coverage.

Underinsurance is a common problem. Even if small increases are periodically made in the amount of coverage, inflation may have outstripped them, especially true if your building is a historic structure. Periodically, have a professional appraisal made of the replacement value of your facility.

Keep an up-to-date inventory of your building's contents. Include photographs and videotapes. The inventory should list, for all furniture and equipment: date of acquisition, description, model numbers, original cost, and general condition. Secure an appraisal of especially valuable items. Store this information in a bank vault or other fireproof storage facility, so that these records are safe.

A coinsurance clause in the insurance policy can limit the size of the claim. These clauses are difficult to understand and easy to overlook. The standard coinsurance clause reads as follows:

> "The Company shall not be liable for a greater proportion of any loss to the property covered thereunder than the limit of liability under this policy for such property bears to the amount produced by multiplying the co-insurance percentage applicable (specified in this policy) by the actual cash value of such property at the time of the loss."

The effect of such a clause is that the face amount of the policy might be recoverable under certain circumstances. If you have a coinsurance clause, it may be necessary to increase the face value of insurance beyond what would be adequate without such a cause.

A committee or knowledgeable individual should be appointed to oversee insurance matters. Find a reputable insurance agent with experience in insuring churches. Someone who handles a lot of congregations not only should be knowledgeable about your particular concerns but may be able to secure a better price or better coverage for you because of their volume of business. Interview several agents and secure several bids when placing a policy.

Related safety issues. Make regular checks of your fire extinguishers and smoke and heat detectors to make sure they are in good working order. Conduct a fire drill at least once a year to make sure all religious education teachers and children know how to evacuate your building safely.

Resources

Atkinson, Harry C. *How to Get Your Church Built.* New York: Doubleday, 1964.

Belknap, Ralph L. *Effective Use of Church Space: Church Buildings in a Time of Energy Shortage and High Costs.* Valley Forge: Judson Press, 1978.

Bieler, Andre. *Architecture in Worship.* Philadelphia: Westminster Press, 1965.

Clark, William S., Ed. *For Church Builders.* Valley Forge, PA: Agora Books, 1969.

Fester, Ruth. *Landscaping that Saves Energy Dollars.* New York: David McKay.

Holway, Bill. *Buildings,* "Growing Series #2," Boston: UUA, 1982. Available from Extension services in the UUA Department for Congregational, District, and Extension Services.

Lynn, Edwin C. *Tired Dragons.* Boston: Beacon Press, 1972.

The Architect and the Congregation. Washington, DC: Guild for Religious Architecture,

American Institute of Architects, 1777 Church St., NW, Washington DC 20036.

Facilities Planning Sourcebook, 1992. Church Development Resources, 2850 Kalamazoo Ave., SE, Grand Rapids, MI 49560.

That All May Worship, 1992. National Organization on Disability, 910 16th Street, NW, Suite 600, Washington, DC 20006.

Unit V

Your Congregation's History, Policies, and Procedures

Fourteen

Maintaining Records and Archives

One cannot overemphasize the importance of maintaining adequate records for the congregation or fellowship. The minutes of meetings, financial records, and membership records comprise the ongoing story of the life of a congregation; they provide the data necessary to short-term and long-range planning as well as the information needed to complete the Unitarian Universalist Association annual report questionnaire. Moreover, these records contain the basic information vital to composing a history of the congregation. Failure to maintain congregation records endangers the harmony of the congregation by resulting in a lack of information on which to base decisions and a consequent confusion over methods and goals. Maintaining congregation records, therefore, should be a priority.

Minutes

Minutes should be recorded for all meetings of the congregation, the governing board, and formal committees. The minutes should provide a source of information about official actions on the part of the congregation, board, or committee without being so detailed that they are difficult to write or read. Here are some guidelines for recording minutes.

- Minutes should always record the date and time of the meeting.

- In meetings of the governing board or committees, the minutes should name those present; for a congregational meeting, it is sufficient to indicate the presence of a quorum.

- Minutes should note the name of the person chairing the meeting and the person taking the minutes; the names of those presenting formal motions may be included if desired.

- Minutes should carefully record the exact wording of formal motions even if not voted on; for motions that are brought to a vote, minutes should record votes for and against as well as abstentions.

- Minutes should also record general understandings or consensus reached at a meeting despite the absence of formal motions or votes. It is not necessary, however, to record the details of every discussion held at the meeting.

- Minutes should include the names of those people elected or appointed to assume various responsibilities.

- The minutes of meetings should be examined by the participants for errors before being accepted as an official document.

- The official minutes of any meeting ought to be available on request to all members of the congregation. Many congregations publish the minutes of important meetings of the board and congregation in a newsletter; other congregations post these minutes where members can view them.

Annual Report

Many congregations publish an annual report in conjunction with the annual meeting of the congregation. Such a document customarily includes a report from the president, the secretary or clerk, and the treasurer as well as a summary of the activities of each committee, interest group, and special task force.

A copy of the annual report should be distributed to all members of the congregation and can be included with the materials given to new members, prospective ministers, and interested others. A copy should also be sent to the Public Information Office of the Unitarian Universalist Association to be included in its congregation files. Finally, additional copies should be kept for future reference.

Electronic Recordkeeping

Many problems inherent in the collection, storage, and transmission of congregation records can be eased through the use of electronic recordkeeping. After surveying available congregation management software, the Unitarian Universalist Association recommends to congregations the Church Organizational Management System (COMS). COMS is an advanced and comprehensive congregational software program that can handle nearly every aspect of running a congregation. COMS allows congregations to track members, prospects, and pledges. Information from this program can be passed to most popular word processing programs (e.g., WordPerfect and Microsoft Word).

COMS is available in both Macintosh and IBM-compatible versions. Questions and orders should be directed to Specialty Software at (407) 728-1199 in Evanston, IN. Other questions about electronic recordkeeping can be directed to the Unitarian Universalist Association Computer Services Department.

Other Important Records

In addition to the minutes of meetings and the annual report, other documents should be carefully preserved.

Preserve all documents that pertain to the congregation's affiliation with the Universalist Church of America, American Unitarian

Association, and Unitarian Universalist Association; the congregation's articles of incorporation; and its bylaws, including all revisions and amendments.

Keep at least one copy of all congregation publications, such as newsletters and brochures, for newcomers to the congregation. These documents will provide essential information for writing a history of the congregation.

Record Storage

All official documents should be kept where they are safe yet accessible. For older records, this means in a fireproof cabinet located in the congregation or parsonage. As noted above, electronic storage of information eases many problems: copies of documents can be stored in the computer and on diskettes to facilitate retrieval and transmission.

Confidential Record: Memorial Service Preferences

Some records may need to be kept confidential in a congregation. One such form is the record of stated preferences for memorial services. Here is a sample form.

Full Name _____   Date _____

Date of birth _____   Birthplace _____

Social Security Number ____ - ___ - _____

Mother's name _____   Father's name _____

Names of brothers and sisters _____

_____

Name of spouse or partner _____

Name(s) of other significant person(s) _____

Name and addresses of children _____

_____

Marital status _____

Date of marriage or service of holy union _____

Place of marriage or service of holy union _____

_____ I wish to have my body cremated and have a memorial service.

_____ I wish my ashes to be _____.

_____ I wish my ashes to be buried in _____ cemetery located at _____.

_____ I wish to have a memorial service with private burial before or after the service.

_____ I wish to have a memorial service with no graveside committal service.

_____ I wish to have a memorial service with graveside committal service.

_____ I wish to be buried in _____ cemetery, located at _____.

I wish to have my service held at:

_____ Unitarian Universalist congregation/____ in my home/____ other: _____

I would prefer, in lieu of sending flowers, that my family and friends make memorial gifts to

_____ Unitarian Universalist Church

other: _____.

I make the following suggestions for material I would like to have used in my service. (Include title, author, and reference, whenever possible.)

Responsive Readings   Songs/Hymns

Poems   Other Music

Speakers (name, address, phone number)   Other Suggestions

Other wishes I have about my memorial service:

Writing the History of Your Congregation

A shared history is a powerful bond and an awareness of history can foster a sense of pride and a feeling of connectedness. The telling of this history, whether in oral or written form, is one of the most important ways that newer members of a family are welcomed into the group.

This sense of history is equally important to a congregation. A sense of who we are is partly dependent on who we were. A history of your congregation can reveal stories of its struggle to survive and prosper, stories replete with setbacks and successes. But this history has no value if it is hidden; it must be shared. While it is important to preserve oral narrative, a written history is essential to the transmission of the story (or stories) of your congregation's past.

When to Write

Anytime is a good time to write a history, but the support needed for such a project is most easily generated as part of an anniversary or commemoration. Many congregations have produced congregation histories on the fiftieth or one hundredth anniversary of the founding of the congregation. The anniversary of a minister's settlement is also a good time for people to cooperate on writing a history. Even a municipal celebration can be a catalyst for starting the work. Keep in mind that research and writing are frequently frustrating and always time consuming, so allow plenty of time to complete the work.

How to Begin

The first step is to involve as many people as possible. A small committee should be created to supervise and coordinate the project; it can decide how the work of research and writing should be divided.

The older a congregation is, the more history it has to be discovered and recorded, but the greater the likelihood that an earlier generation produced a congregation history. Such a document can assist you in deciding what topics are important to your project and can provide starting points for your research. Check the congregation's files or the Unitarian Universalist Association archives.

Divide the research work among the group's members. The personal interests and expertise of researches will suggest ways to apportion the tasks: one person may be interested in the roles that women's groups have played in the life of the congregation; a youth group may want to consider the history of religious education in the congregation; another researcher may examine the congregation's response to major cultural movements such as abolition, suffrage, or civil rights.

The most common way for dividing a congregation's history is chronological, but the overly rigid application of this structure is dangerous. For example, instead of dividing a seventy-five year history into three parts of twenty-five years each, it might be better to divide the parts by a major event (perhaps the settlement of a new minister or the move from one congregational building to another). In this example, it is more effective to have parts that are internally cohesive and logically divided than to have three parts of equal length.

Doing the Research

After deciding how the research work is to be divided, you can begin to collect the pertinent facts for your congregation's history. This information can be found in a variety of places.

Check all congregation records held by the congregation. Start by sketching the broad outline of the congregation's history: When was it founded? Was it the first congregation in that location or were there others before it? Who have been its ministers? Has it always been located at its present address? in its present building?

Move on to more specific congregation records (perhaps with the assistance of the congregation's secretary and treasurer). The minutes of meetings can reveal a great deal about the problems facing the congregation. Treasurer's reports can chronicle the highs and lows of the congregation's history and can show what the congregation considered important enough to spend money on. By examining endowment records, you may also discover important benefactors whose names have been forgotten.

Visit your local library and historical society to enlist the aid of their librarians. These collections may include local histories that refer to your congregation or an earlier congregation history. Local newspapers are also an important source of information. The library's photograph collection may contain photos of an old congregation building that no longer exists, former ministers, or the founders of the congregation.

Explore the congregation's building for lost or forgotten materials. An old trunk in the attic or a dusty box of books in the basement might yield a wealth of materials to examine. Also pay attention to the memorial objects in the building: There may be interesting stories behind who donated the objects and why.

Don't forget to use human resources by spreading word of your research among the members of the congregation. Older congregation members should be asked to share their memories of the congregation; these reminiscences can lead to other avenues of research. Longtime congregants may have interesting photographs and other memorabilia associated with the congregation that can be included in your history.

Further Research

Based upon what you discover in your congregation records, local library, and historical society, and in interviews with congregation members, you may wish to extend your research. Here are some ways to do so.

Contact the UUA Public Information Office and ask how to initiate a search of the archives there. Among these archives are congregation files (including correspondence, clippings, and photos); old directories and yearbooks; and information on worship services. It is not uncommon for these files to include material that individual societies may have misplaced over the years or lost through accident (fires, floods, etc.) If you are in the Boston area, you may be able to arrange to browse through these files yourself; but call at least one week in advance to make an appointment. If not, you can initiate a search by the Unitarian Universalist Association's archival researcher.

The Public Information Office can also arrange for a search of the extensive Unitarian Universalist Association archives held at the Andover Harvard Theological Library in Cambridge, Massachusetts. These resources include files on Unitarian and Universalist ministers; files on individual congregations, deceased ministers, institutional directories and yearbooks; a large collection of photographs; the minutes of various general conventions and assemblies; back issues of the major denominational newspapers (e.g., *Christian Register* and *Universalist Leader*); smaller regional publications, and many other sources of information. There is a charge for archival research done at Harvard and the process can take several weeks.

Other repositories of archival materials are the Meadville/Lombard Theological School in Chicago (after Andover Harvard, the second largest depository of Unitarian Universalist archival materials and the site of the Western Unitarian Conference papers), and the Starr King School for the Ministry in Berkeley, CA. If circumstances permit, you may examine these archives in person; if you send a written request for information, try to make your questions as specific as possible.

Writing the History

After the bulk of the research has been completed, begin to write a draft of your congregation's history. The first step is to hold a meeting where the individuals and groups that have conducted research can present their findings and discuss its significance. Your written history cannot include every detail you have uncovered, so the group must decide which facts are most relevant and significant. You may discover information that is not pleasant: It is just as important to document a scandal or a controversy as it is to chronicle a success. Involve as many people as possible in this discussion to ensure that the finished history reflects the diversity of your congregation.

There are two ways to accomplish the actual writing of your history. The group may want to choose one person to do the writing, especially if that person is experienced. The benefits of a single author (stylistic consistency and less repetition) must be weighed against the fact that this task is time-consuming for one person.

As an alternative to a single writer, the coordinating committee may assign different chapters to different authors based on their interests and expertise (in the same way that the work of research was divided). This method may result in a history that is not quite as polished as one by a single author, but one that better reflects the diverse interests of the group. Whichever method you choose, initial drafts of the history must be discussed before a final version is approved by the group.

Publishing Your History   Present your written history in the most attractive way possible. In the past this meant sending your manuscript to a printer, but today impressive results can be achieved through desktop publishing. This method will also facilitate the storage and dissemination of your work.

After the history of your local congregation is printed, send copies to the local library, historical society, and the Unitarian Universalist Association headquarters. Copies should also be sent to Unitarian Universalist Association archival repositories mentioned above. Plan to hold a publishing party for the entire congregation to celebrate the completion of your work. The many hours of labor required to produce the written history of your congregation bears fruit only when the history is shared by others.